Guillaume d'Orange
FOUR TWELFTH-CENTURY EPICS

NUMBER XCII

RECORDS OF CIVILIZATION

SOURCES AND STUDIES

Guillaume d' Orange
four
Twelfth - Century
epics

TRANSLATED, WITH AN INTRODUCTION, BY
JOAN M. FERRANTE

COLUMBIA UNIVERSITY PRESS
New York and London 1974

The Andrew W. Mellon Foundation, through a special grant,
has assisted the Press in publishing this volume.

Library of Congress Cataloging in Publication Data

Guillaume d'Orange (Chansons de geste)
   Guillaume d'Orange: four twelfth-century epics.

   (Records of civilization: sources and studies, no. 92)
   Includes bibliographical references.
   Contents: The coronation of Louis.—The conquest of Orange.—
   Aliscans.—William in the monastery.
   I. Ferrante, Joan M., 1936– tr. II. Title. III. Series.
PQ1481.A3F4   841'.1   74-4421
ISBN 0-231-03809-7

IN MEMORY OF
JOHN M^CKENNA

SE DE TELS HOMES EUSSIENS A PLENTÉ
RICE SERIENS

Contents

Introduction

History tells us little of the medieval William of Orange, but legend tells us a great deal. From the legends grew the most extensive epic cycle of the Middle Ages. Of the historical William we know only that he was a contemporary of Charlemagne, whom he served as a military leader and provincial administrator in the south of France, and that, towards the end of his life, he retired to a monastery. The legendary hero is the devoted protector of Charlemagne's son, Louis, a lifelong defender of the Christian faith against the Moslems of Spain, the most brilliant scion of a glittering family of heroes, and a divinely guided, if somewhat impulsive, holy man.

Not only did he inspire a complete epic biography in French—seven poems that describe his exploits from glorious youth to saintly death, and seventeen others about his ancestors and relations—but he became a popular figure in other lands as well. The German poet Wolfram von Eschenbach chose William and Perceval as the two French heroes worthy of his attention, for both achieved wordly success and then devoted their lives to God. William's fame as a fighter for Christianity was so great that Dante places him in the sphere of crusaders, beside Charlemagne and Godfrey of Boulogne (*Divine Comedy, Par* XVIII, 46). His adventurēs are recounted in Italian (*I Nerbonesi*), in Norse (*Karlamagnussaga*), in Latin (Orderic Vitalis includes William's story among the lives of warrior saints, in the *Historia ecclesiastica*).

The adventures of the epic hero were attached very early to the saint and they are mentioned with enthusiasm in the *Vita Sancti Wilhelmi* (c. 1125). The heroic adventures are not related in the *Vita* because they do not serve the edifying purpose of the holy recital, but they are well known in any case, the author suggests:

> For what kingdoms, what provinces, what peoples, what cities do not speak of the power of Duke William, the virtue of his spirit, the

strength of his body, the glorious triumphs of his zealous and continual fighting? What chorus of youth, what assembly of people, of military and noble men especially, what vigil of the saints does not sweetly resound and sing in melodious voices what he was, how gloriously he overcame and defeated the barbarians; how much he endured from them and how much he inflicted on them; and how, finally, with victory after victory, he put them to flight and expelled them from every part of the Frankish kingdom? [1]

The evidence of contemporary literature supports this grand claim. The hero of a French romance (the *Roman de la Violette* by Gerbert de Montreuil), when disguised as a minstrel, sings of William's exploits. William is one of the major knights in the *Pèlerinage de Charlemagne* (mid-twelfth century), where he is accompanied, as he usually is in his own cycle, by his nephew Bertrand. The cycle itself is named in a thirteenth-century epic, *Girart de Viane,* as one of the three "gestes" or epic cycles of France, with that of the king, Charlemagne, and that of Doon de Mayence. (Garin is William's ancestor, the first of his line):

> The third geste, which is worthy of praise,
> was of the fierce Garin de Monglane.
> Of his line I can truly swear
> there was never a coward or craven soul
> no traitor nor false flatterer. (11. 1448 ff) [2]

1. Quae enim regna et quae provinciae, quae gentes, quae urbes, Willelmi Ducis potentiam non loquuntur, virtutem animi, corporis vires, gloriosos belli studio et frequentia triumphos? Qui chori juvenum, qui conventus populorum, praecipue militum ac nobilium virorum, quae vigiliae sanctorum, dulce non resonant, et modulatis vocibus decantant, qualis et quantus fuerit, quamque victoriose barbaros domuit et expugnavit; quanta ab eis pertulit, quanta intulit; ac demum de cunctis regnis Francorum finibus crebro victos et refugas perturbavit et expulit? (from the Prologue to the Life of Saint William in the *Acta Sanctorum*).

2. La tierce geste ke moult fist a proisier
Fu de Garin de Montglane le fier.
De son lignage puis je bien tesmoignier
Qu'il n'ot ne coart ne lainnier
Ne traitor ne felon losengier.

epic cycles

The major poems of these cycles date from the twelfth century, the period that produced the philosophical and theological works of the Victorines and the Chartrians and the romances of Chrétien de Troyes as well as the vast number of epic poems, the *chansons de geste*. Unlike the romances, which arose as a new genre in the second half of this century, the epics are the outcome of several centuries of oral composition, probably beginning not long after the time of the heroes and events they describe, but written down for the first time in the twelfth century. Primarily concerned with military feats—Christian heroes battling pagan enemies, rebellious barons fighting each other or their kings—the epics derived much of their popularity during this period from their reflections of the contemporary historical situation—the troubles of the Capetian monarchy in France and the crusades being directed towards the Holy Land.

The first cycle, the "geste du roi," is a loosely related series of poems about Charlemagne—his youth, exploits in Italy and Spain, wars with the Saxons, and journey to the Holy Land. The second group of poems, the cycle of Doon de Mayence, is better known as the "rebellious barons cycle." It consists of a number of works that are connected only by the theme of rebellion against the king and by the common ancestry of the rebel heroes in Doon, who was introduced into the tradition late, an apparent attempt to give some unity to unrelated works. These poems describe the feuds of noblemen either with the king or with their fellow nobles; some are individual feuds, some involve whole families. Pride that is quick to take offense and slow to forgive leads to self-perpetuating and often horrifying violence, of which the most striking instance is in *Raoul de Cambrai*—the burning of the nuns inside their church, innocent victims of the hero's feud.

The William of Orange cycle shares two of the more characteristic traits of the rebellious barons cycle, the weak and often faithless king and the family pride of the heroes. Louis, Charlemagne's son, is in constant need of support from William and his family, but only grudgingly acknowledges his obligations to them. The family of Narbonne, on the other hand, is not only unusually loyal to its king, but it is bound together by an intense devotion of its members to one another. Brothers come with their armies to aid each other; nephews spend years in the service of their uncles. The uncle-nephew bond is much stronger than the father-son relationship throughout this cycle. The uncle-nephew tie is the important one more often than not in *chansons de gestes* and probably reflects an early period of history when sons were attached to their mothers' rather than to their fathers' families.[3] The loyalty within the family of Narbonne is so strong that it draws in even the converted pagans, William's wife Guiborc and her brother Rainoart, who give up not only their religion but their family ties when they are baptized. Guiborc betrays and leaves her pagan husband, Rainoart fights his father and brothers, even kills some of them, out of loyalty to William and Christianity. The love of pagan women for Christian men is a recurrent and related theme (see *Prise d'Orange, Prise de Cordres et de Sebille, Siège de Barbastre, Guibert d'Andrenas, Foucon de Candie, Renier*); their baptism and marriage offsets and complements the slaughter of pagan armies.

It is the causes that the heroes of the William cycle serve which distinguish them from the rebellious barons of the feudal epics; these are loyalty to the king, despite his unworthiness, and dedication to Christianity. The entire family is engaged in a continuous struggle against the pagans, the Moslems of Spain. It might be said that devotion to one cause necessitates devotion to the other. Because the king does not or cannot provide for his loyal vassals, they must provide for themselves. They are too noble to attack his lands or his vassals, so they turn their energies against an outside enemy, the infidel. The Narbonnais accept no lands as direct gifts, neither from the king nor from their fathers. Beginning with the ancestor of the line, Garin de Monglane (the first hero in the family, though a late arrival to the tradition), the heroes carve out their fiefs in pagan territory. Aimeri, William's father, who has himself won Narbonne, sends six of his seven sons off to win their own lands, reserving his for the youngest son, Guibert (*Les Narbonnais*). However, when Aimeri is one hundred-forty years old, he decides to leave Narbonne to a godson instead and Guibert too must win his own lands (*Guibert d'Andrenas*). William serves Louis for many years without

3. W. O. Farnsworth, *Uncle and Nephew in the Chansons de Geste* (New York, 1913).

reward and finally must win his own seat by capturing Orange from pagans, but he needs the support of his father and brothers to secure it (*Aliscans*). The winning of fiefs in foreign territory is a reflection of historical conditions. The French nation, in the eleventh century, was expanding and the younger sons of nobility, in particular, needed to find new lands, which they sought in England, Italy, Spain and, eventually, the Holy Land.

the hero in history

The figure of the hero, William of Orange, is clearly drawn in the poems—his shortened nose and boisterous laugh, his passion for horses and love of disguise, all of which distinguish him from other heroes. The events of his life, too, are known, from his childhood to his death, to say nothing of his family history backwards and forwards for several generations. And yet we know relatively little about the historical figure who inspired the legends, if indeed we can say it was one man. There was a Saint William, a noble who had served as a warrior and administrator under Charlemagne, who was connected with the epic hero at the latest by the early twelfth century. The saint was shown with a horn, a "cornet," clearly a misinterpretation of the hero's epithet "cort nes," short nose.[4]

Orderic Vitalis (1131–41) and the *Vita Sancti Wilhelmi* (1120s) have already been mentioned; both tell the story of the saint and both make references to songs sung about him. But these are relatively late works and they have clearly been influenced by epic traditions: the winning of Orange, which became William's seat; negotiations with King Theodebald; conquests of the Saracens; the spreading of Christian churches across southern France; and the placing of the hero's arms at the altar of St. Julian, where they were worshipped by pilgrims on the way to Santiago. In the *Liber Sancti Jacobi,* a book for pilgrims to the shrine (c. 1139), William's tomb is mentioned as a site to be visited:

> Those who take the Toulouse road to St. James ought to visit the body of the blessed confessor, William . . . the extraordinary stand-

---

4. W. Cloetta, in the introduction to his edition of the *Moniage,* II, 171–72. "Cort nes," "short nose," is probably a corruption of "corb nes," "crooked nose." (See below, p. 38).

ard-bearer, the count of the king Charlemagne, a mighty soldier, most learned in warfare.[5]

Bédier suggests that if William of Toulouse had died before he became a monk, there would have been no epics. But there is evidence in texts which predate the poems by more than a century that William was a well-known hero fairly early. The oldest evidence is a poem by Ermoldus Nigellus, "In honorem Hludovici," from the late tenth or early eleventh century, that mentions a Duke William from Toulouse (l. 137), who offers to lead Louis' expedition against the Saracens in the south. He plays an important part in the siege of Barcelona, he is among the few whose deeds are singled out by the author (see ll. 272 ff, 371–2, 401 ff, 475 ff, 489 ff).[6] He kills Moors, answers their taunts and talks about his horse (l. 147, ll. 405 ff). I do not go so far as to suggest a connection between these passages and the epic William's love of horses, but the fact is intriguing.

William is also mentioned in several Carolingian chronicles, always involved with the struggle against the Saracens in the south: in the *Vita Hludovici,* he replaces Chorso, the Duke of Toulouse, to administer Aquitaine for Louis. When Barcelona is attacked, William goes to Saragossa to meet the Moslem troops from Cordoba and prevent them from relieving the Saracens at Barcelona. The *Chronicon Moissiacense* for the year 793 describes the brutal reign of a Moorish prince, Abderraman Ibin-Mavia (a possible source of the Desramé of the epics), who attempted to take advantage of Charlemagne's troubles with the Avars and sent his troops to lay waste Gaul. He burnt Narbonne, taking booty and prisoners, but on his way to Carcasonne he was met by William and other counts who fought him at the river Orbieu. Although most of the Christians were killed and many deserted, William fought until the Saracens left France. In the *Nota Emilianense,* a fragment from the mid-eleventh century, William is one of the six nephews of Charlemagne to accompany the king and the twelve peers on the expedition to

---

5. Igitur ab his qui per viam Tolosanam ad Sanctum Jacobum tendunt, beati confessoris Guillelmi corpus est visitandum . . . signifer egregius, comes Karoli magni regis . . . miles fortissimus, bello doctissimus (chapter viii).

6. *Monumenta Germanie Historica, Scriptores,* Vol. II.

Saragossa. He is called "Ghilgelmo alcorbitanas," a latinization of the "corb nes" epithet.[7]

There is one further document that suggests the existence of a heroic tradition about William—the Hague Fragment, a résumé of a Latin poem. Although the extant passage does not mention William by name, it provides stronger evidence for such a tradition than the other texts cited. In describing Charlemagne's war against the Saracens, it mentions, among the Christians, several of William's relatives: Ernoldus or Ernaldus, Bertrandus, Bernardus, and Wibelinus, and, among the pagans, Borrel (who appears in *Aliscans*). None of this is conclusive proof that poems about William were recited, but there is no doubt that William was a hero of Carolingian tradition and it is certain that by the late eleventh century he was an important enough figure, in legend, to inspire the forging of various documents by the monks of Aniane in the course of their jurisdictional squabbles with Gellone.[8] William of Toulouse founded the monastery of Gellone in 804 and retired to it in 806, but the extant copies of his Donations have been tampered with. One names his wives, Witburgh (Guiborc) and Cunegune, in that order, the other reverses the order to accord better with epic tradition and adds a nephew, Bertrand, for the same purpose.

If there is one major inspiration for the hero of the poems, it is most likely the William of Toulouse mentioned in the early texts. All we know of him is that he became Duke of Toulouse in 790 and served under the young Louis in Aquitaine while Charlemagne was still alive; he met the Saracens in a disastrous battle near the Orbieu in 793, and took part in the siege of Barcelona in the early years of the ninth century. Having founded the abbey of Gellone in 804, under the influence of St. Benedict of Aniane, he retired to it as a monk two years later and died there in 813. These are few but suggestive details, for the poetic William protects the throne of the young and weak Louis from various traitors (in the *Couronnement de Louis*); he fights Saracens in all the poems and once, at least, suffers severe loss before his victory (*Aliscans*); and, finally, he leaves the world and retires to a monastery (*Moniage Guil-*

7. J. Frappier, *Les Chansons de Geste du Cycle de Guillaume d'Orange* (Paris, 1955), I, 78–79.

8. *Dictionnaire d'histoire et de géographie ecclésiastiques* (Paris, 1924), III, 277–78.

laume). None of the other historical Williams that have been put forth as models (Bédier lists sixteen) has as much in common with the hero. Nonetheless, it is worth mentioning a few, for there are details that may have contributed something to the tradition: there is William VI of Montpellier and William IX of Aquitaine, both of whom fought against the Arabs in Spain in the early twelfth century, when the poems as we now have them were composed; William of Montreuil, a place connected with the hero in the *Couronnement,* who led a Norman contingent into Spain in 1063, and fought for the pope as the hero of the poem does. There are several members of the Aquitaine dynasty: William I, who founded Cluny and whose mother's name was Ermengard; William Fierebrace, who made many pilgrimages to Santiago in the early eleventh century; and another (William VIII) who led the first Spanish Crusade in 1063. There are, of course, numerous "Guillaume Fierebrace" in French history, a common name with a common epithet, but we have no way of knowing whether the poetic hero inspired the epithet of the historic figures or the other way round, or indeed if there is any connection. It is unlikely that any *one* of the various Williams is the hero of the poems, but the fact that there were so many—and particularly southern lords, whole dynasties in some cases—who were necessarily involved in struggles with the Moslems, offers a wealth of material for legend to draw on, and very little hope of sorting it out.

development of the cycle

How the legends evolved into the heroic poems is a question that has intrigued scholars since the romantic period and is likely to do so for as long as there is an interest in origins, for once again there is no single solution. The wisest approach is to synthesize the various theories of oral tradition, literary influence, and pilgrimage routes.[9] Oral traditions persist and grow, even in literate societies. We know that songs were sung about heroes in the Carolingian period—Charlemagne himself had them collected. From the studies of Parry and Lord, we have some idea how these songs develop.[10] Poets work from a collection of stock descriptions

9. For a summary of various theories of origins, see I. Siciliano, *Le Origini delle Canzoni di Gesta* (Padova, 1940).

10. M. Parry, "Studies in the Epic Technique of Oral Verse-Making," *Harvard Studies in Classical Philology,* 41 (1930), 73–147; M. Parry and A. B. Lord, *Serbo-Croatian*

and formulae, which they fit to the subject matter with a degree of success that depends on their skill as well as on the suitability of the equipment. They may sing of contemporary events or of events from the past that have been contaminated in the course of time by extraneous matter. It would be foolish to deny the possible influence of literary works and traditions, monastic or secular, on the formation of such epics. Anything that might interest the audience can accrue to the basic material; stories of comic giants seem to have been piled on the figure of Rainoart in *Aliscans*. No doubt deeds of other heroes, perhaps of other Williams, were attributed to William of Orange as his popularity grew. Certainly contemporary interest influenced the nature of the stories told—the twelfth-century French involvement in the reconquest of Spain would encourage the recital if not the composition of songs about earlier heroes who had fought off the attacks of Spanish Moslems; the enormous popularity of the pilgrimage to Santiago would encourage the relating of feats that had been performed along the route. That relics of the heroes who performed them were in the possession of the monasteries that housed pilgrims was either an added source of interest or a result of that interest. It is impossible to say which, and it seems unimportant—what matters is that the presence of each benefited the other.

What we have in the poems of the William of Orange cycle are the vague reflections of historic events that are set in the ninth century, but may have occurred, if at all, anywhere from the ninth to the twelfth century. The legends grew far beyond the significance of whatever historical figures may be involved. The historical content, as Lot says, may be deformed in the passage of time, while the literary creation is continual.[11] The characters are the combined creation of generations of poets or in some cases the inspiration of one man. The language is made up of stock phrases and descriptions; where the poetic tradition leaves off and the individual poet begins no one can know. We must be content with studying the poems as they have come to us and not attempt to credit the events or poets who were responsible for them.

The full cycle of William of Orange now extant contains twenty-

---

Heroic Songs, 2 vols. (Cambridge and Belgrade, 1954); A. B. Lord, *The Singer of Tales* (Cambridge, 1960).

11.F. Lot, *Études sur les légendes épiques françaises* (Paris, 1958), 257.

four poems, seven about William himself, the rest about members of his family:

"Shorter cycle of William"

Poems about William (mid- to late 12th c.)	[*Chanson de Guillaume*—does not appear in collections with the other poems] *Enfances Guillaume* (EG) *Couronnement de Louis* (CL) *Charroi de Nîmes* (CN) *Prise d'Orange* (PO) *Aliscans* (Al) *Moniage Guillaume* (MG)
Poems about characters from the *Aliscans* material (late 12th to early 13th c.)	*Enfances Vivien* (EV) *Covenanz* or *Chevalrie Vivien* (CV) *Bataille Loquifer* (BL) *Moniage Rainoart* (MR) *Foucon de Candie* (FC)
"Cycle of Aimeri" (mainly early 13th c.)	*Garin de Montglane* (GM) *Girart de Viane* (GV) *Aimeri de Narbonne* (AN) *Les Narbonnais* (Narb) *Siège de Barbastre* (SB) *Guibert d'Andrenas* (GA) *Prise de Cordres* (PC) *Mort Aimeri* (MA)
Works about related figures that do not appear in the larger manuscript collections (late 13th c.)	*Renier* *Enfances Garin* *Bueves de Commarchis* *Galien le Restoré*

Most of these works are preserved in manuscript collections that make a clear attempt to arrange the works in chronological order according to the lives of the heroes, not the dates of composition, i.e., the story of William's childhood precedes his other exploits although the *Enfances* is a later work. The development of the cycle seems to have been roughly as follows: the earliest poems related William's heroic exploits, his de-

FAMILY TREE OF GUILLAUME D'ORANGE

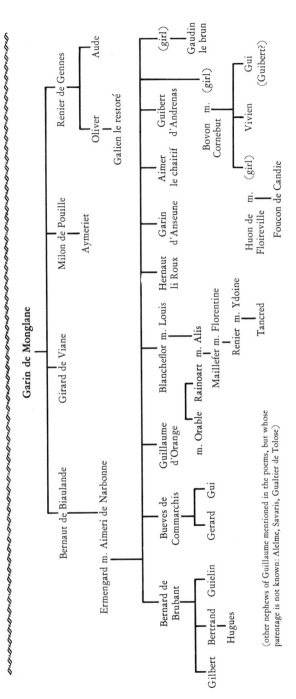

Garin de Monglane

Bernaut de Biaulande

Ermengard m. Aimeri de Narbonne

Girard de Viane

Milon de Pouille — Aymeriet

Renier de Gennes — Oliver — Galien le restoré

Aude

Bueves de Commarchis — Gerard, Gui

Guillaume d'Orange m. Orable

Rainoart m. Alis

Maillefer m. Florentine

Renier m. Ydoine

Tancred

Blancheflor m. Louis

Hernaut li Roux

Garin d'Anseune

Aimer le chaitif

Guibert d'Andrenas

Bovon m. Cornebut (girl)

Vivien

Gui (Guibert?)

Huon de Floireville m. (girl)

Foucon de Candie

(girl)

Gaudin le brun

Bernard de Brubant — Bertrand, Guielin, Hugues

Gilbert

(other nephews of Guillaume mentioned in the poems, but whose
parentage is not known: Alelme, Savaris, Gualtier de Tolose)

PAGAN FAMILY TREE

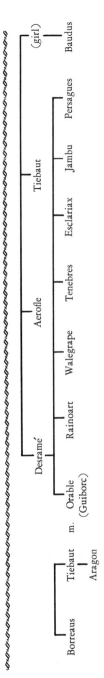

Tiebaut — Aragon

Borreaus

Orable (Guiborc) m.

Desramé

Rainoart

Walegrape

Aerofle

Tenebres

Esclariax

Tiebaut

Jambu

Persagues

(girl)

Baudus

fense of king and pope (CL), his battles against Saracens (CN, PO, *Chanson de Guillaume,* and a later version of the same material, *Aliscans*); then his retirement from the world and his adventures as a monk (MG); eventually, his childhood (EG), made up presumably to explain details in other poems, like William's promises to protect Louis and to marry Orable. Meanwhile other popular figures in the poems, Vivien and Rainoart, gave rise to separate poems about their adventures (Vivien, first in the *Covenanz,* which sets the background for his actions in *Aliscans,* and later in the *Enfances Vivien;* Rainoart in the BL and the MR). The next stage was to fill out the family background: poems about William's father, Aimeri (AN, Narb, GV, MA); his great-grandfather Garin (GM); his brothers (SB, GA, PC); and eventually distant nephews and cousins (FC, Renier, Galien). (For the scope of William's family, see the family tree, p. 11.) Not only are many members of the family heroes in their own right, but other famous heroes are attached to the family— Oliver with his sister Aude, Roland's fiancée, and Tancred, a hero of the first crusade. There is also a strong tendency to alliterative names within the family: Guillaume (William), Guiborc, Garin, Guibert, Guielin.

manuscripts

The relatively large number of manuscripts of these poems testifies to the popularity of the material. With the exception of the *Chanson de Guillaume,* which exists by itself and in only one version, an Anglo-Norman manuscript of the thirteenth century, the poems of the shorter William cycle are found together in nine manuscript collections; the poems of the Aimeri cycle are in three manuscripts with the William poems and in three others as a separate group. For our purposes the important manuscripts are the nine that contain the shorter William cycle in whole or in part. They are designated by the letters normally given them in editions of the separate poems; only the *Aliscans* and the *Moniage* editions use different letterings and those are given in parentheses. There are two versions of the *Moniage,* a shorter one (MG I) and a longer (MG II). The abbreviations refer to the poems as given in parentheses on p. 10.

A [1] Paris, Bibl. nat., fr. 774, 13th c.: CL, fol. 18–33; PO, 41v–52v; Aliscans (A in Halle edition), 81–98, incomplete; also includes EG, CN, EV, CV, MR, MG II.

A ² Paris, Bibl. nat., fr. 1449, 13th c.: CL, 23–38; PO, 47v–60r; Al (Halle, b), 92–142, incomplete; also includes EG, CN, EV, CV, BL.

A ³ Milano, Bibl. Trivulziana 1025, 13th c.: CL, 22–38; PO, 47v–58v; Al (Halle, T), 91–142, incomplete; also includes CN, EV, CV, BL, MR, MG II.

A ⁴ Paris, Bibl. nat., fr. 368, 14th c.: CL, 161–62 (597 lines); PO, 167r–173r; Al (Halle, B), 189–218; also includes EG, CN, EV, CV, BL, MR, MG II.

B ¹ London, Brit. Mus., Royal 20 D xi, 14th c.: CL, 103–12; PO, 118r–124v; Al (Halle, L), 134–84; also includes GM, GV, AN, Narb, EG, CN, EV, CV, BL, MR, MG II, SB, GA, MA, FC. This is the most extensive manuscript.

B ² Paris, Bibl. nat., fr. 24369, 14th c.: CL, 75–90; PO, 100r–110v; Al (Halle, V), 195–240; also includes AN, Narb, EG, CN, EV, CV, BL, MR, MG II, SB, GA, MA, Renier.

C   Boulogne-sur-Mer, Bibl. communale, S. Bertin, 192, A.D. 1295: CL, 21–38; PO, 47v–62r; Al (Halle, m), 93–140, incomplete; MG I (Cloetta ed., B), 301ᵇ–306ᵃ (the first 756 lines agree with MG I in Arsenal MS, the rest of the episode is from MG II). Also includes EG, CN, EV, CV, BL, MR, FC.

D   Paris, Bibl. nat., fr. 1448, 13th c.: CL, 88–89, incomplete; PO, 100r–109r, incomplete; Al (Halle, e), 216–72; also includes GV, AN, EG, CN, EV, CV, BL, MR, SB.

E   Berne, 296, 13th c.: PO, 1r–9r (begins at Laisse XLIX); Al (Halle, C), 23–82; also includes CV, BL, MR, MG II.

There are five other manuscripts that contain a poem or part of one:

C ² Paris, Bibl. nat., nouv. acqu., fr. 5094, 13th c.: CL, 29 lines.

Paris, Bibl. de l'Arsenal, 6562, c. 1225: Al (Halle, a), 1–118; MG I (Cloetta, A), 258r–273v; also includes BL, MR.

Paris, Bibl. nat., fr. 2494, 13th c., Al (Halle, d), 1–165; also includes BL.

Venice, Bibl. Marc., Zan. fr. 8, (252) CIV, 5, 14th c.

Private collection, Phillipps, Cheltenham, mentioned in editions of *Aliscans,* now lost; also includes 1700 lines of CV.

The four manuscripts designated A (^{1}, ^{2}, ^{3}, ^{4}), which are closely related, give the preferred readings for the *Couronnement* and the *Prise.*[12] The B manuscripts attempt to arrange songs from the cycles of Aimeri and of William in chronological order and to connect them so as to give unity to the cycle. A and B are written in a common literary language. C, which is in Picard, is a mixture of different traditions, where assonance is sometimes replaced by rhyme, an indication of later reworkings. In D some songs are strung together, sometimes without indication of where one ends and another begins, and some are incomplete, but the manuscript preserves older readings lost in other versions. The language of D is Lorraine.

The poems in this translation are all from the shorter William cycle. Although they are connected by the main characters and the interests of those characters—devotion to family and the fight for Christianity—the mood of each is distinct. The *Couronnement* is essentially a political poem about a vassal's devotion to his king and the evils a weak king can visit on his land and his subjects. The *Prise d'Orange* is a romantic rather than heroic epic, about the winning of a city and a bride, filled with disguises and recognitions, secret passages, imprisonments and escapes. *Aliscans* opens tragically with the death of Vivien, William's nephew, and the decimation of their army and ends with the heroicomic adventures of William's future brother-in-law, Rainoart, who is a forerunner, if not a direct ancestor, of the comic giant of Renaissance epic. The *Moniage* describes William's primarily comic adventures as a monk and presents a critical picture of life in the monastery.[13]

12. Katz, the editor of the *Prise,* finds B^1,C, D and E widely divergent from A^1; Langlois, editing the *Couronnement,* prefers B^1 to B^2; otherwise the general remarks about the manuscripts are true of both epics. The *Aliscans* manuscripts present a special problem that I have not attempted to handle here. M. Tyssens, *La Geste de Guillaume d'Orange dans les Manuscrits Cycliques* (Paris, 1967), p. 247 ff, studies the relation of the manuscripts at length, but even she hesitates to draw very definite conclusions.

13. There are two versions. I have translated the shorter one and given a summary of the longer, see below, p. 21 ff.

Since the *Chanson de Guillaume* and the *Charroi de Nîmes* have already been translated, these four poems complete the poetic biography of William in English.[14] Only the *Enfances Guillaume* is missing; the *Enfances* is a much later work (from the period of "décadence épique," according to its editor, P. Henry).[15] It is a reworking of another poem, the *Narbonnais,* and was composed to fill in the gap in William's life.

dating

The dates of composition of the other poems cannot be established very closely. They were all written in their present form in the twelfth century—the *Chanson de Guillaume,* the *Couronnement,* the *Charroi,* and the *Prise* toward the middle of the century, and the *Moniage* and *Aliscans* toward the end. Dating of the *Chanson* has varied considerably, some placing it as early as the late eleventh century, but recent opinion is more moderate. Frappier considers it roughly contemporary with the *Chanson de Roland,* with which it has many similarities.[16] Among the other early poems, there are interconnections that suggest a certain order of composition. It is generally agreed that a no-longer-extant version of the *Prise* came first, since there are references to the Orange story in many early texts. The *Vita Sancti Wilhelmi,* c. 1125, mentions William's conquest of Orange from a king Theobaldus; Orable is named in the *Couronnement* as William's fiancée, although the Orange episode should not yet have occurred, but clearly the story was known. There are references in other works (*Aliscans, Foucon de Candie,* the Italian *Nerbonesi*) to the killing of Tiebaut's children during the siege of Orange, by either William or Orable; since no such thing occurs in the extant *Prise,* it is likely that it was part of an earlier telling. The present version is put at around 1160–1165.

14. *Le Charroi de Nîmes, an English Translation with Notes,* by H. J. Godin (Oxford, 1936); *The Song of William, La chançun de Guillelme,* trans. into verse by E. N. Stone (Seattle, 1951).

15. P. Henry, ed., *Les Enfances Guillaume,* SATF (Paris, 1935), xlii. Jessie Crosland omits this chanson altogether when she discusses the "quintet of poems which really constitute the poetic life of Guillaume d'Orange," *The Old French Epic* (Oxford, 1951), 41.

16. For a discussion of the dating of the *Chanson de Guillaume,* see Frappier, I, 150–56.

The *Couronnement,* as we have it, is probably the oldest poem. Van Waard connects the first scene in it with the coronation of Louis VII in 1131. There are various similarities: the presence of the pope and the age of the prince, which accord better with the contemporary event than with the crowning of Louis the Pious that is the historic core of the poem.[17] This puts the poem after 1131 and probably before 1150. It has been suggested that the *Charroi de Nîmes* was a kind of transition between the *Couronnement* and the *Prise.*[18] At the end of the *Couronnement,* we are told that Louis will be ungrateful to William despite his loyal service. The *Charroi* opens with Louis distributing fiefs to his other knights, but not to William, so William decides to take lands in the south which are held by Saracens, and he goes south to win them. This would explain the removal of William's activities from the north, where he is in the *Couronnement,* to the south, in all the other poems about him. Although Bédier attacked this theory, Frappier accepts it in a modified form, and it seems highly plausible. The *Charroi* must follow the *Couronnement,* and therefore should be put between 1140 and 1165.[19]

The dating of *Aliscans* rests on two references in the poem to the king's disposition of Vermendois. This was territory to which Phillip Augustus won the right in 1185, after a war with Phillip of Alsace. The lines in the poem (ll. 2550 ff and 2699 ff) show a marked enthusiasm for the land which suggests contemporary interest. The *Moniage* presents various problems. It was thought for some time that the short line that ends the laisse (MG I) indicated an earlier version, but this position has been seriously questioned.[20] We cannot be sure that the shorter version is either an earlier form of the longer (MG II), as the editor Cloetta thinks, or a later abbreviation, as Tyssens thinks.[21] It seems safest to allow a margin of several decades and place its composition between 1160 and 1190.

17. Ibid., II (Paris, 1965), 160.   18. Ibid., II, 182 ff.

19. Ibid., II, 186.

20. Ibid., I, 56, fn. 1, for bibliography on this issue. The most recent discussion of the subject can be found in M. Tyssens, *La Geste de Guillaume d'Orange dans les Manuscrits cycliques* (Paris, 1967), chap. VI.

21. Cloetta, II, 109; Tyssens, 302. Actually, both critics admit that "original" or older traits are preserved in the versions they consider more recent.

the hero's life in the poems

In order to give a sense of the complete poetic biography of William of Orange, I shall briefly summarize the poems that are not presented in this translation. William's career begins in the *Enfances* when Charlemagne sends for Aimeri to bring his four eldest sons (Bernart, Garin, Hernaut and William) to court to be knighted. They go, although William would prefer to go to Spain and fight Saracens, leaving the mother, Ermengard to defend Narbonne. A spy tells the Saracen king Tiebaut of their departure and he prepares to take advantage. Meanwhile, Aimeri meets a troop of pagans who have been to Orange to ask Orable's hand for Tiebaut. They fight; Aimeri is captured but rescued by William, who also takes the horse Orable had sent as a gift to Tiebaut. This is Baucent, whom William will ride until he wins Folatil in *Aliscans*. Captivated by descriptions of Orable, William sends her a sparrow-hawk and a promise to marry her after he kills Tiebaut. William is captured, by treachery, in the next battle, but he is rescued by his father, a courtesy they exchange several times during the poem. The report of his courage and beauty is carried to Orable. Back at the siege of Narbonne, Tiebaut sets up a statue of Mohammed to help his side, but the Christians knock it down with rocks and the pagans return to Orange. Tiebaut marries Orable, with the consent of her brothers, but Orable unnerves him with a series of visions, and he returns to the siege of Narbonne. Aimeri and his sons, meanwhile, arrive in Paris and William quickly gets into a fight with a baron in an abbey; he is condemned to be burnt and is saved only when his father appears and identifies him. He restores himself to favor, however, by taking on a Breton champion who has challenged the court, and whom the French fear because he has already killed so many of them. William and his brothers are knighted soon after, but the celebration is interrupted by a messenger announcing that Narbonne is about to fall. Charlemagne sends a large army with Aimeri, but, as they leave, extracts a promise from William that he will be loyal to the young prince, no matter what happens. In the battle at Narbonne, William wounds Tiebaut, and once again rescues his father. The poem ends with William accompanying his younger brothers to court to serve the king.

The *Enfances* must fill in a good deal of background to prepare for the *Couronnement,* as well as the southern stories of the *Charroi* and the *Prise.* William commits himself to serve the king and protect the young prince Louis, which will bring him north again for the *Couronnement,* and to win Orable, which leads to the *Prise.* He involves himself in a feud with Tiebaut that will carry through the *Prise* and *Aliscans,* and he wins his most famous mount. In order to get all of this in, the poet is forced into the unusual structure of a double plot, two stories running simultaneously. Normally epics follow a single line of development, moving with the hero from one event to the next. The double plot is found only in rather sophisticated romances, like the Perceval stories.

In the *Couronnement,* William commutes between Paris and Rome, rescuing Louis from traitors and the pope from enemy attacks. Despite all this, Louis forgets William when, in the beginning of the *Charroi,* he distributes fiefs. In an ill-advised attempt to make up for his neglect, he offers William lands that have legitimate heirs, but William indignantly refuses to take them. At the advice of his nephew Bertrand, a constant companion through many of the poems, he asks instead for lands that the Saracens hold, and then sets out to win them: first Nîmes, then Orange. William asks only that Louis will lend his support every seven years, a promise that Louis has to be forced to keep in *Aliscans.* William and his men gain entry into Nîmes by disguising themselves as merchants—William's ability to speak Saracen tongues is a skill that often comes in handy, as in the *Prise* and *Aliscans*—and leading a train of carts into the city.

The *Prise d'Orange* opens at Nîmes, where William and Bertrand are bored with their peaceful life. It was not uncommon for Christian knights who remained behind in the Arab towns they had conquered to succumb to the rich way of life they found there, but these heroes are restless. They are roused by the report of a Christian who has just escaped from imprisonment in Orange and who tells of the magnificent palace and the beautiful queen Orable. It is obvious that William has not heard of her before, despite references in other poems. He decides to go, disguised once again as a Saracen, and after various adventures in towers and subterranean passages, William wins the city and marries the lady (who is baptized and takes the name Guiborc). Her pagan husband is still alive, however, and, furious over the theft of his wife and the loss of his city, he will make war on William on and off for several decades until the final clash of pagan and French troops in *Aliscans*.

The *Chanson de Guillaume* and *Aliscans* tell essentially the same story, but with different emphases. The *Chanson* concentrates on William's nephew, Vivien, his vow never to flee from pagans, and his death at Archamps. *Aliscans* gives relatively more attention to Rainoart, Orable's brother. Rainoart enters *Aliscans* at about l. 3000 and from then on, for the remaining five to six thousand lines, he is the central figure; in the *Chanson*, he is not mentioned before l. 2660 and the poem ends at l. 3554. The *Chanson* begins before the battle, with the news that the pagans are attacking. Vivien's first impulse is to summon his uncle, William, but he is dissuaded by the boasting and drunken Esturmi who insists on facing the enemy, despite the inadequate numbers of the Christian forces. Although Esturmi wants to back down in the morning, when he actually sees the size of the pagan army, Vivien feels that, having shown themselves, they must fight. Esturmi and his own uncle flee the field, leaving Vivien to defend the Christian standards. He fights hard and long, but when he retreats to take a drink at a stream, he is surrounded by pagans and killed. He is later found by William with his hands crossed and a sweet odor surrounding his body; he revives only long enough to receive communion from his uncle.[22] In *Aliscans* the death scene is far more painful. Vivien prays to see his uncle before he dies, but an angel comes to tell him that his prayer will not be answered. William, who has been fighting in a different part of the field, does in fact get to him, and even administers communion but, ironically, although he himself has fled a considerable distance, he cannot comfort his nephew, who has broken his vow never to flee from pagans. Vivien had not gone far before he recovered himself and returned to battle, but he does not know if he went further than the thrust of a lance, the distance specified in his vow, and he dies with that tormenting doubt unresolved. The angel's words may reflect a different version in which William did not find Vivien alive, but the effect in *Aliscans* is to heighten the tragedy of Vivien's death.

22. This passage occurs in the second part of the poem, after line 1981, which is sometimes referred to as G2 or "Chanson de Rainoart," and is considered by most scholars to be later than the first part, the "Chanson de Guillaume" proper.

All that remains in both versions is for William to gather a new army and avenge his nephew. In the *Chanson,* William is ready to give up several times, but Guiborc insists on action. It is she who says better to die at Archamps than dishonor the family, and who refuses to let him retire to a monastery, but sends him instead to Louis for reinforcements. She even gathers an army on her own to support him. In *Aliscans,* Guiborc is less heroic and more human. She blames herself for the deaths of William's men, since his feud with the pagans began when he stole her from them. Knowing he will never have peace unless he defeats them now, she encourages him to go to Louis, despite her qualms that he will meet other women along the way and forget her and she defends Orange with great courage while he is gone.

William's experience at the court is handled quite differently in the two works. In the *Chanson,* it is just a necessary transition from the defeat at Archamps to the victory with new troops. Louis receives William well and promises his support. The only jarring note is struck by the queen, who is afraid that Guiborc is a sorceress and will kill Louis to steal the throne for William. The emphasis here is on the distrust of pagans, rather than the pettiness of the French royal couple, as in *Aliscans.* In the longer work, the king and queen are treated roughly. Their insensitivity and ingratitude to William are contrasted to the loneliness of defeat and misfortune that he suffers from the moment he sets out for the court. He is shabbily equipped and without company; he rides hard, scarcely eating or sleeping, drawing scorn and attacks all along the way. When he gets to court, Louis refuses to receive him because he knows it will mean trouble; the people who had received gifts from William before, scorn him now. Only his family, goaded by his mother's heroic offer to fight, supports him and forces Louis eventually to come through, and even then the queen is ungracious about it.

The rest of the story, brief in the *Chanson* but extensive in *Aliscans,* tells the adventures of Rainoart, whom William has picked up at the French court. Both works describe a number of the same incidents, though in different order: the theft of Rainoart's club; his frequently forgetting it; his moustaches set on fire; forcing the army to rise early *after* a battle; driving the cowards back to battle and taking command of them; rescuing captives, but having difficulty providing them with arms (*Chanson*) or horses (*Aliscans*), since one blow of his club destroys man and equipment; and, finally, his baptism and marriage. In the *Chanson* his bride is an unidentified Ermentrude, but in *Aliscans* it is the French princess, Williams's niece and supporter, Aelis.[23]

At the end of *Aliscans,* William is weary of the long fighting and depressed by the death of his nephew and the departure of his brothers, but his wife, Guiborc, encourages him to go on, to gather workers and rebuild Orange, offering to supervise it herself. They continue, we are told at the beginning of the *Moniage,* to live in peace for many years before Guiborc dies and William is summoned by an angel to withdraw from the world and become a monk. The shorter *Moniage,* the version translated here, presents three episodes: William's life in the monastery, his adventure in the forest with robbers, and his retirement to the desert as a hermit, which is interrupted, as the poem breaks off, by a call for help from Louis. In the longer *Moniage,* the same incidents are recounted and expanded and many more are added. The monks are condemned more severely for their hypocrisy and stinginess. When they send William on a dangerous road, in hopes of getting rid of him, they not only tell him he must not fight; they even promise that if he is killed he will be a martyr and they will ring the bells for his soul. They are stingy to their guests in the monastery, while William is known for his generosity.

After William leaves the abbey for good, in the longer poem, he stays with a hermit, a cousin of his, whose house is too small for the gigantic hero. Attacked at night by a dozen thieves, the cousins kill six of them and hang the others, to the relief of neighboring hermits. In the next episode, William wanders to a cliff overlooking a deserted valley and a serpent-infested rapids, which God clears at his request. An angel tells William he will enter Paradise, but he must suffer first. When he starts to build himself a home, the noise attracts a cannibalistic giant, whom William must fight and kill. Then he completes his home, with a chapel and garden, and lives an ascetic life until he is attacked by Saracens. Though he kills many of them, they finally carry him off to Salerno and put him into a flooded prison cell, filled with serpents. There he remains for seven years, living on bread and water. Another

23. In the M Manuscript of *Aliscans,* Rainoart marries Ermentrut, a niece of Ermengard, when Louis will not allow him to marry his daughter. Tyssens considers this detail an attempt to conciliate divergent traditions (p. 261).

cousin of his, Landry, who had gone to Jerusalem as a pilgrim, had been captured by pagans, ransomed and then captured by pirates, is eventually brought before William's captor, Synagon. The latter offers to free William, now thin and entirely covered by his own hair, if Landry can persuade Louis to bring the French army to fight him. Louis comes to save William, who is kept in a tower when the armies meet so that he cannot help the French. But, when the pagan army is so reduced that only women are left to guard the city, William escapes and, with his support, the French win.

William returns once again to his retreat, but Synagon's nephew, Ysoré, fourteen feet tall, comes to France with sixty thousand men to avenge his uncle, and lays siege to Paris. Louis, surrounded by flatterers and scoundrels, has alienated all his loyal vassals and is unable to defend the city. He sends again for William, but the messenger does not know the hero when he finds him. He does however tell his message to the unrecognized hermit and reports the hermit's reaction—the hermit tore out the good plants in his own garden and replaced them with weeds and thorns. When the messenger relates this incident at court, an old duke, recognizing William from the description of the hermit, interprets the story: the good plants are the loyal vassals Louis has chased away, the weeds are the traitors and liars he supports.

William, of course, does not fail to answer Louis' summons; he goes to Paris secretly, picking up his arms and horse at the monastery where he had left them many years before; the horse has since been used as a draft animal, leading a humble life like his master. When William reaches Paris, at night, he is not recognized and is refused entrance, so he remains outside with a peasant, Bernard, whose house, like the cousin's earlier, is not large enough for William, but is miraculously expanded by God. The hero fights Ysoré and kills him, leaving the giant's head with the peasant. When a cousin of Ganelon claims to have killed Ysoré himself, Bernard shows the head and reveals the truth, but William has already gone.

Back at his retreat, William tries to build a bridge over the rapids, but every night the work he has done is destroyed. One night he waits, catches the devil who is responsible, and throws him into the water, creating a whirlpool. Then he finishes the bridge. He remains there until he dies and his soul goes to Paradise. The place, henceforth, is known as St. Guillaume-du-Désert, a stop on the pilgrimage route to Santiago.

historical background

There are certain obvious similarities in the political background of all the poems in this cycle: the problems that arise from a weak monarchy, the threats from traitors within and from foreign, usually pagan, enemies without. These are situations that were real not only in the period in which the poems are set, the early ninth century, but also at the time they were written down in their present form, the twelfth century, and on and off during the intervening centuries. Although the monarchy was reasonably strong under Charlemagne, it would not be so again until the late Capetians. First there was the problem of succession, which plagued Carolingian and Capetian kings until the late twelfth century. Charlemagne associated his son Louis with him on the throne in order to insure his succession, and most other kings did the same until Phillip Augustus. There was a continual problem of heirs too young or of no heirs at all—some Capetians married three times in order to produce a son—and when there were several possible heirs there was usually fighting among them. In the late Carolingian period vassalage replaced the principle of monarchy as the dominant political force since the Capetian kings were weaker than their vassals. They preserved the monarchy but lost land. Nonetheless, the nobles took the relation of vassal to liege seriously enough to pay homage to the king and to accept his interference in their affairs. But since the king wielded little real power, nobles did not bother to come to his court (under Phillip I, in the late eleventh century, there was only one full assembly), so the royal retinue took over the position of advisors to the king; jealousy and resentment were the result. This is certainly reflected in the court scene in *Aliscans,* where the king is surrounded by men more cowardly and ungrateful than himself, and in the description of the courtiers in the longer *Moniage.*

The king who appears in the poems, Charlemagne's son Louis, has much in common with his historic counterpart. Although he was considerably older at the time of his coronation, he spent much of his reign under the influence of churchmen, particularly his mentor St. Benedict of Aniane. He had been religiously educated and attempted to impose more stringent morals on what had been a fairly lax court under his father; he even made a public confession of his own sins (in 822), in the hope of inspiring his subjects to reform, but this seems to have done his reputation as much damage as good. His religious leanings may well have inspired the remarks in the poem that he might be more fit to be a monk than king.

The problems with foreign enemies were another constant factor in the Carolingian and Capetian periods. France first coped with the pagan Saxons, then with the Magyars in the East, with the Moslems from Spain in the southwest and, by the early tenth century, in Italy as well; with Lombards in the south, and Vikings, first in the north and then everywhere. Later, of course, there were the Turks in Africa and the Near East. But the most continual battle was waged in the south against Moslem invasions and raids. After Charles Martel's victory at Poitiers in 732, there was a continual series of encounters between Franks and Spanish Moslems. Although Charlemagne himself crossed the Pyrenees only once, there were important battles with Moslem forces during his reign at Narbonne and Barcelona.

During the ninth century various Arab and Berber factions that kept the Moslem state in turmoil made expeditions into France less of a threat, but there were occasional persecutions of Christians in Spain by fanatic Moslems. Christians in the northeast, independent, though still thought of by the French as their "marche d'Espagne," meanwhile attempted to rebuild ruined cities and reestablish a Christian nation. By 930 the Arab states of the south were unified in the Caliphate of Cordoba, which proved too strong a force for the Christian princes of the north who were at odds with each other as often as not. In the latter part of the tenth century, the first minister of the Caliph, Mahomet ibn-Abi-Amir, known as Almanzor or Al-Mansur, the Victorious, led a series of impressive attacks on Christian strongholds: he sacked Barcelona in 985, Leon in 987; he conquered Pamplona, destroyed the monastery of Sahagun, and occupied Santiago of Compostela.

The Arabs had their own problems with Moslem fanatics who dominated North Africa from the early tenth century and came to Spain from time to time, summoned either to fight off the attacks of Christians, or to support the more rabid Moslems against the Christian influences that threatened to destroy the purity of Islam within the Moslem states. The

Christians and Moslems who lived together in Arab Spain were culturally compatible, to the distress of their more rigid co-religionists. The Spanish Christian ability to understand and respect the Moslem created problems with the French who came to fight fairly steadily from the early eleventh century until the Albigensian crusade. The Spanish often promised to preserve the mosques and religious freedom of the Moslems they conquered, and generally kept their promises, whereas the French distrusted them, believed them to be an evil race, and preferred to destroy if they could not convert them.

Although one Moslem raid reached Narbonne in 1020, the movement in the eleventh and twelfth centuries was generally in the other direction. This is a period of French involvement, militarily and politically, in Spanish affairs, although by the twelfth century the Spanish Christians were securely established, and the French who wished to find lands for themselves went to the East rather than to Spain. Spain was considered a "Holy War"—Pope Alexander II granted an indulgence to those who fought for the cross in Spain in 1063—but there was more to be gained in the Holy Land.

The Crusades in the East do not figure in the William poems, but there is no question that their existence influenced the treatment of the great struggle for Christianity. The vows that the first crusaders took not to turn back until they reached Jerusalem are no doubt reflected in the rather reckless oaths sworn by so many of the epic heroes, and the fierce devotion to the cause, the willingness to be martyred, the descriptions of monstrous pagan enemies and their vicious treatment of Christian prisoners in the epics suggest the eastern wars more than the Reconquista. The taking of innumerable prisoners for ransom, the swift remarriage of the widows of governing princes in order to maintain a government, although they occurred throughout medieval Europe, were carried on much more frequently and more flagrantly in the East during the Crusades.

Christians and pagans in the poems

The treatment of the Christian-pagan struggle in the poems is simple and unsophisticated. The Saracens are generally presented as monstrous creatures, often physically deformed, brutal to their Christian prisoners, moving in huge hordes that terrify by noise as well as number. Most of them are fit only to be defeated and destroyed; a very few are converted to Christianity (Galafré in the *Couronnement,* Guiborc in the *Prise,* Rainoart and Baudus in *Aliscans*), but curiously, those who convert often turn out better Christians than the Franks. Rainoart's charity puts to shame his Christian companions, to say nothing of the monks. The religious attacks by the pagans on Christianity are contemptuous and violent, but they are not accurate reflections of Moslem positions; they tend to be simply anti-Christian, or, if anything, dualistic. Although Moslems are monotheists, in the poems they worship a small pantheon, swearing by Cahu, Apollo, and Tervagant, as well as Mohammed.[24]

The Christian faith presented in the poems is not so distorted, but it is certainly simplified. It is limited to the use of relics, the appearance of angels, and the credos uttered by the heroes at moments of danger, which are a listing of miracles from the Bible. The treatment of churchmen is somewhat more sophisticated. They are not the ideal counterparts of the evil pagans: the pope is a materialistic and inconsequential figure in the *Couronnement;* the abbot and monks of the *Moniage* and *Aliscans* are greedy hypocrites; all but one priest in the *Couronnement* is a traitor to the king. There is no religious figure of stature except William himself, and his treatment of his fellow monks, however deserved it may be, is startling behavior, even for a warrior-saint.

William's attitude towards pagans, however, is consonant with the context of the poems. They are shown in such an unsympathetic light that we are not shocked at his claim that by killing those who hate God and charity he is destroying evil. When we are told that William takes no Saracen prisoners, that he kills everyone he defeats, we are meant to see that he puts the service of God above his own personal gain; he does not hold them for ransom, as Louis, for instance, would like to do with Rainoart. The pagans, on the other hand, not only capture Christians, but torture them as long as they hold them in prison (see the report of the escaped Christian in the *Prise,* laisse VIII; the treatment of captured

24. Crosland, p. 142, suggests that Apollo may be the Apollyon of the Apocalypse, representing destruction, rather than the Greek god. Frappier posits a connection between Cahu and "chaos" (II, 124), and for the explanation of Tervagant, prefers Grégoire's suggestion that it is a transformation of Diana Trivia (II, 122). Spitzer, in "Tervagant," *Romania,* 70 (1948–49), 397 ff., thinks it might come from the Latin "Terrificans."

Italians in the *Couronnement,* ll. 1329 ff; and of William's nephews in *Aliscans,* laisse XIV).

In their physical appearance as well as their actions, the pagans are hideous monsters, more like inhabitants of hell than human beings. The second part of *Aliscans* presents a fascinating series of such creatures: Aenre, wielding a steel hammer, has strangled and eaten untold Franks; Borrel wears animal skins and is accompanied by fourteen sons, all bearing whips; Baudus, a cousin of Rainoart, is fifteen feet tall, black, with eyes like burning coals, a huge face, and carries the mast of a ship as his weapon; Haucebier, with eyes half a foot apart and red, has more force than fourteen Slavs; Agrapars is only three feet tall but broad, with red eyes, jagged teeth, a swollen mouth, a hooked nose, a hairy body and sharp nails that serve as his weapons; Walegrape, a brother of Rainoart, fourteen feet tall, with long teeth and a tongue of which half hangs out of his mouth, wears a serpent's hide and carries a crook; Grishart, from "beyond the lost isle," wields a hatchet and eats raw human flesh; his sister, Flohart, fifteen feet tall, wearing buffalo hide and armed with a scythe, emits a stinking smoke from her mouth and bites off and swallows pieces of Rainoart's hauberk.

As a group, the pagans are referred to as cowards, pigs, dogs, sons of bitches, or devils. They appear in vast troops of tens of thousands, shouting and sounding horns and drums; however often they are pushed back, replacements keep pouring from their ships. The numbers are particularly emphasized in *Aliscans,* where pagans outnumber Christians sometimes one hundred to one, but never less than fifteen to one. The numbers are wildly out of proportion in the *Prise* as well, where three Christian knights, William and two of his nephews, fight off the entire pagan population of the city and put them to flight.

Although pagans are no more sympathetic figures in the *Prise* than in the other poems, there is more verisimilitude in the description of the luxurious existence they lead in Orange. The palace is magnificently decorated with paintings, marble, and precious metals. The Moslem prince remarks that his father would have done better to stick to boy-lovers than to marry a young wife; this is meant to show the decadence of Arab life, but it also indicates a closer acquaintance with that life than is found in the other poems. The poet is no less biased in his view of the pagans: when they recognize William and reveal his identity to their king, they are not loyal Saracens but treacherous villains, whereas Orable is commended for betraying her people and helping the Christians. Pagan demands that Christians renounce their faith are considered mad, but similar Christian demands are valid and, if refused, justify the killing of the recalcitrant pagan.

There are many pagan taunts thrown at Christians as they fight— "expect no help from your God now"—but only a few instances of direct attack on Christian beliefs. In *Aliscans,* Aerofle, an uncle of Rainoart's, offers peace to William if he will deny the "holy trinity," baptism, Jesus' power, and the humanity of the virgin; when William refuses, Aerofle tells him that the faith of Christianity is based entirely on sorcery, the sacraments are worth nothing, for God is up beyond the firmament, while the earth is under the rule of Mohammed, who provides man with storms and wind, fruit and wine. This hint of dualism, the idea that the earth belongs to Mohammed, which for the poet and his audience was tantamount to saying to the devil, may be a reflection of Cathar or Manichee beliefs, rather than Moslem. The confusion of the two occurs in the *Couronnement* as well.[25] Corsolt, the giant that William meets in single combat, is engaged in a feud with Christians in order to avenge himself on their God, who killed his father with a bolt of lightning and then withdrew to the sky where he could not be pursued. Since Corsolt cannot get Him, he destroys as many of His followers as he can. The giant's object is to rule the earth and confine God to heaven: the earth is mine, the sky can be His (l. 537).

These two pagans, Aerofle and Corsolt, speak for the vast majority of Saracens in the poems; obstinate in their mistaken beliefs, they cannot be saved and are fit only to die. But there are a very few who are willing to be baptized, although they are usually moved by practical considerations. Galafré, in the *Couronnement,* acknowledges the superior power of the Christian God when the Christian champion defeats Corsolt; "Mohammed can no longer help me," he says (l. 1282). From the moment he decides to convert, however, he becomes a zealous defender of the Christian cause, even proposing a way to undo his former comrades. This is perhaps disturbing to our notions of honor, but it is meant as a

25. For a discussion of Cathar elements in the *Couronnement*—the division of spheres and the attack on priests and sacraments—see Scheludko, "Neues über das CL," *ZfSL,* 55 (1932), 428–74, particularly 458.

sign of his devotion to his new faith. Rainoart's cousin, Baudus, refuses all of Rainoart's pleas that he become a Christian, and it is only when he is defeated by him and nearly killed that he agrees to be baptized. Even Orable, who, as Guiborc, is destined to be William's strongest support in the fight for the faith, agrees to become a Christian and to help the trapped heroes if William will marry her. She is not unaffected by the beauty of the hero and his material possessions.

Only Rainoart appears to have a disinterested desire for conversion, but he too, when William overlooks him in the victory celebration, is ready to renounce Christianity, to return to Mohammed and make war on William. In fairness, however, this is meant more to emphasize the enormity of the offense to Rainoart's pride than the shallowness of his Christianity. In general, Rainoart is more Christian than most of the other characters in the poems. He is kind to the poor; he feeds the beggars outside a monastery though, like William, he mistreats the monks within, but they deserve it; he punishes a pagan troop for stealing beans from a poor farmer and he richly reimburses the farmer; he utters a long and moving prayer, not simply for his own victory, but for the conversion of his cousin Baudus, whom he had loved as a child; and he is as fierce in his defense of the Christian cause as any of William's kin. Indeed, like Guiborc, he puts loyalty to William and to Christianity over his old family ties, defeating cousins and brothers and even his father. (For interrelations of the pagans, see family tree, p. 11.)

Rainoart does have some trouble adjusting to Christian ceremonies however; he objects to being held for his baptism and breaks free from his godfathers during the rites. But he has similar difficulties with the formalities of knighthood. He moves slowly from the kitchen oaf wielding a huge club to the giant champion who routs the pagan forces with club and sword. He is, of course, destined to be a great Christian warrior and, like William, even a monk.

On the whole, the converted pagans make a better show in the poems than the Christians whose lives are supposed to be dedicated to God, the men of religion. The pope, in the *Couronnement,* is a vacillating and rather ineffective figure. At first he offers William an excessively comprehensive indulgence if he will fight to save Rome: he absolves William of any sin he may commit in the *future,* except treason; William himself is surprised at this, "no priest ever had such a generous heart" (l. 399). But when the pope sees William's adversary, he loses faith in the outcome and tries to buy off the pagan king with all the wealth of the church. One wonders why he did not use this wealth earlier, and why he has so little faith in God's help; indeed, William must encourage him to trust to God. When the battle goes badly the pope threatens God, vowing to stop all church services if William is hurt, as if God were a minor deity to be cajoled and rewarded; an attitude not very different from Corsolt's, who feuds with a cowardly deity fleeing human revenge. It is surely not coincidental that this pope is not even able to finish the rites he performs: when the coronation of young Louis is interrupted, it is William who finishes the ceremony; when William's marriage is interrupted by messengers from Louis, William leaves both bride and pope at the altar.

The other church figures who appear in the *Couronnement* are engaged in conspiracies against the king, "bishops and archbishops," the poet says, acting probably as political lords, against whom William takes swift and violent revenge inside the church. It is interesting that, whereas in the early part of the poem William would not draw his sword in church against a traitorous nobleman, he does so later against churchmen. The poem's prevailing attitude towards churchmen is scornful, perhaps best illustrated by Charlemagne's remark to his timid son that he might as well go off and become a monk.

In *Aliscans* and the *Moniage,* the only churchmen who appear are monks, but they are no better than the bishops or pope. They treat themselves well and ignore the needs of others. In *Aliscans,* Rainoart finds good food inside a monastery, which he distributes to the beggars waiting, unheeded, outside, having first eaten his fill. When William becomes a monk, he brings great wealth to the monastery; nonetheless the monks begrudge the enormous quantity of food and cloth his body needs, and they particularly resent his attempts to force them to observe their own rules. In desperation, they plot his death, not scrupling to use religious restrictions to further their ends—William is sent on a dangerous trip but forbidden to use any weapons in his own defense. William, however, foils the plot; told he can use only flesh and bone against attackers, he tears the haunch off a pack animal and fights with that. God crowns his victory with a miracle, restoring the animal's limb, and makes it clear which side has the right. When William returns to the monastery, he has to force his way in, and avenges himself furiously on his fellow monks, but when he offers his newly won treasures to the abbot and begs forgiveness, the calculating prelate accepts and absolves him with the somewhat startling remark that it does not matter, new monks are not hard to find. The dead are, in fact, buried and forgotten by dinner. When William leaves the monastery, the monks rejoice and the abbot gives him money to make sure he will never return. The poet loses no opportunity to condemn monks; even the robbers who attack William excuse their raids on monasteries by saying that monks are too rich; they should be giving to the poor and thinking about matins, and leave material concerns to others.

Although William's violence against the monks is shocking from our point of view, it is only fair to recall that there are historic instances of monks shutting their superiors out of monasteries and barring the doors to them, or of deposed abbots forcibly retaking their monasteries.[26] Allowing for the epic exaggeration, William's violence is not unusual. The lax observation of rules in the cloister is probably a reflection of the customs for which religious orders, particularly Cluny, were attacked by the more austere Cistercians in the early twelfth century: luxury in clothing, richness of food and the number of dishes served, general greed and pride.[27] William, unlike his fellow monks, takes his vocation seriously; he learns all the offices and recites them regularly; he does not miss a service, a practice that annoys the other monks, presumably because it shows them up.

The William of the *Moniage* is divinely inspired—an angel was sent to tell him to become a monk, another to tell him to leave the monastery and live as a hermit—but this is not inconsistent with the character of the hero as he appears in the other epics. When he finds the dying Vivien, he does the office of a priest, asking if he has taken communion, then confessing him and giving him the wafer that he carries. When his army is destroyed at *Aliscans,* he worries that Christianity in France may be doomed, that there will be no more masses or matins said if the Saracens overrun the land. There are, of course, moments when William

26. *Life of St. Odo of Cluny,* by John of Salerno, trans. by Dom Gerard Sitwell (London, 1958) Bk. III, chap. viii; and J. Evans, *Monastic Life at Cluny* (Oxford, 1951), 38–39.

27. St. Bernard of Clairvaux, cited by J. Evans, p. 45.

is more worldly than pious: he fights for God but he is also anxious to avoid having bad songs sung about him; sometimes he is more concerned with his own safety than with the fate of captive Christians; but in the main his faith, strong and simple, dictates his actions. He will not shed blood inside a church, so he does not draw his sword, although he has no scruple about killing a traitor with his fist. He drops anything to help his king, but he leaves the king, despite his pleas, to fulfill a vow to go to Rome.

Perhaps the best indication of the simple religion expressed in these poems is in the prayer the heroes utter in moments of grave danger, "la prière du plus grand péril," Frappier calls it.[28] Prayers vary in length from the very short ones in the *Prise* (between four and fourteen lines), to quite long ones in the *Couronnement* (fifty-four and ninety-five lines); in *Aliscans,* Rainoart's, the longest, is forty-six lines, the others from nine to twenty-four. The prayers are part of the stock of epic poetry; they follow the same pattern and draw on the same material with only slight variations. The pattern they follow is to list God's works from creation to the miracles of the gospels and to end with the formula "Si com c'est veir (or 'voirs')," "As this is true . . . defend me from death"; in other words, as I believe in your power, use it for me now. Only the major heroes speak these prayers: William is the only one to do so in the *Prise* and the *Couronnement*; Vivien and Rainoart each recite one in *Aliscans*. Vivien prays to see William before he dies; Rainoart prays for his own safety and the defeat of his cousin Baudus, so that he may convert him. William prays mainly for his deliverance and, in *Aliscans,* to return to Guiborc and his family; there is one exception, while he is watching Rainoart fight Baudus, when he prays for Rainoart.

The events alluded to most often in the prayers are creation,[29] Adam and Eve and original sin, the Virgin birth, the passion, the repentance of Mary Magdalene, the crucifixion and recovery of Longinus, the resurrection and the harrowing of hell, the miraculous rescue of Old Testament figures, particularly Daniel and Jonah. The last three events are victories over the devil, similar to the hero's predicament in his fight

28. Frappier, II, 132.

29. E. Mâle, *L'Art réligieux du 12ᵉ s. en France* (Paris, 1928), 49, on the primitive Christian prayer for souls of the dead, which is similar to the prayers heroes utter in the chansons.

with the infidel. Other events are sometimes featured in a single prayer—Palm Sunday, Judgment, the miracle of St. Anastasia. There is occasional variation in the descriptions of the events, e.g., creation. Compare the single line in the *Prise:* "Glorieus sire, qui formas tote gent" (l. 498) with the following passages from the *Couronnement:*

> Glorios pere, qui formas tot le mont,
> Qui fesis terre sor le marbrin perron,
> De mer salee la ceinsis environ,
> Adam fesis de terre et de limon (ll. 976 ff)

and from *Aliscans:*

> Glorious dex, qui le mont establis
> Et home et feme destinas et fesis
> Osiax et bestes et les grans gaus foillis
> Et ciel et terre, infier et paradis,
> Les egues douces et les poisons petis.

king and vassal

William's devotion to God and his faith never wavers, despite the character of the churchmen he encounters; similarly, his loyalty to his king, Louis, is constant despite Louis' unworthiness. But of the two causes that demand William's loyalty and service throughout his life, Christianity and the monarchy, the monarchy presents many more problems. Although William never wavers in his devotion or in his sense of what he, as a vassal, owes his king, the king's inadequacies often make it difficult for William to carry out his part. When Louis appears in these poems, he serves the poetic function of foil to the hero—his impotence, cowardice, and selfishness set off William's heroism and self-sacrifice. Louis' character, consistent in the cycle, carries a political message, the dangers that a weak king poses for his country: his impotence leaves the way open for attack from outside and for treachery from within. The example he sets produces a court and a retinue of selfish, cowardly men who only weaken his position further. In the *Couronnement,* against the background of the ideal king, Charlemagne, who appears briefly at the beginning, we are shown the totally ineffective Louis, falling into one crisis after another, from which the ever-loyal William must rescue him.

In *Aliscans* it is William who is in need of help, but although it is Louis' obligation to give that aid, it has to be extracted from him by force.

The *Couronnement* opens with Charlemagne's magnificent injunctions to his son, who is about to be crowned, on the duties of a king: he must protect the rights and properties of his subjects, poor and rich alike; he must crush pagans and uphold the church, cherish his knights but show no mercy to traitors, and never indulge himself in greed or vice. For God created kings to govern their people with justice. In the course of his life within the cycle, Louis is destined to transgress all of his father's commands; even at the coronation he is afraid to commit himself and his hesitation invites the traitor Arneis' offer to serve as regent until Louis can govern by himself. This would not have been an unusual situation, although it often led, as the poet clearly means us to assume it would here, to the usurpation of the throne. Indeed, what William does is not so different from what Arneis offered to do. He crowns the young king himself, surely an extension of his rights—the pope, after all, is present and the emperor himself would more properly crown his son than one of his nobles—and takes the responsibility for insuring Louis' reign. He even has the audacity to kill Arneis, whom he alone has proclaimed a traitor, in the presence of the king, a rather shocking instance of taking the law into his hands, and yet the king is thankful for it, knowing William and his family to be devoted servants of the crown. The audience, presumably, accepts William's actions here because, like the king, it knows that he will never fail in his loyalty.

What of the young king, however, who at fifteen hesitates to assume his responsibility, and five years later, when his father dies, is still not ready to defend himself? When the next plot against him breaks out, Louis hides in a church. It is surely not accidental that Charlemagne, in disgust, had threatened to make him a monk when he first demurred; the church seems to be where Louis belongs. But once again, William quells the revolt, establishes order in the land, and restores Louis to his throne. William continues to support Louis and to set him up in positions that he cannot maintain on his own. When he takes the young king to Italy to assert his rights over a German claimant, Louis hides in terror from an enemy attack. Nonetheless, when William defeats the enemy, he makes Louis lord of Rome. In each section of the poem, William carries out a duty that should properly be the king's to perform: in parts I, III, and V he puts down rebellion and establishes order in France; in II and IV he defends the faith, the pope, and Rome from pagans and from Germans and thereby strengthens the French claim to the Western empire. William does all this, as Hagen does in the *Niebelungenlied,* in the service of the monarchy, a concept he believes in, despite the unworthiness of the particular king. But does the poet, albeit he certainly respects William, entirely agree with his blind devotion? One wonders. There are so many reasonable arguments for deposing Louis during the course of the poem: the words of the traitors, Arneis and Acelin, who point out that Louis is a child (William himself refers to him tenderly as a child, even when he is twenty, and certainly he acts like one) and that he does not have the power or skill to govern the country, a fact Louis goes out of his way to prove; also the far more damning words of William's nephew Bertrand at the end of the poem. It was Bertrand who alerted William to Louis' danger at the very beginning of the poem, so his loyalty to the crown cannot be questioned; but by the end he is so disgusted with Louis' failures that he bitterly advises his uncle to forget the king—to leave France to the devil along with her foolish monarch, who will never be able to hold a foot of his inheritance. William has no real answer to this; he simply repeats that he will spend his youth in Louis' service.

Louis' behavior in *Aliscans* suggests that Bertrand was right. In this poem, the king is condemned outright by his every action, as well as by the forceful contrast between the selfishness and luxury of his court and the self-sacrifice and suffering of the Franks at Orange. After the battle at Aliscans, in which William's nephew Vivien was killed, seven other nephews captured by Saracens, and William himself badly abused, the weary, battle-stained hero rushes to Louis' court to ask the help that Louis is required to give him every seven years. This was part of the contract made between liege and vassal when William accepted as his fief the pagan territories that he had to win for himself. The courtiers are both scornful of his shabby appearance, although they had received rich gifts from him in the past, and afraid that he will lead them into further wars. The poet does not need to remind us that if William were not constantly fighting off the Saracens in the south, they would soon threaten the self-indulgent nobles of the north. But the Franks at court are not anxious to lose more men in the south; they wish William dead or far away from France. Their selfish view makes them turn the whole situation upside down: refusing to join William in God's battle, they ask God to take him out of their way; ignoring the pagan threat that he holds back, they see William as the danger to France.

But the ingratitude and self-indulgence of the courtiers is mild compared to the king's. Although he has always been quick to summon William to his aid, when William makes the same request of him, the king curses him as a living devil who brings only trouble, and rejoices in his distress! He sets a guard against William's entrance and attempts to ignore William's presence while he makes a great deal of William's family, the father and brothers, who are his richest and most powerful supporters—they still have something to give whereas William now needs something from him. When William threatens Louis, the latter responds like a petulant child, telling William to go ahead and take everything he has. His behavior is in every way undignified, petty, even effeminate. Not only does he close his court to his most loyal vassal, who has been through a disastrous war, but he has the lack of taste to lean out the window, holding a sprig of mustard in his hand, and scold William for his shabby appearance, telling him to go and get cleaned up and then come back for dinner. Every detail points up Louis' pettiness. When he rides out with William and they discover that the monastery in which William's armor was stored has burnt, the rich king gives fifty pounds for its repair, while his indigent vassal gives one hundred. He keeps a pagan slave, Rainoart, in his kitchen and will not permit him to be baptized, partly because he is afraid of him, and wants to keep him out of the way, but mainly because he hopes to get a ransom for him from his pagan relatives. How short-sighted this attitude is we see when William rescues him from the kitchen and Rainoart becomes the most effective fighter in the Christian army.

Even William's loyalty is strained in the service of such a poor figure of a king, but it takes continued abuse to bring him to the point of violence, and his fury builds up slowly. When he is met with scorn and refused entrance to the court, he sits with his bare sword across his knees, a gesture of defiance (cf. Hagen at the court of Atli, finding himself similarly surrounded by enemies when he has come as a guest), but he confines himself to threats; he does not act. The next day he enters the court with his sword under his cloak, presumably to defend himself, but as the attitude of the king and of the queen, William's sister, remains obstinate, he begins to take the offensive. A magnificent figure of indignation, his clothing in shreds but his head erect, he bares his sword to the king and calls him a coward and his queen a whore, sparing no details in his description of her self-indulgence. This seems to be a rhetorical attack, like the flytings of Anglo-Saxon, the exchange of taunts between heroes in Germanic epics, or the "gabs" of French *chansons de geste;* William does not mean his insults to be taken literally, for later, when he is reconciled with his sister, he apologizes and praises her without qualification. He climaxes his attack on the couple by seizing the queen's crown and throwing it to the ground, a gesture of contempt which one could not have imagined from the young hero of the *Couronnement.* When Louis hesitates to fulfill the promise that has finally been extracted from him, William threatens to withdraw his vassalage, not a startling move by contemporary standards, but shocking in the light of William's previous blind devotion. Even William's father, who supports his son and puts pressure on the king to help him, cannot bring himself to attack Louis' friends, let alone the king himself: I would imprison the great princes of France, *if it were not treason,* he says (ll. 3075–77).

William's loyalty to his king, despite the ill-usage he has suffered, continues through his life. At the beginning of the *Moniage,* he leaves his arms in a church when he prepares to enter the monastery, but with the proviso that if either his godson or his king need his help, he will take up the arms again. The shorter *Moniage* breaks off with a description of Louis' troubles: he has alienated all the men of good birth, who hold him in contempt for his avarice and foolishness, and has surrounded himself with evil councillors who steal from him. There is no one to defend him from the attack of the pagans. Once again William must rescue him.

figure of William

William's whole life is given to the double service of God and king. In the poems that describe his early life, he is a young warrior, fighting for his king and to win glory, lands, and a bride for himself; which he must do twice over (he gives up the first land and bride to return to Louis). In his later life he is a patriarch, upholding the great cause of Christianity, but with lands of his own to defend and a vast family to support him. In the intervening years, we are told at the end of the *Prise,* not a day passed without a Saracen challenge. Like Beowulf, whom we also see move from a young warrior to an old king, and like Charlemagne at the end of the *Chanson de Roland,* William is tired out by the end of *Aliscans.* He is temporarily inspired by Guiborc to go on, but when she dies, he gives up the world. Even in his hermitage, however, the messengers of Louis reach him, and the Saracens continue to threaten.

Despite the passage of time and changes in his world, William's character, like his loyalties, is consistent throughout the cycle. In appearance he is huge (except in comparison to giants like Corsolt), with a powerful arm. Hence the epithet "Fierebrace," which is explained in the *Couronnement:* when William refrains from drawing his sword against Arneis in church, he must rely on his fist; it proves as effective as an axe, hence the name "strong-arm." He is also distinguished by a short or crooked nose, which supplies a second epithet, "corb nes," or, possibly a corrupted form, "cort nes." In an apparent attempt to reconcile the two meanings, the *Charroi de Nîmes* tells how William was wounded and then adds that the doctors who treated him did a bad job and left a bump on the nose. The wound is inflicted by Corsolt in the *Couronnement,* who taunts him with it, for a mutilated nose was a punishment visited on criminals, and therefore a shameful sign. Characteristically, William turns the taunt into a boast: my nose may be somewhat shorter, but my name will be longer . . . from now on I'll be called Count William, the knight of the shortened nose (ll. 1159–64). The nose does indeed become his trademark; his wife refuses to recognize him, in *Aliscans,* until he lifts his visor and shows it to her.

William carries Charlemagne's sword Joyeuse but, unlike Roland, he is far more devoted to his horse, Baucent. William's passion for horses, unusually strong even for a warrior, is one of his most appealing characteristics. In the *Couronnement* he is so anxious to ride the defeated Corsolt's horse, which he has been careful not to harm during the battle, that he mounts it without adjusting the stirrups; they were fitted to the giant's stature, so the hero cuts a comic figure indeed. In *Aliscans* he continually endangers himself rather than strike his enemy in a way that might harm the mount, and he takes horses in preference to any other booty from his defeated opponents; when he can't take one, he cuts off its head rather than leave it to pagans. This may seem cruel, but it is to be taken, like Roland's attempt to destroy his sword rather than let it fall into infidel hands, as love for the creature and disgust for the enemy. He speaks tenderly to his own mount, Baucent, many times during the battle, encouraging him with promises of rest and food and a good deal of sympathy, which Baucent acknowledges with a whinny. He tries not to ride him too hard, not even when he is being pursued by the enemy, and when he wins himself a new horse, Folatil, he sets Baucent free to give him a chance to escape.[30] Even as a monk, William delights in the fifteen horses he wins from robbers along the road and prays God to heal the animal whose leg he used as a weapon, which God does, the single miracle he performs in that poem.

William's obsession with horses inspires some amusing parodies in Rainoart's adventures. Rainoart normally fights on foot but, at one point, attempting to be a knight, he leaps backwards onto a horse and has a very rough ride; he falls off and is dragged around, hanging onto the tail. Finally, in disgust, he knocks the animal down with his fist. In contrast to William's concern to spare animals, Rainoart, even when he tries to get horses for the Christians he has rescued, is unable to keep his club from crashing down through the pagan to the horse under him. He destroys many good mounts, to his companions' annoyance, before he learns to control his blows.

Rainoart's uncontrolled violence, doing harm even when none is intended, may also be a distorted reflection of William, who is quick to take action that often endangers himself and his friends. He undertakes the whole Orange adventure in the *Prise,* despite the warnings of the escaped Christian, and of his nephew Bertrand, because he has to have some action, war or love, and preferably both. When he is recognized inside the city, his first response is to attack, although he is unarmed and surrounded by enemies. He provokes the attack of robbers in the *Moniage* by having his servant whistle, to let them know he is there. When, in *Aliscans,* he is stopped at Orleans on his way to Paris, he cuts a passage through, too impatient to explain or identify himself. In fury at the monks in his cloister for breaking their vows of silence or refusing

30. This, unfortunately, proves to be a futile gesture—Baucent is killed by pagans. In the *Chanson de Guillaume,* the hero's feeling for his horse is less personal, more like Roland's for his sword. When he wins a magnificent horse from a pagan, he kills Baucent rather than let him fall into enemy hands.

him wine, he beats them up, and when they shut the doors on him, he breaks them down. And yet, for all that, he is not insensitive to fear. There are many occasions in the poems—when he sees Corsolt, when he is surrounded by hordes of Saracens, and over and over again during the disastrous battle at Aliscans—when he is very much afraid, but he always determines to sell himself at a high price; sometimes he alternates between fighting and lamenting his situation (see Al, ll. 1054 ff, 1327 ff, 1610 ff). Occasionally, when the odds are too much against him, he flees; though a man of violent action, the poet comments, he was wise enough to know when to flee (Al, ll. 1619–20).

Usually William acts in great self-confidence and pride: he has the temerity to kill the traitor in the presence of the king and crown the prince in the presence of the pope; he chastises the king and insults the queen before the whole court; and he criticizes the behavior of his fellow monks without his abbot's leave. He is very conscious of his family's reputation and his own and does not let the king forget what he has done for him; and yet, when his cause needs their help, he swallows a good deal of scorn and ridicule from the French court before he explodes. He can be tender at times, too. He is moved to tears for the sufferings of Christians he has rescued from Saracens, nostalgic for France; touched by the pleas of his niece Aelis to be reconciled with her mother; saddened by the departure of his family after the second battle of Aliscans; and always thoughtful of Guiborc. He worries about her sorrow when the battle goes badly; he hesitates to leave her alone at Orange when he goes for help; and imposes a strenuous vow on himself to allay her fears of other women. He is grateful for any small kindness done to himself, generous and just with those he encounters. He makes a knight of the loyal gatekeeper in the *Couronnement* and entertains his bourgeois host at a royal feast in *Aliscans;* he makes amends to Orleans for the people he has killed there and, when he makes a bad slip in forgetting Rainoart after the victory at Aliscans, he acknowledges his mistake, begs forgiveness, and bears Rainoart's violent wrath in good humor. Then he appoints him his seneschal and arranges for his niece, the king's daughter, to become his wife.

William is clever, although he is not literate. We are told in the *Moniage* that he knows the services but he cannot read them. Still he is able to speak Saracen tongues and to pass himself off as one of them in the *Charroi,* the *Prise,* and *Aliscans.* He often assumes a disguise or plays a role to gain entrance to a hostile town, either as a Saracen or, in the *Couronnement,* as a friend to the traitors. In the *Moniage* he is smart enough to outwit the abbot who plots his death; when he is sent on a dangerous errand and forbidden to fight, even if robbers take all he has, he persuades the abbot to allow him, for modesty's sake, to fight rather than give up his pants; then he immediately has a special belt made for the pants in order to attract the robbers' attention.

William's nephews Bertrand and Guielin

William is accompanied on all his adventures, until he becomes a monk, by a nephew or two. The uncle-nephew bond, which is often more important for epic heroes than the father-son relation (Roland and Charlemagne, Beowulf and Hygelac, Tristan and Mark), is carried to extremes in the William cycle. William himself, besides the constant and devoted support of Bertrand or Guielin, has a particularly intense affection for a third nephew, Vivien, who seems to have grown up in his care. And there are at least four other nephews who fight for him at Aliscans. Vivien's own nephew, Foucon de Candie, devotes himself to avenging his uncle's death at Aliscans (in *Foucon de Candie*), and even William's father, Aimeri, has several adventures in the company of his uncle Girard de Viane (in *Girard de Viane* and *Aimeri de Narbonne*).

Bertrand and Guielin, who appear with William in most of the poems, share many of his traits: his devotion to duty, particularly in the fight against the infidel, his boldness in the most dangerous situations and, at times, his recklessness. Bertrand encourages his uncle to fight the pagans in Italy without sending back to Louis for help, although they are only sixty Christian knights against an army of thirty thousand; and he curses whoever would dare carry back a request for aid. It is Bertrand, too, who alerts his uncle to the king's danger, first when Arneis attempts to seize the crown, later when Louis is terrified by the enemy attack on the Frank camp. Bertrand shares, up to this point, his uncle's loyalty to the king. But, at the end of the poem, when Louis is in trouble for the third time, Bertrand gives up on him. Let him be, he tells his uncle, he will never be able to defend his own land. Bertrand now shifts his concern to William's good. In the *Charroi,* the news he brings William from the court is that Louis has handed out fiefs without

remembering him; he encourages his uncle to do something about it,
offers the suggestion that he ask for Saracen lands in the south, and then
goes along to help win them. He is always good in a fight he believes
in, but he is not one to pursue the futile defense of a "foolish" king, or
the mad assault on a well-guarded Saracen city and queen. Although he
pushed his uncle into action in the *Couronnement,* he discourages him in
the *Prise,* telling him it is wrong to die or even to be captured for love;
there are more important things to do. He refuses to go along on the ex-
pedition and expects the worst from it—if God doesn't help, it will
bring dishonor and shame on us all (ll. 394–95)—but when the request
comes for his help, he goes immediately, and it is he who kills the
Saracen prince Aragon. He is in the thick of the battle at Aliscans as
well, overshadowed, as are all of William's other nephews there, by
Vivien's heroism and death, but a brave figure nonetheless. He puts a
hundred pagans to flight at a time, goes to Vivien's aid despite the over-
whelming numbers of enemy around him and refuses to leave him even
long enough to summon William. Bertrand is captured, together with
six of his cousins, early in the poem and returns to the action only when
he is rescued by Rainoart; but then, despite his long ill-usage and suffer-
ing, he is anxious as always to fight and pesters Rainoart until the latter
gets him a horse. At the end, he remains with William when most of
the family departs.

Guielin also appears in several poems: [31] he accompanies William
and Bertrand to Rome in the *Couronnement,* and he fights at Aliscans, but
his distinctive role is in the *Prise* where he takes Bertrand's place when
Bertrand refuses to go. He is now the one to encourage his uncle when
the situation is bad, to fight with him against huge odds and to taunt
him about his romance. Time and again, when they are in prison and
awaiting almost certain death, he tells William to look to his lady for
help or to enjoy her embraces which have cost him so much. You used
to be called "Guillelme Fierebrace," "William Strong Arm," he says;
henceforth it will be "Guillelme l'amiable," "William the lover."

31. In the *Charroi de Nîmes,* Guielin uses the excuse of his youth to avoid accom-
panying his uncle on the dangerous expedition, but is forced by his father, Bernart, to
go, and fights hard once he gets there. The timidity is so unusual for him, that one
wonders if this is a remnant of an earlier version, or if the poet had a different Guielin in
mind.

William's wife, Guiborc

The woman for whom William undertakes this dangerous expedition, Orable (who will be baptized Guiborc), proves worthy of it, not only by the help she gives him in the *Prise,* but by her courageous support of him and his cause until her death. We are sympathetic to her from the first description; she is lovely, slender, with skin as white as a flower, but doomed because she does not know God. She is, however, already interested in William, for she asks the disguised Christians about him, and when they speak of his strength and prowess, her response is, "By Mohammed, he will hold great domains/ Happy the lady who possesses his heart" (ll. 731–32). We are prepared, thus, for her to come to his aid when she discovers who he is, and her subsequent conversion to Christianity follows naturally from her commitment to him; a superficial motivation, perhaps, but one that is no more unusual in the poems than it was in life. There is no doubt of her attachment to William and his family; she suffers a great deal because of their losses and she blames herself for the feud between Tiebaut, her pagan husband, and William that leads to the Aliscans disaster, and she does her part in coping with it. She defends the city, with the help only of women and children and, most important, she encourages William when he loses heart. She forces him to live up to the highest standards, refusing to recognize him when he is fleeing, saying that William would not have seen Christians being led off captive and have failed to go to their rescue. Only when, goaded by her words, he rushes off alone against the pagan troop does she acknowledge him, and then she begins to worry about his safety.

Her lion-hearted encouragement is always balanced by tender concern, and once, at least, by jealousy when he goes north to the French court and may meet other women. She always suits her words to William's mood, even when she must rouse him to some action for which he has no enthusiasm. At the end of *Aliscans,* when he is weary and depressed, it is she who suggests that they think about rebuilding Orange, couching the proposal in a speech of resignation to the will of God, of acceptance that it is man's destiny to die, but his duty to live well while he can. William repays her support with devotion and tender concern; in the worst moment of the battle he worries about *her* distress. He even humors her jealousy when he goes north, with a vow not to touch anyone with his lips until he returns. Perhaps the best indication of the kind of relation they have is to be found in the *Moniage,* just before Guiborc dies, when she reminds her husband how they have laughed and joked together, and begs his pardon if she has ever offended him.

Guiborc is one of the most attractive characters in *Aliscans* and perhaps in the cycle, but there are details in her background which, although they are suppressed in most of the poems we have, do occasionally turn up and raise disturbing questions. That she deserts her first husband in the *Prise* is excused by the fact that he is a pagan, but what of her children? The *Prise* does not mention any, but other poems do. When Esmeré meets William in battle at Aliscans, he calls him stepfather and asks about his mother; then he accuses William of killing two of his brothers (ll. 1050 ff). Has Guiborc, then, married the man who killed her children? From allusions in several poems one gathers that she was unmoved by the murders, perhaps even present at them (*Foucon de Candie,* ll. 723–24, ll. 9479–82; and the longer *Moniage Guillaume,* ll. 3068–69); in the Italian version, the author denies the rumor that she herself killed one of the children. The child-killing may be connected with another tradition, in which she was a sorceress; this is mentioned in the early poem the *Chanson de Guillaume,* and is given some play in the much later *Enfances Guillaume,* so it is apparently a strong tradition. The poet of *Aliscans* was probably acquainted with such traditions, indeed he seems to have made a particular effort to counteract them by having Guiborc give in to tender and occasionally weak impulses that otherwise do not suit her heroic stature. It may well be for this reason that he emphasizes her tenderness toward her brother, Rainoart, whom she recognizes instinctively and persuades, in a touching scene, to accept arms that will save his life during the battle at Aliscans.

poetic structure

The poetic structure of the works translated here follows the normal chanson de geste pattern. Each poem is composed of sections or "laisses" of varied length, distinguished and bound by the assonance of the last syllable in each line. Rhyme is found in some later chansons, but only rarely in the early ones. The number of lines per laisse may vary considerably, but the assonance and number of syllables per line is strictly observed. The line is always decasyllabic, with a caesura after the fourth syllable, really two half-lines of four and six syllables.[32] The rigidity of this metrical system demands the constant use of formulae, phrases that will fit easily into either half of the line.[33] Thus the songs abound in pleonasms: "errer ne chevalchier," "pelerins ne palmiers," "et cercies et tentes," "rostee et escaufee"; in epithets: "beau pere dreiturier," "glorieus pere," for God; "le marchis au vis fier," "Guillelmes au cort nes," for William; "le palazin Bertran," "ses nies Bertran," for his nephew. Certain patterns of words evolve of necessity. If the name Rainoart appears in the first half of a line, the other word must be a monosyllable—"dist Rainoars"; with a two-syllable name, a different verb is needed—"respont Bertran"; but never "respunt Rainoars" or "dist Bertran."

Descriptions are stereotyped, sometimes in single phrases: "le blanc halberc," "le bon espié," "l'espié trenchant," "un fort hauberc doublier"; to describe bad wounds, "de la menour mourust un amiralz," "the least of which would have killed an emir"; for punishment, "ardeir en feu ou en aive neier," "to burn in fire or drown in water," a conventional phrase for punishment, which is rarely meant to be taken literally. The standard descriptions may also run to long passages, e.g., the arming of a knight, the appearance of armies, hand-to-hand combats, laments for the dead. Rychner lists twenty-four such motifs in epic poetry.[34] They can be varied in effective ways, but generally they are changed only slightly to suit different assonances:

> 1) Vait s'en li cuens, de neient ne se targe.
> De ses jornees ne sai que vos contasse;

32. This is true for all the poems in this collection, with one exception: in the text of the *Moniage* (MG I), the last line of each laisse is a short line of six syllables. Although, generally, the songs of the cycle follow the pattern, there are exceptions in the *Chanson de Guillaume,* which is unusual in many ways: lines often break after the sixth, rather than the fourth syllable, and occasionally there are extra syllables, probably the result of corrupted transmission.

33. Parry, "Studies."

34. J. Rychner, *La Chanson de geste: essai sur l'art épique des jongleurs* (Genève, 1955), pp. 128–39. For a good example of motif variation, see the *Chanson de Roland,* the landscape motif that begins "halt sunt li pui," but ends differently depending on the scene it introduces: dark and foreboding for the loneliness of the rear-guard, rushing waters for the hastening army, etc.

> Montjeu trespasse qui durement le lasse;
> De ci a Rome n'aresta Fierebrace (CL, ll. 268–71).
>
> . . .
>
> 2) Vait s'en li cuens, qui de riens ne se targe,
> Montjeu trespasse, qui durement le lasse.
> De lor jornees ne sai que vos contasse;
> De ci en Brie n'arestent ne ne targent.
>
> Vait s'en Guillelmes al Cort Nes li marchis (new Laisse)
> De ses jornees ne sai conte tenir;
> De ci en Brie ne prist il onques fin (CL, ll. 1446–52)

In the second passage, the first four lines repeat the formula almost verbatim. The next three begin a new laisse and must therefore be varied to end with a new sound; however, the first part of each line is preserved, and the substitutions are made within the pattern of stock six-syllable phrases. The variation is due to technical exigencies, not to subtleties of meaning.

Sometimes a poet repeats formulae verbatim even when they create inconsistencies within a context. A striking example of a misapplied formula occurs in the *Prise:* when Bertrand, who has been left at Nîmes to defend it, climbs the palace, the poet says: "Monte el palés Otran le deffaé,/ Qu'il ot conquis par sa ruiste fierté," "he climbs the palace of the heathen Otran, whom he had conquered with his fierce courage" (ll. 1660–61). Although Bertrand did take part in the conquest of Nîmes, it was William who gave the final blow to Otran; and indeed, in the first part of the *Prise,* the formula is properly applied to William, in lines 46–47, which are identical with ll. 1660–61 but with the right reference.

The oral presentation of the poems necessitates a good deal of repetition, in order to remind the audience of details or events. It may be done in different ways, either by a recapitulation at the beginning of a new laisse of what has occurred in the previous one, with the words or word order varied to suit the new assonance (as in the Montjeu example above); or by the introduction of a messenger who recounts events to characters within the story. There is also a good deal of foretelling of events, either to add pathos, by announcing the tragic outcome, death or betrayal, before it occurs, or simply to induce the audience to pay up in order to hear more. Many pitches of this kind are made in the long poem, *Aliscans:*

Por ce est bone la chançon a oïr

. . .

Molt bon essample i puet l'en retenir.
Bien en devroit avoir a son pleisir
Henax et robes et bliäuz a vestir
Qui de Guillaume set chanter et servir; (ll. 640 ff)

and later, put more strongly:

Prodon ne doit jougleor escouter,
S'il ne li veut por dieu del sien douner.
Car il ne sait autrement laborer (ll. 4579 ff)

that is, you have no right to listen to me unless you are willing to pay for it, it's the only work I know how to do. Several times the poet advertises another song altogether (see Al., ll. 3013 ff, 7811 ff, 8340 ff, 8425 ff) and at the end of *Aliscans* he looks ahead to the poems about Rainoart. The hero himself is conscious of his reputation in song:

Ja n'en avront honte mi ancisor,
N'en chanteront en mal cil gogleor,
Ke en ma vie perde terre plain dor (ll. 436–38).

The most appealing plea for "jongleurs" occurs in the *Moniage.* William has forced his servant to sing, in order to attract the attention of robbers in the forest. What he sings, incidentally, is a version of the *Prise d'Orange* (MG I, ll. 446–50). The robbers then argue whether to attack, saying that minstrels should not be troubled, but rather loved and honored and given money, clothes, and food. One cannot help feeling that this is the poet's plaintive idea of how things ought to be; life is different, however, and the robbers do attack.

Couronnement de Louis

The structure, tone and quality of the four poems vary considerably, a strong indication that they are the work of different poets. In the *Couronnement* there are five distinct parts, which has led critics to posit the traces of five separate stories: *I,* the Coronation of Louis and the Treachery of Arneis, laisses I–XIV; *II,* the Combat with Corsolt to save Rome, laisses XV–XXXIII; *III,* Suppression of the Norman Treason, laisses XXXIV–LVI; *IV,* the Conquest of Rome from Guy d'Allemagne, laisses LVII–LXII; *V,* Suppression of a Barons' Revolt, laisse

LXIII. One can see a certain pattern through the poem; the action moves back and forth between France and Rome, which represent the two focuses of William's loyalty, king and church; and the episodes alternate in the type of enemy encountered, internal enemies or traitors, in *I, III,* and *V*; foreign aggressors in *II* and *IV*. As Frappier points out, each episode presents an aspect of the king's duty that William carries out for him: to protect the pope and Christianity, to put down rebels and establish order and justice in France, and to affirm the rights of the French king to the western empire. The attempts made to connect the parts of the poem, aside from the general problems of a weak monarchy, are only superficial: the messengers who come to Rome in the third part appeal to William to remember the duty he had assumed in the first part, and those who come from Rome in the fourth, remind him of the lady he left waiting in the second, but there is no internal connection of episodes. The name of William's betrothed, Orable, is brought in (l. 1433) in an awkward attempt to reconcile the poem with others in the cycle, or as an unsatisfactory excuse for William's failure to marry the Italian princess to whom he is betrothed in the second part and whose lands he returns to save in the fourth part. The marriage is never carried out and nothing more is heard of the girl.

But despite the episodic nature of the poem and the transparent attempts to fuse them, there is an artistic progression from beginning to end, in the mounting up of William's responsibilities and the increasing hopelessness of his ever fully discharging them. In the first part, the duties of a king are set forth by Charlemagne, only to be systematically transgressed by his son, throughout the poem and beyond it. William assumes the responsibility for carrying out those duties in the first part and does so from then on. In the second part, he goes on a pilgrimage to Rome, finds the pope endangered by an infidel invasion, rescues him, converts the pagan king, and accepts half the land and the daughter of the Christian prince. He is unable to receive them, because of his previous commitment to Louis, who sends for him. Louis is now threatened not just by one traitor or one family of traitors, but by rebellious nobles, clergy, and townsmen. William rescues him again, punishes the traitors, but makes peace with one of them. This leads to more trouble because, unlike the converted pagan of the earlier episode, the defeated

Christian does not keep his word. When William finally disposes of him, William is called back to Rome where he now has the added obligation of saving the lady to whom he is contracted, as well as the pope; he does not only that, but also crowns his own king, Louis, king of Rome, thus making manifest the connection between his Rome adventures and his service to Louis. But Louis is still unable to take care of himself, and the poem ends with William pledged to spend his youth in his defense, having renounced, for the time being, all chance of enjoying the fruits of his labors himself.

The poem reflects both the political conditions of twelfth-century France, in the conflicts between vassals and king, and various historical events from other periods. There are historical analogues for most of the branches, particularly the first, which purports to relate Charlemagne's coronation of his son Louis at Aix in 813. Several Latin sources have been suggested for the description, but it seems more likely that the poet superimposed a contemporary event—the consecration of Louis VII le Jeune in 1131—on poetic tradition.[35] Details of the description in the poem are closer to the twelfth-century event: the presence of the pope, who did not attend the coronation in 813 but did in 1131, and the youth of the new king, Louis VII, whereas Charlemagne's son was thirty-five in 813. The Carolingians had actually won the pope's blessing for their dynasty by supporting him against the Lombards and the Byzantine emperor (albeit not consistently), and although the pope did not come to France to crown Charlemagne, he did crown him Emperor of the Romans in Rome in A.D. 800.

In the other branches, real events are only remotely suggested by the incidents: the attack on Rome in the second part has been connected with the Saracen attack on Gaifier of Salerno in 873,[36] with the siege of

<hr/>

35. Curtius thinks Theganus' Latin chronicle is a definite source, "Zum *Coronement Loois*," *Romanische Forschungen*, 62 (1950), 322–49. Scheludko lists Theganus with two other sources, a prayer from Martane's *De antiquis ecclesiae ritibus*, and Wipponi's *Vita Konradi*.

36. A. Jeanroy, "Le *Coronement Loois*," *Romania*, 25 (1896), 357–59; D. Scheludko, p. 440; L. Willelms, *L'Elément historique dans le Coronement Loois* (Gand, 1896), p. 12. For a discussion of various theories, see Mario Roque, "L'Elément historique dans la Branche II du *CL*," *Romania*, 30 (1901), 176–81.

Rome in 846, and with the Norman landing at Salerno in 1016. The fact that pagans had at some time threatened Rome would probably be sufficient to give rise to legends. The historical confusion of the next two branches is hopeless: there was an Acelin, bishop of Laon, c. 987, who betrayed, among others, the heir to the throne, Charles de Lorraine, but Acelin had nothing to do with Normandy or with a Louis or a William. There was also a Richard, duke of Normandy from 943–946, who lived under Louis IV and Louis V, but he was not involved in conspiracies. Guy l'Allemand may be Guy of Spoleto, a great-grandson of Charlemagne and king of the Italians, but he was not a German. Charlemagne did get the Duke of Spoleto to shift allegiance to him in 773—Spoleto was one of the three major dynasties of Carolingian Italy. Pope John VIII had trouble with Saracens and with the Duke of Spoleto in the late ninth century, and in the twelfth century Louis VI supported the pope against the German emperor Henry V. However, there is no connection between these events or these people, and there is little to be gained from pursuing the analogies. The final branch is short and vague; it simply picks up the theme of the first and third parts, the rebellious vassals.

There are as many analogues in popular literature for the stories told in the *Couronnement* as there are in history: the prisoner delivered by a true friend who hears of his misfortune and comes from afar to save him, entering his prison by a trick and then summoning the aid he left outside; the banished councillor who returns in time to save his master from traitors; the hero who defends another's land from foreign invasion and is offered the princess in reward; the boy-king who remains a child through years of adventures; the invulnerability of the hero in all but one part of his body (in this case his nose, the only part that is not touched by the arm of St. Peter). There are conventional epic motifs which readers of the *Chanson de Roland* will recognize: the hero's dream of his enemy as a boar-hound; the pope's promise to the Christian troops that they will go to heaven if they die in this battle; and the argument between William and his nephew over whether they should send to Louis for reinforcements or meet the overwhelming odds on their own.

Prise d'Orange

There is no historical basis whatsoever for the *Prise d'Orange,* although the story was connected with William at least by the 1120s, since it appears in the fifth chapter of the *Vita Sancti Wilhelmi.* The Duke of Aquitaine was reputed to have taken Orange from a Saracen chief, Theobaldus, during the reign of Charlemagne. The name Theobaldus is not Saracen. Grégoire believes that it comes from a Roman monument at Orange, a triumphal arch celebrating a victory over a German chief, Teutobodus.[37] Since, during the Middle Ages, Roman monuments were sometimes thought to be the work of Moors, Grégoire further suggests that the palace of Gloriete is modeled on a Roman ruin. Indeed, he suggests that the whole story is set in Orange because of the ancient monuments there, and that the historic William of Toulouse becomes William of Orange because of the romantic tales associated with that city. Orable, the wife of Tiebaut in the *Prise,* is not mentioned in the *Vita.* Presumably a separate bride-quest story was added to the original Christian-pagan battle; her name, Orable, may well be derived by alliteration from the name of the city, Orange.

The plot of the poem, particularly in the motivation of the hero, is frivolous compared to the other epics. William is bored at the beginning of the poem and longs for battles or sex. A Christian, just escaped from prison in Orange, describes a city that holds both, and William makes a rash vow to take that lady and city or never fight again, an oath which is more in the nature of a "gab," a boast that must be proved, than the serious oaths taken by others in the cycle. This quest leads William into a series of unlikely situations: disguised as a Saracen, he makes his way into the tower of the Emir's wife, where he is recognized by a Saracen who had once been his prisoner; he and his two nephews fight off troops of pagans, who finally capture them by sneaking into the tower through a secret passage; the queen rescues them from their dungeon and sends for the entire Frank army through underground tunnels. The structure of the poem, in contrast to the situations, is very simple; it is two parallel parts, with a short opening and closing scene:

37. "Les monuments inspirateurs. Comment Guillaume de Toulouse devint Guillaume d'Orange," *Provence historique,* I (Marseille, 1950), 32–44. Frappier accepts Grégoire's suggestions, adding that the underground passages in which much of the poem's action occurs may well be the ruins of Roman aqueducts or sewers, II, 274 ff.

boredom of French at Nîmes

heroes leave Nîmes, enter Orange in disguise	Orable rescues them, sends messenger to Nîmes secretly
recognized by infidels	overheard and betrayed by infidels
close themselves in Gloriete and fight	close selves in King's palace and fight
pagans arrive secretly, capture them	Franks arrive secretly, rescue them

baptism of Orable, marriage

Many critics have complained that the *Prise* is not a major artistic achievement,[38] but the story is amusing and there are some charming touches—the boredom of the French at the beginning of the poem, when they find themselves without the pleasures either of civilized life or of war; the cynical attitude of William's nephews towards the whole romantic exploit, the foolishness of which they never let him forget; the suspense of William's disguise; the terror of wanderings through underground passages.

Aliscans

Aliscans is no more historical than the *Prise,* although it may have its orgin, vaguely, in the battle at the Orbieu, but the tone of the poem is quite different. One might better say the tones—pain and despair in the early passages, frustration and anger in the middle, and exuberant farce for the remainder. The poem has three large sections, with a great variety of incident through them. The first is the battle at Aliscans, sometimes called Archamps or Archant,[39] of which Vivien's death is the central scene but William's suffering the predominant theme—for the loss of his nephews by death and capture, his thwarted attempts to flee, to

---

38. L. Gautier, *Les Epopées françaises,* 2nd ed. (Paris, 1882), IV; R. Weeks, "The Primitive *Prise d'Orange,*" *PMLA,* 16 (1901), 361–74. Frappier admits that there are "invraisemblances," repetitions, and melodramatic elements, but finds it amusing none the less, II, 280.

39. Aliscans, from *Elysii campi,* was presumably an ancient cemetery; Archant, of disputed etymology was probably a river port. See G. Rolin, ed. *Aliscans* (Leipzig, 1894), xlii–liv; Rolin suggests that Archant was Vivien's battlefield, the site of defeat and death, whereas Aliscans is William's, the place of victory and revenge (liv).

guard his nephew's body, to save his own horse, to get back into his city. Each time he is at the end of his strength, he must pull himself together to fight off new crowds of Saracens, until he reaches home and his own wife demands a further proof of him. The second part of the poem, William's journey north to seek help, is filled with frustrations of another sort: first he is impeded by the townspeople of Orleans, and then rebuffed by the French king and court, and gets his way only by threatening the king and insulting the queen. He is rewarded, finally, in the last part, with total victory over his enemies of several decades, but the victory is mainly due to the unusual exploits of the pagan giant Rainoart, whose adventures dominate the poem from the moment he appears. Rainoart's combats are catalogued and described in detail, but the poet is equally concerned with his actions at the monastery, his defense of the bean-farmer, the troubles with his club, and finally the social vindication, his baptism, knighting, and marriage.

The change of mood in the course of the poem suggests that at least two stories have been fused, the tragic death of Vivien and the comic adventures of Rainoart. These are the two most dramatic figures in the William cycle, apart from the hero himself, and to treat both of them in the same song, despite the vast difference of character, must have been an overwhelming temptation. There are obvious attempts in the version we have to connect the two stories: references to Rainoart in the early part of the poem—as the strongest hero (289), as the only man who will be able to rescue William's nephews (1488), as the eventual conqueror of the pagans (1547)—and references to Vivien towards the end of the song, when his death is avenged (6678[a]) and his body is finally buried (7364 ff). It is no accident that it is Rainoart who defeats Haucebier, the pagan who delivered the death blow to Vivien, thus completing, at the end of the poem, the battle for Orange and the revenge of Vivien. As in the *Chanson de Roland,* the final victory completes the story of the early defeat, but in *Aliscans* the character of the hero who dominates that victory, Rainoart, is strong enough to change the tone of the poem.

There are many interesting aspects of this huge work: social and political overtones, odd characters, but perhaps the most obvious is the similarity with the *Chanson de Roland.* [40] The poet himself points this up with several allusions to Ronceval: of Bertrand's fighting he says, there

40. Frappier discusses this in I, 156 ff.

was no need there for Roland or Oliver (l. 138); and of the battle: they had no such battle at Ronceval (l. 559). The basic elements of the situations are the same: the courageous struggle of young Christian heroes against overwhelming numbers of Saracens; the death of the finest of them; the massing of a larger army, an older generation of heroes (in this case William's father and brothers replacing his nephews) to avenge the young; and the fate of Christianity in France resting on the encounter between the forces of Christendom and the forces of the infidel. There are echoes of Roland even in the smaller details: the ritualized mourning, laments, and fainting of William over Vivien's body, like Charlemagne over Roland's; the personal feud that brings on the battle, in this case between William and the pagan whose wife and city he stole, as Ronceval has its roots in the feud between Roland and Ganelon; and, finally, the reckless pride of the young hero Vivien, the vow never to flee a lance-thrust before pagans. There is considerable pride behind this vow, as there is behind Vivien's fear that he has betrayed it, but like Roland's pride in fighting without calling for help, Vivien's evokes a considerable amount of self-sacrifice—he has been so badly wounded that he must tie himself up with his standard in order to keep his guts from running out, but he continues to fight, helping his friends or fighting alone when his cousins are captured. When he is forced to stop, he dismounts, confesses himself, and prays only to see William before he dies. An angel comes in response to this prayer, another echo of Roland's death, but only to tell him that it will not be answered, that William will not arrive in time. There is apparently some confusion here with another version, since William will in fact arrive; there are conflicting traditions about the death scene, as we know from the *Chanson de Guillaume,* where Vivien dies before William arrives, but revives later in the poem when his uncle finds him. In *Aliscans,* William finds him alive, talks to him at length, and gives him communion before he dies. In any case, the angel's words contribute to the young knight's distress in his last moments; he is already tormented by the fear that he has betrayed his vow, although he repented almost as soon as he began to flee, and quickly turned back to fight. But he does not know how far he went before he turned and that doubt is left unresolved when he dies. Even William's assurances to the contrary do not help. This adds a tragic element to his death which is very different from Roland's; Roland assumes the position of conqueror, facing the enemy, before he dies, clearly untroubled by doubts about his actions.

There is a strong need to fulfill the letter of one's oath in this poem, not only in the character of Vivien, but in Aimer, who has vowed not to be distracted from his fight against the infidel by good food or comfortable lodging and therefore refuses his brother's hospitality and tries to remain aloof from the family reunion, although in any case, he cannot fight until they are ready. But the most touching instance of such a vow is William's not to touch any mouth with his lips until he returns to his wife, a promise he makes to allay her jealousy of other women, but keeps scrupulously, even turning his head from his parents and brothers when they greet him.

The poet means us to be entirely sympathetic to Vivien's fate, despite the vow that may or may not have contributed to his death but which, in any case affects only him (his cousins are not killed, only captured and eventually rescued); he is caught in a situation that is none of his making. Unlike Roland, who refuses to summon help until too late, Vivien tries to persuade Bertrand to go for William, but Bertrand refuses to leave him alone, as much out of devotion as from a heroic determination not to leave the battlefield. There is a stronger sense of fate overwhelming the young hero in *Aliscans* than in the *Chanson de Roland,* and there is never a question of personal honor interfering with public duty in the William cycle.

The poet of *Aliscans* has other serious concerns that are not common in epic. He is disturbed about certain aspects of social injustice, the abuse of the poor and defenseless, particularly their helplessness in the face of events over which they have no control but which do affect them. I do not know another instance in *chansons de geste* in which the poet mentions the plight of the poor farmer whose crops are destroyed in the course of a great war. Even though it is the pagan army that pillages the bean fields, it is the war they are engaged in that makes it necessary. The beans were to be sold to buy food for the man's children, who must now go hungry, Rainoart tells the pagans when he forces them to pay for what they have taken—the man worked hard to cultivate those beans, which he hoped to sell at a small profit. The pagans excuse themselves, saying they were not really stealing, because no one tried to stop them, hardly a valid excuse but one that has the ring of authenticity to it, in the attitude of an invading army. Rainoart is instinctively moved by the plight of the poor—it is surely no coincidence and a strong indictment of hypocritical Christianity that the only example of this kind of Christian charity is in the actions of a pagan before he has been baptized—as we see when he feeds the beggars outside the monastery doors; the monks, whose responsibility they should be, have ignored them while indulging themselves. The poet also comments several times during the poem on the inequity inherent in the scorn the rich show for the poor; his point, whether it applies to William at the French court or to Rainoart in his kitchen clothes, is that shabbiness and temporary material distress do not preclude nobility. Again it is no accident that the two figures who are ridiculed for their outward poverty are the two greatest champions in the poem, William and Rainoart.

Rainoart is probably the most interesting character in *Aliscans,* and a very complicated one. He begins as a foolish kitchen boy, huge and dirty, but able to wield a tremendous club. His early adventures consist mainly of the revenge he takes on his tormentors, but he is zealous when he begins to fight for William and for Christianity, even against his own family, and he becomes a heroic figure in his own right. After *Aliscans,* epics are composed in which he is the hero (*Bataille Loquifer, Moniage Rainoart*), and he wins himself a place in Dante's heaven with the crusaders. It is his line that is destined to produce Tancred, the hero of the first crusade and of Renaissance epics.

We do not know where the figure of Rainoart comes from. There have been inconclusive attempts to trace the giant with the huge club to a God of thunder,[41] but it is more likely that he is related to folktales of the unknown hero who is confined to the kitchen until he gets a chance to prove himself.[42] Within the poem *Aliscans,* the comic force of the character, drawn with the same exuberance and heroic stature as William and Guiborc, is sufficient excuse for his presence. It is not necessary to interpret him, as Friscia does, as a precursor of the "sans-culotte," the lower-class revolutionary who accomplishes what the feudal class, i.e., William, cannot.[43] One cannot deny certain suggestive details in his

41. J. Runeberg, *Etudes sur la geste Rainouart* (Helsingfors, 1905).

42. E. R. Curtius, *European Literature and the Latin Middle Ages,* trans. W. R. Trask (New York, 1953), Excursus IV, §6, on Kitchen Humor.

43. A. Friscia, "Le Personnage de Rainouart au Tinel dans la *'Chanson d'Aliscans',''* *Annales de l'Université de Grenoble,* Bk. 21 (1909), 43–98.

background and character: as a child he ran away from his family because he killed the tutor who beat him; he served seven years in Louis' kitchen, and never afterward feels at ease in more formal surroundings. He is uncomfortable at feasts; although he is anxious to become a Christian, he is annoyed by the ritual of his baptism—failing to understand why he has to be *held* by his godfathers, he breaks away from them; he is bemused by the idea of jousting, although, as he points out, he is willing enough to take on a real enemy. These traits, along with the championing of the poor, do suggest that the poet uses him to attack the hypocrisy and empty forms of contemporary noble life. But to see in this a class conflict is to go too far, for the poet does the same thing with William, whose suffering and distress also point up the hypocrisy and sham of the French nobility, his own class.

It would also be a mistake, in all this talk of social concerns, to lose sight of the comic aspect of Rainoart's character. The scenes in which he is the butt of the kitchen staff, whom he treats roughly in return, are pure farce of the broad, boisterous, excessively violent kind one associates with epics. Rainoart's strength is so great he cannot control it; he kills anything, man or animal, that crosses his path. When he strikes opponents in battle, his force is such that he crushes the horse as well as the man, and has difficulty providing mounts for the knights he rescues. All this is comic. So, too, Rainoart's attempts to ride a horse, which he mounts backwards, falls off, and eventually punches in disgust; or to sail a boat—not knowing what to do with the sails, he pushes with a pole and sinks the craft; and his devotion to his club, similar in its intensity to Roland's feeling for his sword or William's for his horse, but comic in its object. He caresses the club, hugs and kisses it, and wipes it with his coat; when he kills his brother, he lets the club take the blame for the act.

Despite his early oafishness and uncontrolled violence, Rainoart shows human delicacy: he does not want to kill his father and is relieved when their battle is interrupted; he is anxious to convert his cousin, Baudus, whom he loved as a child; he is tender with Guiborc, and accepts her gifts rather than hurt her feelings, promising to defend William for her; and he loves the French princess, Aelis. He eventually learns to control his strength, when he thinks about it, and even to use the outer trappings of knighthood. When his club shatters, he is forced to try the sword and is delighted to find that it works; when he goes to defend the bean-farmer, he carries a shield; when he is knighted, he finally mounts a horse, but all this is meant more to reconcile the presentation of the character with the Rainoart who is the hero of other epics, than it is essential to his nature in *Aliscans.*

We cannot leave *Aliscans* without mentioning two other figures, who play small roles but make an impression. William's mother, Ermengard, is the first to speak out in support of her son at the French court.[44] Berating the Franks and even her husband for their lack of courage, she pledges all her treasure to buy soldiers for William and promises that she herself will ride into battle with them—My hair may be white, but my heart is bold. And William's niece, Aelis, the daughter of his sister and of King Louis, but, unlike her parents, wise and just. Mindful of the debt they owe William, she persuades her mother to apologize to him and thereby effects a general reconciliation. She also recognizes the worth of Rainoart and asks his forgiveness for anything she might have done to offend him, a delicate way of apologizing for the way her father had treated him. Both Aelis and Ermengard, like Guiborc, exemplify the woman's function of persuading and encouraging others to noble action; they are worthy members of the family of Narbonne. Only Blancheflor, William's sister, falls short, and this is apparently because of the man she married, the weak and selfish Louis. The other women are the counterparts of their heroic husbands.

Moniage Guillaume

The last of the epics presented here, the *Moniage,* has probably the most solid historical basis for its central theme, of William as a monk, though there is more legend than fact in the incidents recounted. We can be fairly certain that William of Toulouse built the monastery, retired to it, and died there in 813. There are documents that tell more, but we no longer possess the originals and the copies that remain seem to have

44. Some of the traits attributed to this attractive character may well be based on a contemporary figure, Ermengard the Countess of Narbonne. She inherited her father's lands in 1134 and ruled them, despite attempts by the Count of Toulouse and others to take them from her, until 1192, when she abdicated in favor of her nephew. While she ruled, she led her own troops and she exercised all the powers of a ruler, even judicial. See A. Lehmann, *Le rôle de la femme dans l'histoire de France au Moyen Age* (Paris: Berger-Levrault, 1952), 278 ff.

been falsified by the monks of Aniane (see above, p. 7). There are no re-
liable historic sources for the three basic episodes in the poem: William's
troubles inside the convent, his defense of his breeches from robbers, and
his withdrawal to a hermitage which is interrupted by the Ysoré com-
bat. In fact, the story of the robbers and the pants is told about other
heroes.[45] But there are reflections in the poem of the twelfth-century
struggle over monastic reform, in the descriptions of the monks' luxuri-
ous clothes and concern with their food, in their resentment of Wil-
liam's strict adherence to the rules of silence and attendance at all serv-
ices, and even in their barring the doors of the monastery to him,
forcing him to fight his way in. There are at least two historic instances
of the latter, in one case against Odo of Cluny, whose reforms were
feared—he eventually made his way in, alone, on a donkey, without
violence—the other, Pons de Melgueil, a deposed abbot who fought his
way into the old monastery and forced the monks to accept him or to
leave.[46]

There are also some notable monks whose lives offer analogies with
the matter of the poem. Odo, the second abbot of Cluny, was also a
monk and a hermit who had encounters with robbers, though never vio-
lent; had the doors of a monastery shut to him; and had trouble with
rebellious monks he tried to reform. Gerald of Aurillac was a nobleman
who became a monk, secretly, but remained in the world for a time in
order to carry out his secular duties.[47] He was known for his defense of
the poor and helpless, and he was connected with William I of Aqui-
taine who founded the monastic house of Cluny.

Although the poet of the *Moniage* is clearly on the side of Wil-
liam—as is God, who sends angels to him and performs a miracle in an-
swer to his prayer—and although the monks are selfish and petty and
deserve to be shown up, still William's actions are not entirely blame-
less. We might excuse his violence against the monks who transgress the
rules of the order, but what of his brutal attack on the cellarer who re-
fuses to give him wine? The amount each monk was to receive per day
was specified in monastic rules: William, for his huge bulk, may have

45. In the Novalese chronicle, c. 1027, II, chaps x–xi, and in the *Fecunda Ratis* of
Egbert of Liège, c. 1023, I, ll. 1717 ff, Walter of Aquitaine is the protagonist.
46. See footnote 26.
47. Life of St. Gerald of Aurillac by St. Odo of Cluny in *St. Odo of Cluny*, II, ii.

had a right to a larger share, but that is not stated in the poem and the implication is that he was perpetually seeking food and drink. Certainly, when he goes to buy fish, he spends part of the money on good food and lodging for himself, hardly proper conduct for an ascetic. And he goes out of his way to provoke a battle with the robbers in the woods. He cannot be excused on the grounds of self-defense, for he has a rich belt made for his drawers in order to tempt the robbers, and he has his servant sing to attract their attention when they do not appear. He is fixing for a fight and he manages to get it. Naturally, the scene is a slap at the monks who thought they could so easily rid themselves of him, but it is hard to believe that the poet was so naïve he failed to see the impropriety of William's behavior. Perhaps this is to belabor the point, however. It may well be that the poem simply combines criticism of the laxness within the cloister with the boisterous, exaggerated action that William is known for—the popular hero, even as a monk, must perform in the way that won the audience.

translations

In the translations I have attempted to follow the metrical pattern of four- and six-syllable lines when possible, though the English versions do not begin to approach the regularity of the original. The verse is free, except in the translation of the oldest song, the *Couronnement,* where I have maintained the assonance—the same vowel sound at the end of every line in a laisse—to give some idea of the effect in Old French. This necessitates some free renderings as well as distortions of the normal word order; it makes, at times, for a stilted style, but that is also characteristic of the original text. The tenses of verbs follow no logical order in the French, pronouns are often unclear in their attributions; I have not regularized them in the translation. Variant readings are translated only when they are particularly interesting or when they seem to clarify difficult passages. The editions used for the translations are: [48]

---

48. These are the standard editions, but they are not without problems. Tyssens attacks the first part of the Halle edition of *Aliscans,* because it does not include the variants of two manuscripts, (e) and (V), and the Katz edition of the *Prise,* because it fails to take B[1] variants into account. Frappier also finds some fault with the Katz edition, errors in variant readings (II, fn. p. 257). However, the Halle edition is still the best available for *Aliscans.* There is a new edition of the *Prise,* by Claude Regnier, in

E. Langlois, *Le Couronnement de Louis,* 2nd rev. ed. (Paris: Honoré Champion, 1966).

B. Katz, *La Prise d'Orange* (New York: King's Crown Press, 1947).

E. Wienbeck, W. Hartnacke, P. Rasch, *Aliscans* (Halle: Max Niemeyer, 1903).

W. Cloetta, *Les Deux Rédactions en vers du Moniage Guillaume,* 2 vols. (Paris: Firmin Didot, 1911).

The translation of *Aliscans* is abridged. Passages that are similar to material in the *Chanson de Guillaume,* or that are repetitious within the poem, have been omitted. Brief summaries have been inserted for the missing passages. I have retained the numbering of lines and laisses from the Halle edition so that the reader can locate passages in the original. In some cases I have included variant readings of particular interest, distinguishing them, as in the Halle edition, by letters rather than numbers.

For help with difficult passages in the original texts, I owe particular thanks to Professor Lawton P. G. Peckham, and for advising, correcting, and encouraging these translations, I am grateful to Professors William T. H. Jackson, Carolyn Heilbrun, Frederick Goldin, and Daniel Penham.

Bibliothèque française et romane, le Centre de Philologie romane de Strasbourg, Sèrie B., 5 (Paris, 1967), which came out after this translation was completed. I have, however, checked my translation against it and found only a half dozen cases where the meaning is affected by a difference in the text. In two of these I have adopted Regnier's reading (l. 999, *brisent for bessent;* l. 1568, *cuens for dame*).

The Coronation of Louis

i

Hear me, my lords, may God grant you his aid.
Will it please you to hear a noble tale,
a tale that is sung with charm and grace?
The base minstrel makes his boast in vain—
he speaks no word that has not been prepared.
Of Louis the king I shall sing the tale
and of William of the Short Nose, the brave,
who suffered so much from the Saracen race.
Of no better man could one sing the fate.

ii

Lords and barons, will you hear this example   10
in words well sung with grace and charm?
When God laid out nine and ninety lands,
all that was best he gave sweet France;
and the best king, that was Charlemagne,
who in love and justice ruled sweet France.
God made no land to ignore his command.
He gave his law to Anjou and Alemagne,
Bavaria, Lombardy and Brettagne,
to Normandy, Tuscany and Navarre.

iii

A king of France who wears the crown of gold   20
must be strong of body, brave and noble;
and if any man tries to do him wrong,
he must be pursued through plain and grove
until he is dead or begs to atone.

France's honor is lost if the king acts not so.
He was wrongly crowned, as the story shows.

iv

When the holy chapel was built at Aix
and the church consecrated in god's name,
such court was held that will never be again:
fourteen counts kept the palace gates.   30
For justice the poor never sought him in vain;
no man was denied who had a just claim.
Right was done then, but has not been sustained,
the wicked have turned all right to their gain;
by false flattery and fees, just pleas are stayed.
God is good, he governs all he creates;
the evil in Hell will suffer their fate
in the fetid well of infinite hate.

v

On that day there were ten and eight bishops,
ten and eight consecrated archbishops,   40
and mass was sung by the holy pope.

vi

On that day mass was magnificent.
France has never again seen such brilliance,
it glorified all who were then present.

vii

On that day there were six and twenty abbots
and four royal kings wearing crowns had come.
On that day Louis was raised at the font;
above the altar was the crown held aloft,
which the king his father to him held forth.
Then to the pulpit climbed the archbishop   50
to preach to all Christians; he spoke these words:
"Hear me well," he said, "barons and lords:
Charlemagne has ruled us well and long,

he can no longer his duties perform.
He can bear the golden crown no more,
he would give it now to his son, our lord."
With great joy they all received his words,
all their hands they raised high to God:
"Father of glory, you have saved our honor,
we need never bow to a foreign lord."   60
His son then came before our emperor:
"Fair son," he said, "mark well my words.
Behold the crown that lies here before.
It will be yours, on this pledge, before long:
never shall you commit sin or wrong,
nor against any man allow treason,
nor seize the fief of a young orphaned baron.
If you are ready to give me your word,
receive the crown and praise be to the lord.
But let it be, my son, if you are not.   70
Remember then, it is forever lost.

viii

"Louis, my son, do you see the crown?
You are emperor of Rome if you take it now.
You shall have troops of a hundred thousand
when beyond the Gironde you choose to ride out.
Pagan peoples you shall crush and confound,
and all their lands you shall unite with ours.
If you are ready, receive the crown;
it will never be yours if you refuse it now.

ix

"If you would ever, fair son, accept bribes,   80
in excess and arrogance waste your life,
indulge your lust, favor evil and crime,
seize the fief of an orphaned child,
or four pennies from a widowed wife,
I forbid you this sacred crown of Christ.
Louis my son, you will lose it for life."

Speechless, motionless, stood the child;
for him wept many a worthy knight.
But the emperor burned in sorrow and ire;
"Alas," he said, "I was deceived by my wife—   90
a lowly valet lay at her side
and begat on her this cowardly child.
He will have no more from me in his life.
To crown him king would have been a crime.
Rather we shall cut his hair with a knife
and shut him in church to be a prior,
to pull the ropes and follow the rites;
only his food, lest he beg, I shall provide."
Arneis of Orleans sat at the king's side.
He was fierce in his strength and in his pride.   100
Ruses and flattery he began to devise:
"Just emperor, make peace now, be wise;
my lord is young, it might cause him to die—
he is fifteen—if you made him a knight.
In me, if it please you in your need, confide;
grant for three years, lay your anger aside,
if he become a fit heir, bold and wise,
I shall return his lands to him as is right,
protect and increase them as in my power lies."
The king answered: "Be it so prescribed."   110
"We thank you sire" all the flatterers cried,
they were of Arneis d'Orlean's line.
He would be king had William not arrived,
in haste from hunting in the wilds,
summoned by his nephew Bertrand, afire
with rage: "Whence come you, fair nephew, and why?"
"In God's name, from church, sire,
where evil and treason have been devised.
Arneis deceives his true lord by his guile;
he will be king, the Franks approve his design."   120
"To his misfortune" William the fierce replied.
Wearing his sword, he entered the shrine.

Before him a path opened through the knights.
Arneis stands before him, splendid and bright;
William draws his sword, anxious to strike,
but he thinks on the glorious Lord of the sky—
to kill a man is a mortal crime.
He thrusts his sword in its scabbard, still wild
with rage, forward in fury he strides,
grasps the hair in his left fist, with his right   130
raised high, on his neck he strikes,
breaks the bone, tears his throat wide;
throws him on the ground at his feet to die.
When he had killed him, he began to chide:
"God torment you for ever, traitor!" he cried,
"Why would you your true lord beguile,
when you should have loved him and raised him high,
protected his lands, spread his dominions wide.
There will be no reward for your ambitious pride.
I had thought only a little to chide   140
but you are dead, worth no more than in life."
He sees the crown; on the altar it lies.
The count resolutely lifts it high,
sets it gently on the head of the child:
"Bear it, fair lord, as a burden divine,
may God give you strength to uphold his right."
The father looks on his son with pride:
"William, rich thanks to you and your line,
fair lord, for saving mine from this plight.

X

"Ah Louis, my son," said Charles, "be it known: 150
my realm now is yours in honor to hold,
if you never in life renounce your oath
not to grasp an orphan's land or his gold,
nor to steal the pennies of a poor widow,
and holy church to love and uphold,
that the devil bring no shame to your throne.

Take care to cherish the knights of your host,
they will honor you, in your service be bold,
and through all lands your fame will be known."

xi

And that day Louis became their king.   160
The court retired, when their rights were determined,
and the Franks returned to their daily habits.
Five years and no more, then, did Charles yet live.
Charles the king came to the palace to visit
his son; he spoke these words when he saw him:

xii

"Louis, my son, I would teach you the truth.
The rule of my realm you must soon assume,
when I die, if God bless me. Be assured
what wars I have faced will be renewed,
who hated me will never love you.   170
Him you must, by the Virgin's son, pursue,
refuse him ransom, deny him a truce;
unless you destroy him, he will cause your ruin.

xiii

"Louis, my son, the truth will not be concealed;
for his people God made kings, justly to lead,
not to oppress them with false decrees,
countenance sin or commit adultery,
nor seize of an orphaned child his fief,
nor from a widow her pennies steal,
but he must trample evil under his feet,   180
crush and destroy it, and never fear
the cause of a poor man to honor and heed,
be not annoyed when he makes an appeal.
You should him with patience and wisdom hear,
for the love of God, and his troubles relieve.
Toward the proud you must ever be fierce
as a leopard is eager his victims to eat;

when he makes war with no just cause to plead,
summon all noble knights in France, levy
a host, thirty thousand and more, to lead   190
against his stronghold, his castles besiege,
lay waste and destroy the lands of his fief.
And when by your forces the traitor is seized,
let him not move you to faint-hearted mercy,
but rather hack all his limbs to pieces,
burn him in fire, or drown in the sea.
For if ever the Franks see your defeat,
they will call you a Norman, cowardly, weak:
'Of such a poor king, we have no need.
May the crown of his head be covered with grief   200
who would wait on him at his palace seat,
bear arms for him, his distress relieve.
To redress our wrongs his lands we must seize.'
Of one thing more, my son, take heed,
That, if you live, may spare you grief:
never a peasant in your council receive
nor the son of a provost or overseer;
for small rewards they would often deceive.
But if William, the warrior of valiant deed,
the son of Aimeri of Narbonne the fierce,   210
and his brother Bernard of Brabant bespeak
a will to defend you, you need not fear;
in their loyalty you can firmly believe."
The child replied: "By my head, there is truth in your speech."
He came to the count, fell at his feet.
William hastened to lift him from his knees,
asking him: "Fair squire, what do you seek?"
"In God's name, sire, kindness and mercy.
My father says you're a knight of great deeds,
under heaven's mantle, you have no peer.   220
To you I would entrust my lands and fiefs
to hold for me, noble knight, in your keep,
until I can defend them with sword and shield."
The count replied: "By my faith, willingly."

He swears to him by the saints and their creed,
what little he has, if Louis had need,
he would give of his own will, happily.
Wishing no more to delay, he appealed
to the king, before him fell to his knees:
"True emperor, my lord, I ask your leave,   230
for I must wander, and ride far to seek
Saint Peter and the Pope in the Holy See.
It is fifteen years, I will not conceal,
the promise I made then I must still keep,
I can no longer put off this journey."
The king let him go, but in anger and grief;
he sent sixty armed knights on powerful steeds
and outfitted in silver and gold thirty beasts.
The king and the count kissed, their affection deep.
With this the warrior took his leave;   240
he was not to return, so involved was he
in others' plights, before death had released
Charles and all his lands were left to Louis.
But before William could his weapons wield
in defense of his lord, or his kingdom reach,
Louis was wrongly shut away and concealed,
with no hope but to lose his hands and his feet.
William might have waited too long to appear.

xiv

In the church was William of the Mighty Arm,
he asks leave of the emperor Charles   250
who put sixty men at arms in his charge,
and thirty beasts with gold and silver-filled bags.
Anxious not to delay, the count departs,
Louis escorts him with many a man,
weeping he implores William Fierebrace:
"Ah, noble count, for God's sake, don't go far,
my father will soon from this world depart;
he is old and weak, can no longer bear arms,
and I am young, I cannot take my part.

If I have no help all will come to harm."   260
The count replies: "My lord, do not lose heart,
for, by the apostle I seek in the ark,
while I am away on this pilgrimage,
if you send me a letter sealed by your hand,
or a trusted messenger to call me back,
I shall not be hindered by any man
from aiding you with all my baronage."
Anxious not to delay, the count departs.
Of those days, I don't know what to recall:
Montjeu, he was sad and distressed to pass;   270
not before Rome was there rest for Fierebrace.

XV

So departs William the noble and brave,
with Guielin and Bertrand of great fame;
their inscribed swords they wore beneath their capes,
even with that, to be armed they took care
with gold helmets and good hauberks arrayed.
The squires who followed were, from the strain
of bearing great swords and shields, almost faint.
Of their days I know not what to relate;
Montjeu they were sad and distressed to forsake.   280
They traveled through Romany on their way;
not before Rome did their speed abate.
That night to an inn the squires repaired;
Ciquaire was their good host called by name,
who for their comfort all his wealth displayed.
that night the count was in honor detained.
They went soon to rest, after they ate,
the weary count sleep quickly embraced.
But he dreamt a dream, he was sore afraid:
from Russia a raging fire came   290
it set all of Rome burning in flames.
A boar-hound came at him in wild haste,
first with other hounds, then separate.
Against a leafy tree, William was braced,

before the beast he was dread afraid;
the blow of his paw caused William such pain
before the boar-hound he fell prostrate.
When the count awoke, he began to pray.
No dream ever better revealed a fate,
for Saracens were making haste,   300
the king Galafre and the king Tenebré,
the king Cremu and Corsolt the caliphate,
the main defense of Capua to take,
whose king Gualfier they had there restrained
with his daughter and wife, for beauty famed,
and thirty thousand captives all afraid
their heads would be torn from their trunks in that place.
But God did so love William the sage
that by him all were led from prison safe.
Corsolt, from beyond the Red Sea, for these stakes   310
he fought, the strongest man who was known by fame,
he cut off the nose from William's face,
as you will hear before day fades,
if you give me to think you like my tale.
With these words we are brought to break of day;
Count William rose early and made his way
to the church to hear mass and adore the saints.
All his armor on the altar he laid,
with Arabian gold he would buy it again.
The pope was noble and widely praised;   320
to sing the mass he was richly arrayed.
When the service was said, there suddenly came
two messengers riding hard, all in haste;
with such dark tidings for all to relate
that many a good man was then dismayed.

XVI

To church came William Fierebrace, the bold,
to hear mass sung by the wise pope of Rome.
When it was said, up two messengers rode,
bitter tidings in that church then were told:

great harm was done by the Saracen host,   330
the city of Capua by force they hold,
thirty thousand captives or more they boast;
without help they will suffer a fatal blow.
The message they brought terrified the pope.
Seeking William Fierebrace, swiftly he goes,
who rested below on the marble stone,
praying to God, our father and hope,
to give him honor, courage, and force,
and to the son of Charles, Louis his lord.
The pope does not hesitate to approach   340
the count, or with his staff strike him a blow;
the count looked up and quickly arose.

xvii

Count William swiftly rose to his feet;
the pope then began anxiously to speak:
"Noble knight, for God who rules us justly,
say if only you will now help me.
For pagans and devils are our enemies,
king Galafré is their leader and chief.
He is in distress who was once our shield,
the rich king Gualfier, led off in defeat,   350
with his daughter and his noble queen
and thirty thousand prisoners meek;
they will be killed if they are not soon freed."
"Ah, God help us," said the count of fierce mien;
he crossed himself for so many kings' grief.
But his nephew, Bertrand, began to speak:
"My uncle, are you by madness seized?
For no man before have I seen you fear."
"For the love of God, fair nephew, have mercy.
It would be mad to let our forces meet;   360
to strengthen our side we must first seek,
sending a messenger to young Louis.
Let him with his aid quickly appear,
while Charles remains to uphold his decrees,

for he cannot ride forth, he is old and weak."
Bertrand cried: "By God who rules us justly,
let him by death and madness be seized
who such a shameful message carries;
his shield will be shattered, his armor pierced,
his hauberk torn, gashes long and deep,   370
his body struck down by a mighty spear,
before he dare such a message reveal!
Hundreds and thousands of pagans seek
us in battle; let us arm with speed,
rest our defense in our sturdy shields.
From the men of Rome what shall we fear?
Should we of a hundred thousand take heed?"

xviii

The count of fierce visage stood in the shrine,
and heard the pope's words, courteous and wise:
"Noble lord, for God who defends the right,   380
protect us against these savage tribes."
"Ah, God help us," count Fierebrace replied,
"to Rome but as a pilgrim did I ride,
I have only a few well-armed knights,
no more than sixty rode at my side.
Against so many kings how can we fight?"
"God help us then," said the pope so wise;
"if the keeper of souls, Saint Peter, inspire
you on this day in his service to strike,
you may eat flesh all the days of your life   390
and take women, as much as you like, to wife.
There is no sin so bitter, no vice,
but for treason, that you can devise
that can balance this deed the rest of your life.
You will rest forever in paradise
with all who love God in eternal delight.
The archangel Gabriel will be your guide."
"Ah, God help us," the count Fierebrace cried,
"no priest had ever a heart so fine;

for no man on earth will I be denied,   400
for no pagan, howso monstrous his crimes,
meeting these miscreants in murderous fight.
Bertrand, fair nephew, make ready to ride
with Guielin and the other knights."
William Fierebrace for his weapons cries.
He arms where he stands, he loses no time,
dons the hauberk, laces the helmet bright,
girds on his sword in a sheath at his side.
His piebald steed is led out, his head high;
with no need of stirrups the count leaps astride.   410
From his neck hangs a shield red as fire,
in his firm fist, a spear swift to slice,
fixed by five golden nails its pennant flies:
"My lord pope," asks Count William the wise,
"how many men can you summon to fight?"
The pope answers: "In truth I can provide
three thousand armed men and you may rely
on the strength of their spears and swords swift in strife."
"That's a good beginning," the count replied.
"Have the foot soldiers armed and assigned   420
to hold the barred gates for us with their lives."
He answered: "This seems fitting and right."
Then were assembled all of Rome's knights,
full armed for battle and ready to ride.
The pope blessed them with the sign of Christ:
"My lord barons," began the pope so wise,
"whoever in battle on this day dies
will live forever in paradise
with all who love God in eternal delight.
Saint Gabriel there will be your guide."   430
The men all seize their weapons as they rise
to go forth against proud and savage tribes,
hurtling themselves, with furious cries,
through the great gate which was wondrous high.
"My lord barons," says the pope so wise,
"wait here with your assembly of knights.

I shall go to Galafré and devise
how to persuade him, with wealth of great price
to sail with his barks and barges, retire
with his mighty host that along our shore lies.   440
He shall have the great treasures of our shrine;
all the ark holds I shall sacrifice,
gold and silver, chalices, jewels bright,
before I see such noble men die."
"This is meet and just to say" they reply.
The pope goes, a sole abbot at his side.
To the tents they hasten, they waste no time
until the rich king Galafré they find.
They do not greet him, it would not be right.
The rich king regards them, fierce in his pride.   450
The pope speaks softly, to move him he tries:
"I am come as a messenger of God, sire,
and Saint Peter, who keeps all souls divine,
on their behalf, this message I recite:
sail off in your barks and barges, retire
with your mighty host which on our shore lies.
You shall have the great treasure of our shrine,
all the ark holds I shall sacrifice,
gold and silver, chalices, jewels bright,
before I see such noble men at arms die.   460
Noble king, of good birth, be well advised."
The king answered: "You are not very wise.
I am come for my heritage, Rome is mine.
By my fore-fathers it was colonized,
Romulus, Julius Caesar; far and wide
they flung the walls, built the barriers high.
Down by force these pillars I would strike,
all that is God's I should sacrifice,
bring sorrow and shame to the priests of his rite."
The pope, when he heard, was terrified.   470
For the gold of Carthage he would not abide.
Safe conduct of the emir he required;
three Saracens to protect him were assigned.

Then king Galafré a new truce invites:
"You of the great cloak, stay, speak with me, sire.
I have never yet a just plea denied.
For the city which is my inherited right
choose any man who is valiant in fight
and I shall choose one of my noble line.
Then we shall of our champions make trial.   480
If your God has the power to inspire
the defeat of my champion by your knight,
then you will hold Rome free and for life;
no other man will you ever find
who dare take from you the smallest prize.
But if you suspect me of treacherous guile
I shall let both my sons as hostages ride.
No fortune so great will ransom their lives,
you shall hang them both from a tree to die."
When the pope heard his words, he deemed them wise,   490
all the gold of Carthage no happier prize;
for he sees count Fierebrace in his mind
standing armed before the ark of the shrine.
To bear arms there was no worthier knight.

XIX

For wisdom and learning the pope was revered.
He saw that God wished to bring him relief,
his rights were to rest on one man's deeds.
But he demands all his rights of the enemy:
"Sire," he says, "this should not be concealed:
Since our cause rests on two men it is meet   500
that your champion I be allowed to see,
who would challenge God for Rome with his spear."
The king replies: "I am glad to agree."
King Corsolt was summoned, on foot he appeared,
squint-eyed and ugly, hideous as a fiend;
his eyes like red coals or burning steel,
his head was huge, his hair bristly.
Between his eyes a half foot sweep,

a fathom from shoulder to waist he seemed,
no more hideous man ever ate meat.   510
He rolled his eyes at the frightened priest,
and cried aloud: "Little man, what do you seek?
Are you required to have your head sheared?"
"I serve God, sir," he said, "in his church freely,
and Saint Peter who on earth was our chief.
On his behalf I make this appeal
that you, with your hosts, make ready to leave;
I shall give you all the church treasury,
not a chalice nor censer shall I keep,
nor gold and silver, a single piece   520
shall I attempt from you to conceal."
The king answered: "You are not very wise, I see,
if you dare for God before me to plead.
No man in the world has so angered me.
My father was killed by the lightning he wields;
he was all burned, there was no relief.
When God had killed him, He did as you teach;
he rose to heaven, which He will not leave.
I could not pursue, He was beyond reach,
but I take revenge on His servants and priests.   530
Of those who were baptized by His decrees,
thirty thousand I have crushed in defeat,
burned in fire and drowned in the sea.
If God in battle on high I can't meet,
here below none of His men will I leave.
Then with your God, I will have made my peace;
He may have heaven, but leave earth to me.
If I by force can conquer this fief,
whatever is God's, I shall ravage and steal,
and by the knife make His servants pay dear,   540
and you who are in His church the high priest,
shall be roasted on coals in racking heat
until your liver falls in a brazier deep."
When the pope heard the king's violent speech,
it is not strange, he was seized with great fear.

Some solution with the abbot he seeks:
"By Saint Denis, this Turk is a mad fiend!
A wonder there is earth still at his feet,
that God has not cast him in Hell's fire steep.
Ah William, baron of countenance fierce,   550
may He who hung on the cross be your shield,
against his power you will be in need."
He asks safe conduct of Galafré the fierce,
who entrusts to him his wife's sons dear
to lead back to Rome as they had agreed.
Count William came forward the pope to greet,
the iron of his stirrup he courteously seized.
"Sire," he asked him, "what have you achieved?
Tell me, have you seen the enemy
who thinks to take Rome by God's defeat?   560
Gentle lord, in all this did you succeed?"
"Hear me, fair lord, I will nothing conceal,
this is no man, but a black-hearted fiend.
If Roland and Oliver were now here
with Hates and Berengier, Yvoire and Yve,
the archbishop and the young Manessier,
Estolt of Lengre and Walter the courtly,
Gerin and Engelier, and ranged with these,
those who were killed in battle, the twelve peers,
and if there were the warrior Aimeri,   570
your noble father, whose name is revered,
and all your brothers, knights brave in their deeds,
none would dare this man in battle to meet."
"Tell me, by God," cried William, "who is he?
For now I see how false is the clergy.
First you tell us that if God holds us dear,
he will always help and support us in need,
shamed and dishonored we cannot be,
burned in fire nor drowned in the sea.
But by the apostle whom at Rome we seek,   580
did he into the sky twenty fathoms reach,
I should fight him now with iron and steel.

If God intends to destroy our decrees,
I shall be killed despite my brave deeds.
But if, instead, he will aid and support me,
no man under heaven could cause my defeat,
burn me in fire or drown in the sea."
The pope was heartened when he heard him speak:
"Ah, count," he said, "noble chevalier,
may He who hung on the cross be your shield;   590
no knight has ever made a braver speech.
Jesus will help you whenever you are in need,
whom in thought and desire you always seek."
He had brought from the church the arm of St. Peter,
from its gold and silver cover torn free,
the count kissed the main joint, then the priest
blessed him with it, over his helmet of steel,
over his heart, before and behind, as was meet.
Those jewels would serve him soon in his need:
there was no man who might cause his defeat   600
or inflict harm more than a coin's width deep,
but even for that the brave man would be teased.
Quickly he mounted his battle steed,
hanging at his neck a quartered shield,
and in his fist a swift cutting spear.
Boldly he rode to the hilltop with speed,
grimly watched by his pagan enemies.
They told each other: "What a fine knight is he,
bold and wise, educated and courtly.
Were he to fight today with his peer,   610
to begin combat he would be fierce,
but against Corsolt no force will serve his need.
He could do no more, were he fourteen."

XX

King Galafré came forth from his tent,
a majestic figure in elegant dress,
towards the hill and the count his look was bent.
"The Frank has come," he remarked to his men.

"There on the hill—he bears his armor well.
He must do battle with Corsolt the dread
against whom he is pitifully impotent.   620
Not even Mohammed or Cahu can help;
King Corsolt will soon bring this to an end."
The champion appeared, for the king had sent.
He went forth to meet him with arms outstretched:
"You are welcome, fair nephew," the king said,
I have seen the Frank on the battered ascent,
he will not withdraw, this is his intent."
Corsolt replied: "He is destroyed and dead.
I have seen him, now let me quickly dress.
Bring me my arms, why delay our success?"   630
Seven kings, fifteen dukes, ran to attend,
beneath a broad tree his armor was set.
But these arms now exist only in legend.
Could another man ever carry them,
he would not take all the world's gold in their stead.

XXI

Fourteen kings helped arm the pagan foe,
on his back they placed a shirt of steel cold,
then a white double hauberk to guard from blows.
He girds on the sword that has wreaked such woe,
a half foot wide and long, heavy to hold.   640
He carries his laced quiver and long-bow,
his crossbow and square-headed steel arrows,
darts that were sharp and ready to throw;
his steed was led up, Alion the bold.
The horse was marvelously fierce and noble
and spirited as I have been told.
Even at a distance he let none approach,
but the one man who always rode.
Before him four darts were attached to the horn,
behind hung an iron mace from the saddle-bow;   650
by the stirrup mounted the king Corsolt.
At his neck hung a shield of purest gold,

a quartered-shield of great breadth, with huge bolts;
a lance he had ever refused to hold,
but double arms on him they bestowed.
Oh God! What a horse king Corsolt rode,
however he checked him the steed would bolt,
that neither hare no hound could come close.
Then he turned to his uncle and spoke:
"The terms of peace," he cried, "you may compose.   660
Let your seneschals quickly approach,
prepare a feast, have the tables disposed.
For this poor Frank there is little hope,
sooner will he be dead and overthrown
than you can on foot half an acre cross.
My sword I should have no need to hold,
if with my mace I can strike one good blow;
unless I crush him and his steed below,
let no man again give me food to swallow."
"Mohammed help you!" cried the pagan host.   670
Through the vast army the champion rode,
in Mohammed the pagans put their hope.
Count William watched his opponent approach,
heavily armed, hideous to behold.
It is no wonder the count's fear grows;
God his true father he praised and extolled.
"By Saint Mary," he cried, "this steed is noble!
He must be good when his rider is bold.
I must spare him and gain him for my own;
may God prevent, who is judge of all souls,   680
that with my sword I harm such a horse."
These are not words of a coward's boast.

XXII

William climbed the hill, there he remained
with fine weapons and armor well arrayed,
and watched as the furious pagan came.
It is not to his shame that he was afraid.
He alit from his waiting steed to pray.

Towards the Orient then he turned his face
and said a prayer of such goodness and grace
that no man born of woman under heaven's gaze,   690
if he said it with good will and deep faith
in the morning when he arose each day,
could ever be by the devil betrayed.
With great humility he sought God's aid:
"Glorious God, who set me in this place,
and the earth to your will did once create,
enclosing it round with great rushing waves,
Adam you formed and then Eve as his mate,
led them to live in the Eden you made,
the fruit of all trees you gave them to taste;   700
from the apple alone they were to abstain,
which, in their folly, they desired and ate.
They could not conceal it—it brought them shame.
Paradise they were bound to forsake;
to plow and labor the earth they came,
to endure and suffer mortal pain.
Cruelly was Abel murdered by Cain;
then the earth began to weep and wail,
a cruel gift they were given that day:
nothing leaves earth but to return again.   710
Oh God, those who were born of this race
were never to give you honor or praise;
you destroyed them all in ravaging rains.
Noah alone, no other escaped,
with his three sons and their wives, he was saved.
Of every beast, to fill the world, a pair
he had set in the ark, female and male.
Oh God, from this people was born a race
from which the virtuous Virgin came
in whose womb to hide your body you deigned.   720
There in flesh and blood was your body made
and your holy blood that had a martyr's name.
Bethlehem, city of wondrous fame,
you were pleased, true God, to make your birth-place

on the night of Noel which we celebrate.
Saint Anastasia you caused to be raised;
to care for your body she had no hand,
but all she could wish, you freely gave.
Then came three kings who wished homage to pay,
myrrh, gold and frankincense before you laid.   730
For you they followed a tortuous way,
that they might the cruel Herod evade,
eager to murder and mutilate.
He caused the Innocents to be slain,
thirty thousand, as learned men relate.
Thirty two years as a man you remained,
wandering the earth, to spread far the new faith.
You went forth to fast in the desert wastes,
and there you remained full forty days;
you suffered the devil to tempt you in vain.   740
On White Easter, with palms, now we celebrate,
you were pleased, true God, to go your way
to Jerusalem of wondrous fame,
where they opened for you the famed gold gate.
You scorned the rich in their great estate,
your heart to the poor, simply, you gave.
With Simon the leper you chose to stay;
the twelve apostles there did congregate.
Mary Magdalene silently came,
sat at your feet, not a word dared she say.   750
With her bright tears your feet she embraced,
she wiped them dry then with her rich hair.
There all her sins you gently forgave.
Then by Judas you were cruelly betrayed;
in his folly he sold you, to his shame,
for thirty coins from Methusalah's day,
to the false Jews when he kissed your face.
Beaten and scourged you were bound to a stake
until morning of the next day
when to a hilltop they led you, in pain,   760
Mount Calvary, I have heard it named.

At your neck a great cross they made you bear,
they covered you with a hideous cape,
and let you not move one step on your way,
that you were not struck or beaten again.
To the holy cross your body was nailed,
your blessed limbs exhausted and strained.
Then Longinus of happy fortune came,
he had not heard you, nor yet seen your face,
he thrust his lance, renewing your pain,   770
blood and water ran down his arm and his face,
he wiped his eyes, by great light he was dazed.
He beat his chest, ashamed and afraid,
in your goodness all his sins you forgave.
Nicodemus later with Joseph came,
stealing silent like thieves in the night's shade,
down from the cross they took your body pale,
to final rest in the sepulchre laid.
When you arose at the third day,
you descended to Hell's fire and flames   780
to cast those you loved forth; long had they stayed
for your coming in that sorrow-filled place.
As this is true, king in majesty great,
defend my body, that I may escape
death at the hand of this devil incarnate.
He is so huge, so hideous, so in haste,
holy Mary, please come to my aid,
let me not be the cause of a dreadful disgrace
through cowardice on all of my race."
He stood up and made the cross on his face.   790
The Saracen approached with troubled gaze,
he saw William and did not hesitate:
"Tell me now Frank, don't be slow to say,
whom you addressed in this long tirade."
"I'll tell you the truth," said William; "I prayed
to the God of glory, in majesty great,
that he would me in his goodness sustain,
that I might all your limbs from your body tear,

and leave you to lie on this hilltop slain."
The pagan cried: "You are mad with raving.   800
Do you really think your God will be able
to protect you from my furious rage?"
"Monster," cried William, "God will be paid,
for if He will only grant me His aid,
your great pride will be crushed in disgrace."
"Fierce in your folly," said the Turk, "you rave,
if you will Mohammed adore and praise,
your other God deny and forsake,
you shall such honor and wealth attain
that has never been seen by all your race."   810
"Monster," said William, "God bring you pain!
Never by me will He be betrayed."
"In truth," said the Turk, "you are fiercely brave.
Since you can no longer your body spare
from this combat, tell me, what is your name?"
"That," said William, "I can proudly say.
From no man have I ever kept my name.
I am William the marquis, by God's grace,
the son of Aimeri, whose beard is now gray,
and Ermengard, renowned for her bright face.   820
Bernard is my brother of Brabant fame,
and Hernaut of Gironde on the sea, and brave
Garin, whose deeds will ever be praised,
Bueves of Commarch, who leaves terror in his wake,
Guibert of Andernas, the youngest in days,
Aimer, too, is our brother of noble grace,
who enters no lovely home, but remains
outside in the wind and breeze all the day,
so he helps to destroy the Saracen race;
for your people he has nothing but hate."   830
The pagan listened fuming with rage,
he rolled his eyes wildly, his eyebrows raised:
"You have gone too far now, cursed Frank, to be spared.
Too many of my people have by yours been slain."

XXiii

Fiercely the Saracen berated the youth:
"Can't you see, William, you speak like a fool?
You believe in a God who is of no use.
From beyond the firmament, what can he do?
Here on earth no one accepts his rule,
it is Mohammed's laws we execute.   840
All your sacraments and holy books,
your weddings and masses, all your priesthood
are as a gust of wind in a typhoon.
Christianity is only for fools."
"Miscreant," cried William, "God will destroy you
and crush forever your unholy rule.
For Mohammed—the world knows this is true—
was a prophet of our lord Jesù.
He crossed the mountains preaching the truth
and came to Mecca where he abused   850
our faith with drinking and pleasures crude
and fittingly ended as pigs' food.
If you believe in him you are deluded."
The pagan said: "Your lies are base and rude.
If you would do as I advised you
and freely accept Mohammed's truth,
I should give you honors and lands to rule,
greater than any your line ever knew,
for I know you are of noblest issue.
I have heard oft of your courageous youth;   860
it is not right that you should die so soon.
Tell me quickly, if you accept this truce.
You will die in torment if you refuse."
"Miscreant," said William, "may God destroy you!
Now I see you are not what I assumed—
there is no courage in threats and abuse."
William mounted his steed, handsome and sure,
neither stirrups nor saddle-bow does he use.

His quartered shield at his neck hung loose;
he brandished his spear fierce and resolute,   870
from his lance his defiant standard flew.
The Saracen watched him in grim fury,
speaking to himself so that no one knew:
"By Mohammed, who is my soul's greatest good,
this is a man with fierce courage imbued."
Had William suspected the pagan's mood
and wished to accept the offered truce,
he would have found peace easy to conclude.

xxiv

"Tell me then, Frank," asked Corsolt the wild,
"by your God for whom you must fight,   880
do you claim Rome as your inherited right?"
"You shall soon know," count Fierebrace replied.
"On horse and with arms I must now fight
in the name of God our spiritual sire.
Our emperor Charles holds Rome by right,
Romany, Tuscany and Calabria wide.
Saint Peter is its protector divine
and the pope in whose governance it lies."
The king answered: "You are not very wise.
If you would seize this heritage by might,   890
then it is meet that we settle in strife,
but I'll give an advantage to your side:
hold fast your arms, and raise your spear high,
and strike my shield, I shall stand still behind,
to put your valor a little to trial
and see how a small man in battle can strike."
William said: "I would be mad to decline."
Spurring his horse, a long acre he rides
from the mountain that was immense and wide.
Holding fast his arms, in his saddle he rises,   900
the Saracen makes no move to retire.
The pope cries out: "Now we shall see a fight.
Wise men and fools, now quickly alight.

Let each pray God with his whole heart and mind
to bring William Fierebrace back alive,
safe and sound within the walls of Rome high."
The noble count chose barons to recite
prayers for him. Why should he longer abide?
He spurs his horse, drops the reins at his side;
brandishes the lance and the silk standard flies.   910
On the red shield of the pagan he strikes,
beats and crashes—the blow's force was dire.
It pierced and tore the hauberk white,
the old mail-shirt is not worth a dime.
The sharp spear cuts through him like a knife,
the broad banner appears at the other side
flying from the iron, a dreadful sight.
Such was count William's overwhelming might.
He tore his good spear out of his side.
But the pagan's spirit was still high;   920
he said softly that none might know his mind:
"By Mohammed, whom I have glorified,
only a fool would scorn a man for his size
when he sees him undertake a great fight.
This morning in the field, little did I prize
his valor, when I saw him, or his might
and yet I must have been out of my mind
when I gave that advantage to his side.
Never did I think to pay so high a price."
His pain was so sharp he could scarcely rise.   930
Count William hastened once more to strike.

XXV

William was most powerful and strong.
He struck the pagan with all his force,
he tore out the spear with such ardor
it ripped the shield at his neck from its chord,
his good shield of gold fell beneath the horse.
The men of Rome raised an excited roar:
"Strike again, bold count, with the aid of the lord!

Saint Peter, sire, be still our protector!"
The noble count William spurs on his horse   940
when he hears their words; he thrusts himself forth,
he brandishes his lance, his banner aloft,
he strikes the pagan's hauberk with such force
that it opens wide, all mangled and torn,
not two nails was the old mail-shirt now worth.
He sends the spear deep in his body soft,
on the other side the iron came forth.
A lesser wound in another would have cost
his life. The Saracen was not daunted.
A javelin from his saddle-bow he shot,   950
it struck count William with such great force
lightning could not have burned his neck more.
The count falls forward, afraid he is lost,
he was struck on the back through his armor.
God protected him, his flesh was not torn.
"God," says the count, "who gave life to Saint Loth,
will you keep me, dear lord, from dying wronged?"

XXVI

The Saracen knows his wound is deep.
In his chest lies still the count's dark spear,
the blood runs down from the wound to his feet.   960
He says softly so that no one can hear:
"By Mohammed, whose pardon I entreat,
no man has ever dealt me such a defeat.
What a fool I was to be so deceived,
that I gave him an advantage over me."
A dart from his saddle-bow he seized,
threw it at William with furious speed,
like an eagle, burning, his neck it pierced.
The count turned from the traitor he feared,
for he had cut through his lion shield,   970
and his old mail-shirt for defense was weak;
it passed his side with such force and speed
that it struck deep into the sand two feet.

William bows his head at what he sees,
God by his most holy name he entreats:
"Glorious father, who formed earth and the spheres,
who set the earth on a marble seat,
and girded it round with the salt seas,
Adam You made of earth and clay, and Eve
for his mate, as the holy books teach.   980
You made them a gift of paradise sweet
and offered them all the fruits of the trees,
one apple alone You forbade them to eat
but they disobeyed to their lasting grief.
For God imposed such a cruel penalty:
in Hell in the well of Baratron deep,
Belzebut and Neiron their overseers.
One Easter You came on the back of a beast,
the child of an ass You chose for Your steed,
little children followed in procession, meek.   990
On White Easter since then, clergy and priests
a sacred procession in Your honor lead.
With Simon the leper You chose to sleep. ⁷
There Mary Magdalene came for mercy
she wept so sore with her eyes at your feet,
washing them with her penitent tears,
You lifted her gently, touching her cheek
and pardoned her sins with infinite mercy.
Then Judas committed his treacherous deed:
he sold You and was brought to lasting grief;   1000
thirty coins for You the traitor received.
You were hung on a cross between two thieves.
As evil wretches were the Jews revealed;
in Your resurrection they would not believe.
On Ascension You rose to heaven's spheres, ⁒
thence the great redemption, sire, will proceed,
on the Judgment day when we all appear.
Then the father will no longer the son precede,
nor the clerk follow after the priest,
his page will then be the archbishop's peer;   1010

the duke the king's; the count the overseer's;
but no traitor will then receive mercy.
You confessed the apostles by your decrees;
placed Nero's meadow in Saint Peter's keep,
converted his friend Saint Paul to your creed;
You saved Jonah, whom the great fish did eat,
and the hunger of Saint Simon relieved,
rescued Daniel from the den of the beast.
Simon Magus You crushed in defeat;
the flame in the bush You made Moses see,   1020
that did not burn or make coal of the tree.
As it is all true, and we must believe,
my body from death, Lord, and prison keep,
let not the evil Saracen kill me.
He bears so many arms I cannot draw near,
a great cross-bow at his side he carries,
at his saddle-bow hangs an iron mace fierce.
If He who forgave Longinus does not heed,
so many weapons I cannot defeat."
Three words in reproach of him Corsolt speaks: 1030
"William, like a coward's your heart is weak.
I wonder that you such a champion seem;
you are not shy your weapons to wield,
but your arms will no longer bring you relief."
He turned around on his Arragon steed
and drew the sword at his side from its sheath.
He struck William with a blow so fierce
he tore the helmet, the nasal was pierced.
He cracked the hood of the hauberk that gleamed,
and crushed the hair on his forehead lean,   1040
cut the end of his nose with his sharp steel,
for which the count would much ridicule hear.
The blow struck the saddle-bow beneath,
and hacked in two halves the noble steed.
The blow was huge and it came with much speed;
it cast three hundred rings on the ground at his feet.
The sword from the monster's hand was thrown clear.

Count William quickly leapt to his feet
and drew Joyeuse at his side from its sheath;
to wound his foe on the helmet he seeks,   1050
but so large and immense and long was he
for all the world's gold he could not succeed.
The blow fell on the hauberk that gleamed,
it cast three hundred rings on the ground at his feet.
But the old mail shirt protected the fiend,
not a spur's worth of damage did he feel.
Corsolt shouted three words in his fury:
"William, like a coward your heart is weak:
your blows are worth no more than a flea's."
The men of Rome cried as one in their grief,   1060
with the pope who was shivering in fear:
"Saint Peter, lord, help your knight in his need,
if he should die there will be no relief;
in your church, while we live, no one will hear
the offices or the mass of our creed."

XXVII

Count William stood, his look noble and strong,
on the mountain, fully armed, as he fought;
he saw that the pagan had lost his sword
with which he had cleft the spine of his horse.
The Turk goes the length of a cross-bow or more,   1070
brandishing his mighty mace aloft,
he charges William his head low before;
at the mouth, like an angry beast, he froths,
in a wild wood, chased and hunted by dogs.
The count saw him and held his shield forth.
The Turk struck him a blow of such force
from his head the length of his body it tore,
cut through the armor where the buckle was wrought;
and passed swiftly into the hole it had bored,
unhindered and violent in its course.   1080
Near the helmet the mace passed all along;
his head bowed at the blow, his suffering sore.

For his part Rome would then have been lost,
without the blessed Virgin and her lord.
The cries of all Rome to the heavens soared:
"Where are you, Saint Peter?" the pope implored,
"if he dies it will be a cruel fate and wrong.
In your church your rites will not be performed
as long as I live and remain strong."

XXVIII

The noble count William was stunned and dazed,   1090
overwhelmed by the sharp blow and his pain;
troubled by something he could not explain,
that the Turk so long on his horse remained,
although the loss of his blood had been great.
Had he wished, he might have unhorsed him straight
but he was more anxious the steed to spare,
for his thought was, that was something to gain
which might often later come to his aid.
The Saracen charging in fury came;
when he saw William he began to rage: 1100
"Miserable Frank, you have made a mistake,
half of your nose has been cut from your face;
by Louis now you must be maintained
and your line will suffer taunts and disgrace.
Now you must see that you cannot escape;
I must return with your body in haste,
for the emir's court at dinner awaits;
he will wonder that I am so delayed."
Over the saddle-bow he bent his face,
thinking on the neck of his steed to lay   1110
William's body fully armed and prostrate.
William watched him, and forgot his dismay;
he readied himself for this blow with care,
he struck the king, nothing did he spare,
on his helmet of gold richly arrayed.
Flowers and jewels fell to earth in a blaze
then he cut through the great hood of iron-mail;

the good head-piece he had to forsake,
for the crown had been opened a palm's space.
He fell over the neck of his steed in pain.   1120
He could not rise, his arms heavy on him weighed.
"God," said William, "I've avenged my nose's shame!
Never by Louis shall I be maintained,
my family will never be so disgraced."
He drew his arm out of the broad shield's stays
and threw it off in the field a short way;
no knight was ever so daringly brave.
If the Turk had been whole and sound and safe,
· for his folly, it would all have begun again.
But God would allow the Turk no more aid,   1130
and Count William no longer need hesitate.
With his two fists the steel sword he raised
and struck the king—he would nothing spare.
He cut through the brilliant helmet's stays,
the head with the helmet flew four feet in the air;
the body staggered and fell—the Turk was slain.
Count William would no longer delay;
the good sword which had disfigured his face
he would gird on—it was too long to bear,
he went to the saddle-bow and hung it there.   1140
The stirrups a foot and a half longer again,
when they had been half a foot shorter made
Count William mounted with the stirrup's aid.
He drew his spear, as the Saracen lay,
from his body where it still remained;
the whole of the lance was dark with blood stains.
"Oh God," said William, "what thanks I should say
for the horse that in this combat I gained!
Montpelier's gold I would not for him take.
Long have I coveted him today."   1150
From there to Rome William rides in great haste.
To receive him and greet him the pope came
and kissed him when his helmet was unlaced.
How his nephews, Guielin had wept and prayed

and count Bertrand and Walter the fair!
Never beneath heaven were they so afraid.
"Uncle," he asked, "are you well then and safe?"
"Yes," he answered, "by God's heavenly grace,
only the nose is shorter on my face,
but I am sure that will lengthen my name."   1160
The count baptized himself there again.
"Henceforth, by all who love and would praise,
by Franks and Lombards, I shall be named
Count William Short Nose, the warrior brave."
Never after was the name to be changed.
Then all rode on, to the great church they came.
Who then held his stirrup, his joy was great.
The noble count all night they celebrate
until the morrow at the dawn of day.
They had many other things to debate.   1170
Then Bertrand cried: "To arms, knights, once again!
Since the field by my uncle has been gained
from the giant of whom all were afraid,
against the weak let us try what we may.
Uncle William, to rest now you should stay,
for you have struggled and suffered much pain."
William listened and laughed, his feelings to feign:
"Ah Bertrand, sir, do you seek my disgrace?
Your attempt, you must know, is bound to fail,
for by the apostle whom pilgrims praise,   1180
by Montpelier's gold I could not be stayed
from leading our army into the fray
until I have struck with my steel sword and slain."
When the Romans had heard him so declaim,
the most cowardly grew agile and brave.
Let the perfidious villains take care,
that they do not too long hesitate,
while the Romans now for battle prepare.

XXIX

King Galafré has come forth from his tent,
a majestic figure in regal dress.   1190

"I have lost much," he said to his men,
"that Corsolt is thus defeated and dead.
The God they believe in deserves their respect.
Take care now quickly to strike all my tents;
we must all flee, what good can we expect?
If the Romans now in attack descend,
not one of our army will escape them."
They answered: "We will do as you suggest."
Then sounded together fourteen trumpets,
the host mounted, rode off like a tempest.   1200
But William had heard the roar of movement.
"We've waited too long," he cried to his men,
"the pagans—miserable wretches—have fled.
For Jesus, our king, quickly after them!"
The men of Rome charged in roaring torrent,
William kept his place always at their head,
the noble count, though he was exhausted.
By the sharp spurs Alion was impelled
to charge with such force he could scarce be checked,
so light the rider he now carried felt.   1210
Between two hills the pagans were pressed.
What a battle might you have seen there then,
how many breasts struck, how many trunks and heads!
Count Bertrand exacted a price, though he bled.
His lance broken, he drew his sword instead.
Whomever he struck, he pierced through the breast,
hauberks were not worth a straw in defense.
Many blows he received, but more he dealt.
Guielin struck many with fatal success,
Walter of Toulouse caused much blood to be shed;   1220
but William was held above all in dread.
When he saw King Galafré William pressed
forward his horse, with his shield at his neck.
When King Galafré perceived his intent,
in his heart he called on Cahu and Mohammed:
"Lord Mohammed, see how I am oppressed!
If you will it, then grant me the strength
to restrain William, his ravages check."

With his sharp spurs his steed forward he pressed.
Count William saw him, he was not distressed.   1230
Mighty blows high on the shields they direct;
the bucklers are broken over the breast,
white hauberks mangled and torn in the stress.
Along their bodies the cold iron is felt.
William the terrible by God was helped
and by Saint Peter whose cause he upheld,
for the pagan king did not wound his flesh.
But the noble count such a fierce blow dealt
that neither stirrup on the horse was left.
The animal shied at the blow's great strength,   1240
and the king fell to the earth as if dead.
Stuck in the earth was the point of the helm,
two of the stays were broken from the stress.
Count William then over the body bent,
he drew his sword of sharp steel; his intent
was to sever from that body the head.
But God performed a miracle then
by which many sorrowing captive men
free from prison on that day were led.

XXX

Count William was a knight of worthy deeds: 1250
when he saw the king prostrate at his feet
he might have cut off his head had he pleased,
but the king cried out for gentle mercy:
"Baron, if you are William, don't kill me,
take me alive, you will be paid richly.
The rich king Gualfier shall be set free
with his noble wife and his daughter meek,
and thirty thousand prisoners released,
who, if I die, will be killed horribly."
"By Saint Denis," said the count of visage fierce,   1260
for this alone I must grant your appeal."
Into the stirrup Count William leaps.
The king surrenders his rich sword of steel,

which the count sends to be in the pope's keep
with three hundred prisoners they have seized.
When the Saracens, perfidious beasts,
see their rightful lord so crushed in defeat,
along paths and roadways they flee in fear,
rushing to the Tiber with furious speed.
They must find their ships, they are in great need;   1270
they enter them, they would soon these shores leave.
Count William from the field turns back his steed.
The kings disarm beneath an olive tree.
The noble count to the conquered king speaks:
"Ah noble king! For God who rules justly,
how will the captive prisoners be freed
who in your barges lie bound and concealed?"
The king answers: "It is in vain you plead,
for, by the cross that holy pilgrims seek,
not one gold piece will you receive from me   1280
until I am baptized by your decrees,
for Mohammed can no longer help me."
"Thanks be to God," said William, "for this deed!"
The gentle pope hastened to make ready
the baptismal fonts that he might receive
the king in the sacrament of their creed.
As godfather, William the knight stood near,
with Guielin and Walter the courtly,
and thirty knights, powerful, worthy peers,
each one of them born noble and free;   1290
his name they wished not to change, but to keep
and renew, as for a Christian was meet.
They asked for water and sat down to eat.
When they had enough to serve all their needs,
Count William swiftly arose to his feet:
"Ah, gentle king, by God who rules justly,
my noble son, come and tell me in peace.
How will the captive prisoners be freed
from your barges where they lie bound and concealed?"
The king answered: "My advice you must heed;   1300

for if the Saracens and pagans hear
that I was raised and baptized in your creed,
to be flayed alive they would rather leave me
than give any treasure for my relief.
Now take away my fine garments and clean
and set me to ride on a mangy beast.
Send with me a group of knights and conceal,
close to the Tiber where they can hear me,
all your men armed with their weapons and steeds
under this wall, among the olive trees.   1310
If the Saracens should with armed might seek
to bring me aid and secure my release,
you will all stand ready with lowered spears."
"God," said William, "by your holy mercy,
no nobler convert could break bread and eat."
They swear him an oath they will surely keep
to spare him from blows, he need have no fear;
but they sprinkled hare's blood from his head to his feet.
From there to the Tiber they rode with speed.
King Galafré shouted as he rode near,   1320
aloud he cried: "Champion, my nephew, hear,
son of a baron, and bring me relief.
Let the captive prisoners be released;
know, if they are, that I shall be freed."
Champion answered: "Mohammed had mercy
on you, if wealth can your body reprieve."
They make fast the dromont at the shore, lead
forth the captive prisoners now free,
whom the pagans had so cruelly beat
because they were conquered in war and seized.   1330
There was not one whose arms did not bleed,
shoulders and head and body. For pity
William the warrior wept gentle tears.

XXXI

When the captives from the barges were cast
there was not one whose face or whose arms

and body did not bleed from the lash.
For pity wept Count William Fierebrace;
he went to the pope, his counsel he asked:
"Sire, by God in whom we hope," he began,
"many nobles bare at the breast here stand. 1340
Let us put fine gowns and furs on their backs,
gold and silver and whatever we have
that they may return as lords to their lands."
The pope said: "You are a noble, good man;
let all generously extend their hands.
It is right that we redeem their mischance."
They rode on to Rome, they never looked back.
The captives' ills were redressed at last;
in gowns and mantles of fur they were clad,
gold and silver and whatever they had 1350
that they might return as lords to their lands.

XXXII

When all the host to Rome had retired,
on a marble step sat Count William the knight.
Of a sudden the rich king Gualfier arrived.
He threw himself down at his feet and cried:
"Noble man, sire, you have given me my life,
you have saved me from the fierce pagan tribes
who would have led me into bitter exile,
never to see my lands and honors wide.
I have a daughter, there is no gentler child, 1360
whom I would gladly give you to wife;
if you always hold her in honor high,
you shall have half my lands now, and in time,
you will be my sole heir after I die."
The count answered: "I must be advised."
He went to the pope and drew him aside:
"Sire," he asked him, "shall I take her to wife?"
"With great joy, fair lord, for it would be wise.
You have no land, you are still a young knight."
"Then I shall give my pledge" the count replied. 1370

He was taken to see his promised wife.
No man of flesh, pilgrim or palmer, might,
should he through the whole world wander and ride,
a more beautiful lady ever find.
William the warrior was so struck at the sight,
that to leave her sadly oppressed his mind,
as you shall hear before sun sets this night.

xxxiii

Would you now hear her fair beauty extolled?
No man of flesh, however far he rode,
might a more beautiful woman behold.   1380
When duty forced William of the short nose
to forsake her he suffered deep sorrow,
as you shall hear before the sun is low,
two messengers, riding hard, now approached;
from France they come; furiously they rode
their weary horses until they reached Rome.
Long for Count William they have searched and sought
until in the holy church they behold
the count with his lady before the host,
to be married there by the gentle pope,   1390
arrayed for the mass in his finest robes.
The ring to marry the lady he holds
when the messengers rush in and bow low:
"Have mercy, William, for God's love, on our souls.
Do you forget young Louis and your oath?
For Charles is dead, who was noble and bold;
his rich heritage Louis now holds,
whom traitors are plotting to overthrow.
They would set another king on the throne,
the son of Richard of Rouen, the old.   1400
All the land has been struck down with sorrow,
noble man, sire, you are our only hope."
William heard them, then he bowed his head low.
He drew to one side, for counsel, the pope:
"My lord," he begged, "make my real duty known."

The pope answered: "God be praised, by my soul!
Who seeks counsel in faith, should truly be told.
As a penitent I would have you go,
Louis, your lord, to relieve and uphold.
Great ills will come when he is overthrown."   1410
The count answered: "If you would have it so,
your good counsel will not be opposed."
William kissed the lady whose bright face shone
and she kissed him but her gentle tears flowed.
So, in sorrow, they abandoned their oaths;
they were never after to fulfill their hopes.
"William, my lord," said the most noble pope,
"since to sweet France once again you must go,
Galafré the emir will stay to hold,
on your behalf, the rich country of Rome."   1420
The count answered: "That was madness you spoke.
I could never such rank treason condone,
while the rights of my lord I yet uphold."
"William, my lord," said the most noble pope,
since to sweet France once again you must go,
you shall lead a thousand knights in your host,
thirty beasts laden with silver and gold.
You won it all—it is yours to dispose."
The count answered: "Your goodness shall be known."

XXXIV

On a Sunday, fifteen days after Lent,   1430
William Fierebrace was in Rome, his intent
to take a wife, a king's daughter to wed.
His lady Orable he seemed to forget,
when two messengers from France were sent
with bitter news to Count William to tell:
that his emperor and lord, Charles, was dead.
All his lands to his son Louis he left.
But traitors, may God's body have revenge,
the bearded son of Richard of Rouen would set
on the throne with all the barons present.   1440

For sad pity William Fierebrace wept.
He took his leave of the wise pope, who sent
a thousand armed knights, William to attend,
thirty beasts with gold and silver they led.
When he departed many barons wept.
He could not delay, the count quickly left,
he passed Montjeu, he was deeply distressed.
Of their long days I know not what to tell;
they rode to Brie, they did not stop to rest.

XXXV

William of the short nose left Rome in haste.   1450
Of his long days I know not what to say;
until he came to Brie, he would not stay.
He saw a pilgrim walking on his way,
staff in hand, a purse at his neck, he came,
so fine a pilgrim you would not see again;
his beard was white like April's gentle sprays.
William saw him and spoke without delay:
"Where are you from, brother?" "Saint Martin of Tours, of late."
"Have you no news that you might relate?"
"Yes, my fair lord, of the young Louis' fate.   1460
For the king of Saint Denis, Charles, lies in his grave
and the country was left to Louis' care.
But traitors, God curse them, would in his place
the son of old Richard of Rouen name
to be king of France and her lands maintain.
But a noble abbot, God give him grace,
to a crypt in Saint Martin's has escaped
with the young child and so far they are safe;
they think not of the hour they will be slain.
God help us," the noble pilgrim despaired,   1470
"where are the noble knights and the brave
of the valiant Count Aimeri's race?
They were ever swift their lord to sustain.
By the cross on which God suffered such pain,
if I were a man who could offer aid,

the foul traitors I should have so disgraced
they would no more think their lord to betray."
William heard him and laughed at his rage.
Then he called Bertrand to his side to say:
"You'll not see so noble a pilgrim again.   1480
If he were a man who could offer aid
no evil plots would ever have been laid."
Ten ounces of gold to the pilgrim they gave,
in good spirits they sent him on his way.
William goes on, the long road he sustains.
He who has friends was born with a good fate.
At the road that lies before, William stares;
seven score knights he sees riding straight,
on fine chargers, in bright armor arrayed.
Gualdin the dark, riding before them came,   1490
and at his side rode Savari the brave,
they were nephews of William, on their way
to France to offer young Louis their aid.
When they all meet they are stunned and amazed;
as nephews and friends they kiss and embrace.
They will surprise the abbot of noble race
who has the little Louis in his care.
If he can, for a short while, keep him safe,
and Alori's family somehow evade,
before three days are past he will have aid.   1500

XXXVI

On rides William the warrior fierce.
Twelve hundred knights in his army he leads.
To the whole host he has sent a decree:
that each man spur on his charger or steed,
and he tells them to ride with utmost speed,
of sparing the horses not to take heed;
for a lost dray he will give a fine steed.
"I would be there at the start of these deeds.
I wish to find out for myself and see
who would be king and give France his decrees.   1510

For by the apostle whom pilgrims seek,
whoever now would be so proud and fierce,
on his head I shall set a crown indeed;
his brains will be crushed down into his feet."
The Romans say: "This man's heart is most fierce.
If we fail him may God bring us to grief!"
I know not what to tell of their journey;
from here to Tours they ride on with all speed.
Wisely the count has chosen to proceed:
a thousand knights in four corps he concealed,   1520
only two hundred well-equipped, he leads,
wearing white double hauberks hard to pierce,
beneath their hoods laced helmets bright and clean;
they girded on their polished swords of steel.
With their arms, close behind their squires keep,
carrying the strong shields and cutting spears
for the knights to call on when they have need.
On to the gates they ride without relief.
They order the gate-keeper to appear:
"Open the gate, let us quickly proceed.   1530
We are come with the aid Duke Richard seeks.
Today in the church his son will receive
the crown as king, the Franks have so decreed."
The gate-keeper rages at what he hears.
To God our righteous father he appeals,
the courteous keeper cried: "By Saint Mary,
how poor your defenses, my lord Louis!
Unless he, who is judge of all, take heed,
you will not escape with your hands and feet.
Ah! God help us!" said the courteous keeper,   1540
"where are the valiant knights and fierce
of the line of the warrior Aimeri
who were wont to help their lord in his need?"
He told William: "You shall not enter here.
There are too many traitors and thieves;
I will not have their numbers increased.
I wonder the earth such evil carries;

for if God in his glory had so pleased
He could have opened the earth beneath your feet
and brought Louis back to his rightful fief.   1550
And the world would be avenged on the fiends."
William rejoiced and was glad at his speech.
He called Bertrand: "Sir nephew, now tell me
when have you heard such a gate-keeper speak?
Who would a courageous heart reveal,
he may well serve us today in our need."

XXXVII

"My friend, fair brother," said William the knight,
you were rash my entrance to deny
for if you knew what land gave me life,
of what people I am born, of what line,   1560
if from your words I can perceive your mind,
you would with joy our entrance invite."
His words made the gate-keeper quickly arise,
open a window to look with his eyes:
"Noble man, sir, if I dared to inquire,
I would ask of you what land gave you life,
of what people you were born, of what line."
"I shall tell you the truth," William replied,
"my name to no man have I yet denied.
I am William, from Narbonne-sur-mer I ride."   1570
"Praise be to God," the good gate-keeper cried.
"Lord William, I know well what you desire;
no cowardice could ever touch your line.
The traitor Richard has already arrived,
he brought with him seven hundred armed knights.
My noble lord, your resources are slight,
you cannot endure or suffer their might."
But William said: "We have men to suffice.
Outside the wall in four groups hidden lie
ready and armed yet a thousand good knights.   1580
Two hundred I have well-armed at my side,
beneath their robes they wear strong hauberks white,

beneath their hoods are jeweled helmets bright.
We have left our weapons not far behind,
if we need them, in the care of our squires."
"Praise be to God," the good gate-keeper cried.
"If you were to ask what I would advise,
send for your men now wherever they hide
by messengers, silent and swift to ride.
All the traitors are locked safely inside.   1590
Why seek elsewhere what here you can find?
On this day, in truth, sire, if you would strike,
before the dawn brings the morning light,
on them you may wreak all that you desire.
A man who would to such glory aspire,
must be more fierce than a boar in the wild."
William listened, his head bowed for a while.
He called Bertrand: "Did you hear his design?
When have you heard a keeper so inspired?"

xxxviii

When the keeper learned William was the man   1600
who before him in all his boldness stands,
towards the palace he turned his head and cast
defiance; a glove high in his right hand
he shook; in a voice loud and clear he called:
"I defy you, Richard, you and your land.
I will no longer serve you as your man.
When you would pursue treason with your plans,
it is God's will you should be crushed at last."
Before William the gates were thrown apart.
They quickly unlocked every bolt and latch.   1610
William and his fair company pass;
the gate-keeper softly bids them to arms:
"Noble knights, vengeance is yours to exact
from the betrayers of your king and land."
William heard him, his head bowed, then began
to summon a squire and send him far:

"Go to Sir Walter of Toulouse, impart
the news, and Garin of Rome, to ride hard;
the gates have been opened for us to pass.
There is wealth here to be pillaged and sacked   1620
if silent and swift they answer my call."
The squire rides off, he does not look back.
Quickly the four corps prepare to charge,
through the gates that opened to them they pass.
Those who look down from the windows and walls
think they have come to fight on their behalf,
but they are shortly to learn how they stand;
the news for them will be cruel and sad.

XXXIX

Count William called the gate-keeper and said:
"Advise me if you will, fair brother friend,   1630
how to find lodging for so many men."
"In the name of God, sire, I cannot help;
there is no great hall, no cellar or shed
where weapons and chargers are not now kept
and in the apartments the warriors rest.
But yours is the force of the greatest strength.
Seize their equipment, destroy their defense,
if any be bold enough to object,
let him not come forth but to lose his head."
"Indeed," said William, "you advise me well,   1640
by Saint Denis, what more can I request?
The gates no more shall you have to protect,
but at my side you shall offer counsel."
He called Bertrand: "Sir nephew, tell me when
you've heard a gate-keeper speak so well?
As a noble knight I would have him dressed."
"Most happily, fair lord" young Bertrand said.
He looked at him carefully, body and head,
admired his nobility and strength.
In the arms of a knight he had him dressed,   1650

a good sword, and hauberk over his chest,
a cutting spear and a fine steel helmet,
his squire on a horse, on a steed he was set,
a palfrey, a mule and pack-horse he led;
for his service the count had paid him well.
For Walter of Toulouse, Count William sent
to make known to him his plan and intent.
He was his sister's son, noble descent.
"The gate which leads to Poitiers you'll defend,
son of a noble woman, with your men.   1660
Twenty good knights on your orders depend.
See that all passage through the gate is checked,
no clerk or priest, whether he prays or begs,
shall pass, but at the price of limbs and head."
"Most willingly, fair lord," his nephew said.

xl

Marquis of the short nose, William the brave,
summoned Sehier of Plessis to his aid:
"On the road to Paris, guard the high gate,
noble and valiant knight, go there and take
twenty armed knights who are gallant and brave.   1670
See that no man born of woman escape
from the city but he be killed or maimed."
And he answered: "We shall do as you say."
There was no bolt, no barrier, no gate
where knights of Count William had not been placed.
Then the count rode to the church all in haste.
There he left his horse in the open space,
entered the church, made the cross on his face.
On the marble William the marquis prayed,
kneeling before the crucifix, for aid   1680
that God who was hung on the cross sustain
his lord Louis and send him there safe.
Meanwhile Walter, a clerk of the church, came.
Well did he know William the marquis brave.

On his shoulder firmly his fingers laid,
he tapped him until the count was aware.
The count stood up and showed Walter his face:
"What do you seek, brother? Do not delay."
"Tell me the truth," the clerk said, "if you came,
my lord William, to bring Louis your aid.   1690
At Saint Martin's church make fast all the gates.
Within are four score canons and prelates,
bishops and abbots most worthy of fame
who for riches have wickedly betrayed
king Louis; he will lose his crown today,
if you and God do not keep it safe.
Cut off their heads, I beg you, for God's sake.
For the crime in church I assume the blame
for these cowards and traitors must be slain."
William heard him and laughed at his rage: 1700
"Happy the hour such a priest was raised!
Can you tell me where my lord Louis stays?"
"Truly, my lord," the clerk said, "in God's name,
I'll fetch him, if God please and I escape."
He went to the monastery in haste,
and entered the great crypt without delay.
There he found his young lord Louis still safe.
The noble priest took his hand, he was pale.
"Son of a good king, be no more afraid,
may God help me, you have more friends today   1710
than you knew of when this dark morning came.
William the marquis is here in this place
with twelve hundred valiant knights in his train.
To see you the count in the church now waits.
There is no bolt, no barrier or gate
where knights of Count William have not been placed."
Louis listened, and happier he became;
together they went to the church in haste.
The noble abbot spoke to him again:
"Son of a good king, be no more afraid.   1720

William is here who once pledged you his faith.
Kneel at his feet, give him thanks for his aid."
The child answered: "I shall do as you say."

xli

The noble abbot told him to take heed:
"Son of a baron, put aside your fear.
There is William, go and fall at his feet."
The child answered: "Yes, my lord, willingly."
Before the count the child hastened to kneel;
embracing him, humbly he kissed his feet
and the ground he trod, his gratitude deep.   1730
William the warrior could not see—
it was dark in the church—who knelt at his feet.
"Stand up, my child," said the valiant marquis,
"God made no man who could so anger me
that if he should kneel at my feet to plead
I would not pardon him quite willingly."
Then the abbot began for Louis to speak:
"In God's name, sire, I would not conceal
Louis, son of Charles of countenance fierce.
He will be killed today, his body pierced   1740
if God and you do not bring him relief."
William heard him, lifted the child at his feet
in both his arms, and embraced King Louis.
"In the name of God, child, I was deceived
by the abbot who told you to kneel at my feet;
before all men I should help you in need."
He summoned his noble knights to speak:
"I would have you give me your decree.
If a man is crowned by the church a priest
and should spend his life with a psalter to read,   1750
should he then commit treason for a fee?"
The knights answered: "He should not certainly."
"If he do so, what should he then receive?"
"He should be hung like a miserable thief."
The count answered: "Well have you advised me,

by Saint Denis, what better could I seek!
I would not humble God's order or priests
and yet for their crimes they will pay most dear."

xlii

Count William in his heart was firm and strong;
he has heard the judgment of his barons.   1760
He came to the chancelry where he sought
in great haste, the bishops and the abbots
and the clergy by whom the king was wronged.
To his rightful lord, Louis, every cross
he gave, which he had from the priests' hands torn.
The good count on both sides embraced his lord
and four times he kissed him on his face soft.
Count William then would not wait any more.
He came to the chancelry where he sought
in great haste, the bishops and archbishops.   1770
For fear of sin he will not use his sword
but with clubs and sticks they are beaten, forced
to run from the church, their only recourse
to commend themselves to devils four score.
Who would commit treason against his lord,
it is right he be made to suffer sore.

xliii

Count William was a most valorous knight.
He called on Louis his lord to decide:
"Listen, sire," he said, "what I would advise:
we must summon a messenger to ride   1780
to Acelin to say that you desire
he come and name you his lord as is right."
"We are in accord, sir" Louis replied.
He summoned Alelme the baron to his side:
"Go and tell Acelin in his bold pride
to come and acknowledge his lord as is right,
in good speed, for the sorrow he inspires."
Alelme answered: "All alone shall I ride?"

"Yes, fair brother, with a staff to hold high.
If he ask you on what strength we rely   1790
then tell him we number forty brave knights.
If he refuse to renounce his designs
let him and his companions be advised
they will be so shamed before evening tonight
they would not be there for Arragon's gold bright."
Alelme answered: "We do as you desire.
By the Saint who in Nero's field abides,
we shall not lose by this messenger's ride."
On the back of an Arragon mule he climbed
and spurred him on through the streets, low and high,   1800
until at the lodging he finally arrived.
Acelin with his companions he finds;
in the hearing of all, aloud he cries:
"Sir Acelin, noble and gentle knight,
William the brave would make known his desire,
Count Fierebrace, with the heart of a lion:
that you name Louis your lord as is right,
in good speed, for the sorrow you inspire."
Acelin listened, his chin lowered, and inquired:
"My friend, I know what your uncle desires.   1810
Tell me on how many men he relies."
"In God's name, sire, he has thirty good knights."
Acelin answered: "Blessed be God on high!
Go and tell William the bold I advise
him to do as the others, if he is wise.
The crown of the kingdom is now my prize.
France has been lost from the hands of this child;
Louis' power is now very slight.
Count William is a brave man and fine
but without lands and defence he is no knight.   1820
I shall give him whatever he desires;
a fief he shall have to rule as he likes,
ten mules with fine gold and riches piled high,
he will be wondrously rich all his life."
"Indeed," said Alelme, "you are ill advised.

He would not accept for Arragon's gold bright.
And he would further make known, why deny,
a more cruel fate than has yet been described:
if you refuse to renounce your design,
you'll be so shamed before evening tonight   1830
you would not be there for the world's riches bright."
Acelin said: "Blessed be God on high!
Neither peace nor love in him can I find,
tell him therefore his challenge is defied."
And Alelme said: "We have heard your reply.
Nonetheless I shall tell you we defy
you and all your traitorous barons and knights."

xliv

Acelin was a man most proud and fierce;
he observed Alelme from his head to his feet
and saw how fair, straight and handsome he seemed;   1840
he knew this man for a squire indeed.
"Friend, fair brother, in bad taste you appear
to insult me, when all my knights may hear.
For your uncle I'd not give a silver penny.
In him I find neither friendship nor peace;
I shall cut off his head at his defeat.
Today I shall tear all his limbs to pieces
for I have seven hundred such knights here
and four counts who are greatly to be feared,
not for their limbs will they fail me in need.   1850
Had you not as a messenger appeared
I would have your head cut off for your speech,
and your body ravaged and torn and pierced."
Alelme answered: "Damned be he who would fear!"
He went out of the court, he took no leave.
Acelin had his people prepare in speed
while the noble Alelme mounted his steed
and rode at a gallop through the long streets.
He was met by William the warrior fierce,
who, anxious, asked: "What did you achieve?"   1860

"In God's name, sire, I found no wish for peace.
He will not acknowledge his lord Louis.
When he heard the number of knights you lead
then you were threatened with dreadful defeat,
your head cut off, your body torn and pierced.
Had I not as a messenger appeared,
he would have cut off my head for my speech,
burned me in fire or drowned in the sea."
William heard him and his anger was fierce.
Through all the hostels they searched and they seized   1870
all the armor, which they piled in a heap.
If any were bold enough to object
he lost his head, there was no relief.
The bourgeois of the town began to flee,
but the count had them pursued and seized.
The traitors, may God overwhelm them with grief,
who began and inspired the evil deed,
were driven to flight on their mighty steeds.
They rode to the gates with furious speed
but they found the keepers obstinate and fierce.   1880
They were compelled there such tribute to leave
that never again could they wage war in need
for any man who might make an appeal.
Count William begins to spur on his steed,
the home of the townsman Hungier he seeks.
He finds Acelin on a marble seat
but the man is so very proud and fierce
that he does not rise Count William to greet.
William sees him, his anger is fierce.
Since he cannot alone so many meet,   1890
he has sounded his trumpet, shrill and clear.
What a rush from the ambushes was seen!
Bertrand and Walter ride in at great speed,
a thousand good knights in their troop they lead.
What a battle you might have seen there fierce,
so many lances broken and shields pierced,
so many hauberks torn and gashes deep.
When they saw the battle would bring defeat,

the wretched traitors were struck with fear.
They knew their strength was no use in their need   1900
they threw down then their bared swords at their feet
and with clasped hands they begged for mercy.
The count ordered them all to be bound and seized,
but Acelin at a wild gallop flees.
Count William follows, close at his heels,
and taunts him with a merciless speech:
"Sir Acelin, come back, we entreat,
the crown in the church you must receive.
We shall place a crown on your head indeed,
your brains will be crushed down into your feet."   1910

xlv

Of fearsome aspect, William the count
sees Acelin and in fury he shouts:
"Traitorous thief, may God crush and confound
who would his rightful lord wrong and renounce.
Richard your father never wore the crown."
Bertrand appears with his broad sword and stout.
William sees him and fiercely he cries out:
"Fair nephew," he says, "advise me how
we may best destroy this traitor foul."
And Bertrand says: "Fair uncle, on his brow   1920
shall we set, what do you think, such a crown
that his brains will be crushed down through his mouth?"
He came forward waving his broad sword about.
Before a hundred men he would strike him down
but his uncle cried out, William the count:
"Fair nephew," he said, "do not touch him now.
We would offend God, who made seas and mounts,
if he by a bold knight's arms be struck down!
I should rather see him lie in shame on the ground,
so disgrace to all his line will redound."   1930

xlvi

Count William was a good knight and brave.
Fierce towards the proud he had always remained

like a leopard who would eat those he slays.
He would not touch him with the arms he bears.
He sees a sharp pike standing in a grate,
he goes forward, tears it out with disdain;
he strikes Acelin on his head with the stake,
down to his feet pour his blood and his brains.
He struck him dead, he would no longer wait:
"Montjoie," he cries, "Saint Denis bring me aid.   1940
Louis is avenged on this king today."
Count William spurred his horse and rode away
to the great church, he did not hesitate.
To Louis there, his rightful lord, he came;
the child on both sides he ran to embrace.
"My young lord, sire, why would you still despair?
I have crushed the son of Richard in shame;
he will never wage war in need again
for any man in the world who may pray."
"God," said the child, "my gratitude is great!   1950
If his father were now brought to disgrace
I could then be truly happy and gay."
"God," said William, "who can show me the place?"
They told him Richard in the church remained;
the count rode furiously after him there
and four score knights followed behind in haste.
He found Richard at the altar in prayer,
although in church he was not to be spared;
with his left hand he seized him by the hair
and forced him to the ground where he lay.   1960
With his right fist he struck his neck with pain
and threw him down at his feet, stunned and dazed,
so that none of his limbs might be spared
and neither his hands nor his feet remain.
William saw him and in disgust exclaimed:
"Wretched traitor! May God bring you to shame!"
He asked for scissors to cut off his hair,
on the marble he left him bald and bare.
Then he cried to all the knights who were there:

"In this way should a traitor be disgraced   1970
who would his rightful lord wrong and betray."
But the counts and barons begged him and prayed
until peace between William and Richard was made.
Pardon for the death of his son he claimed.
Before they left church the peace was proclaimed;
before many knights they kissed and embraced,
but peace between them did not long remain
for soon they plotted to murder and slay
the count in the woods with their swift steel blades.
But God would never his servant forsake.   1980
Count William no longer wished to delay,
he called the good abbot Walter to say:
"To the kingdom of Poitier I must in haste
where many traitors in safety now stay,
but, if God wills, none of them shall escape.
My rightful lord I would leave in your care.
Keep him well; when he rides to sport or play,
a hundred knights let him take in his train,
for by the apostle whom pilgrims praise
if when I return someone should relate   1990
that Louis has been harmed in any way,
your sacred orders will not keep you safe,
your limbs will be torn from your body in pain."
The abbot answered: "You threaten in vain.
He will be kept better than the church's saints."
Count William was a valiant knight and brave.
He sent letters through the land with great haste
to summon the knight barons to his aid.
In less than the term of fifteen days
more than thirty thousand eagerly came.   2000
They rode off together then to Poitiers.
For three years there was not a single day
that William the count, so noble and brave,
his dark helmet on his head did not lace,
girt on his sword, while his charger strained.
There was no feast when all Christians should pray

or Christmas day that we should celebrate
that he was not in his armor arrayed.
The knight suffered great hardship and pain
to maintain king Louis and give him aid.   2010

xlvii

Three full years William the baron performed
great deeds in Poitiers, Louis' rule to restore.
There was no holy day that we honor,
Easter or Christmas, when we praise the lord,
nor the feast of all saints that we adore,
that William did not gird on his sword,
fasten his dark helmet and mount his horse.
The hardships were many that the count bore
to guard and protect his young emperor.

xlviii

Count William of fierce and daring person   2020
rode off to Bordeaux along the Gironde.
There he conquered the strong king Amarmonde
and received the crown from Charlemagne's son
and the wide and broad fiefs which he had won.

xlix

Count William with a heart bold and steadfast
left Bordeaux and went on to Peralade.
There he conquered Dagobert of Carthage.
Of Louis the wise he held those lands
and the great broad fiefs were in his command.

l

Count William of wise look and strong will   2030
made his way to Andorra, secret, swift.
He attacked Saint Gile at once, in a morning,
took the city before it could resist.
Then what was pleasing to Jesus he did:
he saved the church from ravage and ruin.

He held Julian who ruled the land, until
he gave all the hostages William wished.
So he achieved the peace he had promised.
Count William summoned his people to him
and told them what was most pleasing and fit: 2040
"Mount up now Franks, you have served well your king.
Let each go back to his land now to live
with his wedded wife whom he has long missed."

li

Count William of the short nose, with his men
to ride once more to sweet France now is bent.
Many of his knights in Poitiers he left
to guard the great castles and fortresses.
Two hundred well-armed in his train he led,
he marched through all Brittany at their head;
they would stop only at Mont Saint Michel.   2050
There for two days and no more might they rest.
Toward Costentin, on the third day, they went.
Of their long days I know not what to tell,
until Rouen they lost not a moment;
in the great city their lodgings are set
but the count is foolhardy. He forgets
that the old Duke Richard is not his friend,
and in his own land may plot to avenge
his son whom William in their battle left dead.
The noble count William did not suspect,   2060
he thought their strife had been brought to an end.
But the peace they had made was not long kept
for they thought to murder and ruin him then.
"Truly," said Richard, "I should lose my head
that I see in my land this knight enter.
By him, of the best heir, I am bereft,
ever born to govern a land and defend.
By the apostle pilgrims seek for help,
before he leaves he will repay me well."
"In the name of God, sire," his knights all said,   2070

"in this city his blood will not be shed,
for the townsmen would come to his defence.
This treason will have no chance of success."
Richard cried: "My anger is all the more intense.
I shall prepare a message to be sent
that I too will ride to sweet France as his friend.
We shall be sixteen very well-armed men;
if from his own people he can be led
they will thrust their steel knives into his breast.
His body will be ravaged, his life spent."   2080
Fifteen bold knights then promised him their help.
Had they not gone it would have been best
for it brought them only shame and distress.
God! The count of fierce look knows nothing yet.
He rises early to ride with his men
to Lyons and luxuriant forests.
There on a heath they dismounted to rest
and ate food that was brought them by peasants.
When the noble knights had dined and drunk well,
some fell asleep, they were all exhausted.   2090
William watched them with pity as they slept.
He called for his armor, he would not rest.
It was brought to him and he quickly dressed;
he dons his hauberk, laces the steel helm,
girds on the sword with its gold sculptured head.
Before him his charger Alion is led;
the count mounts by the stirrup on the left.
A huge quartered shield hangs down from his neck,
in his fist he takes a cutting spear dread,
where with fifteen nails a standard is set.   2100
With him ride only two knights to attend.
They go to sport where the river bank ends.
Then the old Duke Richard rides down to them;
he had had him watched all day by his men,
fifteen bold knights on whom he could depend.
William sees him and is quite distressed.

lii

Count William is riding along a mountain;
when he sees Duke Richard the Red above,
riding towards him with fifteen companions,
William sees him, he is greatly frightened.   2110
He quickly calls on both his companions
to tell them his fears of Richard's intentions:
"What shall we do?" he asks of his barons.
"Do you see how Duke Richard the Red now comes?
In hatred he would demand a ransom
as you well know, for the death of his son,
although we made peace after it was done.
We made a peace in the church at Tours once."
They answered: "Then why do you fear treason?
Ride to the bridge with no hesitation   2120
and greet the count in good faith and true love.
If he should then give you any reason
to doubt him, hold up your shield with the lion.
Despite the world's gold you can rely on us."
William answered: "My thanks, noble barons."

liii

Straight to the bridge Count William then rode.
He addressed the duke thus as he approached:
"Duke," said the count, "God keep watch on your soul!
Do you stand before me still as a foe?
We have pledged our peace forever to hold,   2130
in the church at Tours we uttered that oath.
There we kissed for many knights to behold."
"Truly," said Richard, "with much art you spoke.
You took from me the best heir, all my hope,
ever born to sit on a kingdom's throne.
But, by the apostle all pilgrims know,
you shall pay dear for him before you go.
God cannot help you now nor all your host,

I'll cut off your head and tear out your bones
for the death of my son you will atone."   2140
"Vile wretch," said William, "may God bring you woe!
You are a mad dog beyond control"
He pricks Alion with spurs of pure gold
and strikes Richard's shield a powerful blow.
Beneath it the buckler was pierced and broke,
the white hauberk torn and shattered below.
Into his left side he thrust the steel cold
until from both sides his blood flowed.
The good horse was overwhelmed by the blow,
the spurs of the duke towards the heavens rose,   2150
the helmet's point stuck in the ground below
with such great force that two of the stays broke.
With his sword drawn, Count William then approached,
he had grabbed his hair, as I have been told,
when the fifteen, God strike them, down the slope
charged Count William the warrior bold.
Had anyone seen what spirit he showed
with his steel sword to return their rich blows,
he would have pitied the good man alone.
But then his companions took up their posts   2160
and each struck his man a mighty blow.
The heavenly father such help bestowed
that they killed and destroyed ten with their strokes.
The other five fled wounded, their blood flowed.
But Count William at their backs followed close,
shouting insults and abuse as he rode.

liv

The five fled wildly through a stretch of wood;
Count William followed them in close pursuit,
crying aloud sharp insults and abuse:
"Lord barons, for God who in heaven rules,   2170
how can this shame and disgrace be endured?
Your rightful lord will be led off, subdued.

God, what a deed, if he could be rescued!"
They answer: "For God, William, don't pursue!
Noble knight, you might well be king, in truth,
or have a rich land as emir to rule.
May God help me, we should be conquered soon,
our intestines lie on our saddles loose.
The least wounded would never be captured."
William listened and gave up the pursuit.   2180

lv

When William heard how for mercy they begged,
for Montpelier's gold he would not still press.
Quickly he turned and rode back to his men.
They had taken the weapons from the ten,
Duke Richard lay bound without defense;
like a trunk on a mule, he had been set
on a charger; to the camp he was led.
Quickly back to the main army they went.
The men were awake to receive them;
"Uncle William," Bertrand the warrior said,   2190
"by your sword's blade I see blood has been shed
and your shield has been broken and bent.
You must have been in a rather bad mess."
William answered: "Thank God, fair nephew, for his help!
When, this morning, to ride out I had dressed,
I saw you were weary and exhausted,
so leaving you to sleep and dream I went
alone with only two knights to attend.
Duke Richard the Old on the way I met,
a watch over me all day he had set   2200
and fifteen bold knights beside him he kept.
He hated me still for Acelin's death.
He would have cut off my limbs and my head
but our righteous father gave us his help
so that we killed and destroyed ten of them,
the other five, wounded and bleeding, fled.

Here are the arms and war-steeds of his men,
and Duke Richard bound and tied we have led."
"Thanks be to God!" Bertrand the baron said.

lvi

"Uncle William," said Bertrand the brave,   2210
"you look as though you could take no more strain."
"Nephew," said William, "I shall ask your grace
for I would suffer all my youth great pains
until the king has all his land again."
Then they prepared to ride; they would not stay.
They marched and rode at a very swift pace
until to Orleans city they came.
There Count William found his king, Louis, safe.
He delivered Richard into his care,
he had him thrown in prison in disgrace,   2220
where, as I have heard, for so long he lay
that there he died of sorrow and despair.
Now William thought to rest from his cares,
in the woods, by rivers, to spend his days.
But he was not long at rest to remain.
Two messengers then were riding in haste.
They lost no time, direct from Rome they came,
their horses weary, destroyed by the strain.
Of King Louis had they long sought a trace,
when they found him and Count William the brave.   2230
They bow low at his feet to beg his grace:
"Have mercy on us, good count, for God's sake!
Do you no longer remember the maid
to whom vows in the church at Rome you made?
Gualfier of Ypolite lies in his grave.
Counts, lords, and peers seek the lady with claims,
but to you alone her love she gave.
And we are oppressed by still greater cares:
Galafre the noble emir lies in his grave,
whom you once baptized at the font and raised   2240
and the gentle pope, death has embraced.

Guy of Alemagne assembled forces great
to seize Rome's main strongholds and shut her gates.
All the country around will be laid waste,
noble lord, sire, unless you bring us aid."
William listened, his head low, his thought grave,
then Louis began to weep in despair.
William saw him, went almost mad with rage:
"Ah, poor king, my hope was foolish and vain,
I thought forever to defend you against   2250
all of Christendom, your throne to sustain;
by all the world's hatred you are betrayed.
To serve you I would give all my young days,
all you desire before you to lay.
Send for your men and your barons today,
let all the poor bachelors ride in haste,
on ill-appointed steeds, mules, unshod drays,
with armor torn and in need of repair.
Let all whom poor lords in service maintained
come here to me, they will be amply paid   2260
with gold and silver and coins of great weight,
with Spanish steeds and mules richly arrayed,
as I brought them here from Rome in my train,
and the many riches I won in Spain;
I cannot dispose of a tenth of my gains.
That I am a miser no man will say,
I shall give all I have and then again."
And the king said: "God keep you ever safe!"
They sealed the charters and letters and gave
them to the sergeants and messengers to bear.   2270
Before they were gone even fifteen days
so many men were assembled and arrayed,
they seemed to be fifty thousand in that place.
There were well-armed knights and stout sergeants brave;
of all those none went on foot, for in haste
they wished to arrive in Rome with their aid.
Of their journey I know not what to say;
they were saddened to leave Montjoie on their way,

from there to Rome they did not delay.
But the Alemand would not open the gate.   2280
Outside the walls they were forced to remain.
King Louis ordered his camp to be laid,
his tents were pitched and his pavilions raised,
the kitchens set up and the fires made.
Count William led the foragers away,
they rode through the land and laid it waste,
they robbed the earth and pillaged the plain,
they paid and enriched the host with their gains.

lvii

Count William leads the foragers far and wide.
Guy of Alemagne to his feet arises   2290
to tell a peer of Rome what he devised:
"Noble lord, make peace and hear me, sire.
I would have you summon a thousand knights.
Before the tents are pitched you must arrive
to throw them into confusion and strike.
If you need me, I shall be at your side."
He answered: "This seems a good plan to try."
Quickly he and his men prepare to ride.
They don their hauberks, lace the helmets bright,
mount their steeds and gird swords at their sides.   2300
At their necks hang quartered shields strong and wide,
in their fists their cutting spears swift to strike.
They charge through the gate, eager to fight.
Then a mist begins to fall from the sky
so that none of the men can see to ride.
The Franks have no way to defend their lives
while the Romans attack the tents with fierce cries.
They lead off the horses and kill the squires,
they carry off food from the kitchen fires
and kill the chief steward before they retire.   2310
And Louis runs wildly about in fright
from one tent to another trying to hide.
"Bertrand, William, where are you?" he cries.

"Sons of barons, come and protect my life.
God help me, how I need them at my side."
William leads the foragers far and wide.
Count Bertrand his nephew hears the wild cries:
"Uncle William, you must some plan devise.
From our host I hear terrified shouts rise;
God help me, their distress must be high."   2320
Count William answers: "We must quickly ride
against Rome, lace on your helmets bright.
If we close them out, take the gates by surprise
and entrance to their own army deny,
we can gather all the booty inside,
the greatest wealth since Gualfier was alive."
Then Count William began to Rome to ride.
The haze grew ever thicker in the sky,
the Romans had no way to defend their lives
and William began to shout to his knights: 2330
'Montjoie," he cried, "for our emperor strike!"
There you might have seen a battle wild,
spears were splintered, shields shattered in the strife,
so many hauberks with gashes torn wide!
The dead, one over another lie!
The Roman host had no chance to take flight,
they closed in on them before and behind.
Of the thousand men of Rome, the Frank knights
spared none, all were left sore wounded to die
or tied and bound were led off still alive.   2340
Then the lord who led them tried to take flight.
The count follows him up a mountain side.
Furiously he shouts: "Come back, sir knight,
or like a miserable wretch you shall die."
Along his leg the count's steel blade slides,
he falls; across the neck of his steed he lies.
Sword drawn, William goes for the head of the knight
when for mercy and pity he cries:
"Don't kill me, if you are William, be wise,
you will gain more if you take me alive.   2350

I shall give you wealth and goods of great price."
Count William had come up to his side;
he surrenders his sword, polished and bright.
To Louis he brings the conquered knight,
then with his foragers again he rides.
Guy of Alemagne to his feet now rises
and tells his men: "Hear what I have devised.
My men wounded, bleeding in the field lie;
if I cannot prove myself now in strife,
hand to hand take on one of their knights,   2360
all our strength will not assure even our lives."

lviii

Guy of Alemagne a messenger seeks,
sets him upon an Arabian steed,
at his neck a sable pelt he carries,
in his hands a staff where a spear would be.
Guy of Alemagne made his messenger this speech:
"To the tents of silk quickly proceed,
tell, on my part, the son of Charles, Louis,
that he does me wrong to ravage and steal
in my lands—Rome is not his, nor her fiefs.   2370
If he thinks by such outrage to seize
what is my right, in combat I shall meet
the king or whoever for him appears.
If in the combat I am crushed in defeat,
Rome and her lands will be his clear and free,
there will be no man whose challenge he need fear.
But if I should conquer with my swift steel,
he will regret the smallest coin he steals;
he shall return to Paris, or Chartres and leave
Rome, that is my inheritance, to me."   2380
He answered: "This is a fitting appeal."
He turned, through the wide gate he disappeared.
From Rome to the tents he rode with great speed.
Beside the tent of silk he left his steed,
he entered the huge tent swiftly to seek

the son of Charles, king of the Franks, Louis.
He called him for all the barons to hear:
"Good emperor, listen to what I speak.
It is not fitting that I should you greet.
For Guy of Alemagne I have come here,   2390
his message to you I shall not conceal:
you have no right to Rome nor to her fiefs,
if you think by outrages to seize
what is his right, in combat he would meet
you, or a knight who for you will appear.
If in the combat he is crushed in defeat,
Rome and her lands will be yours clear and free;
there will be no man whose challenge you need fear.
But if he should conquer with his swift steel,
you will regret the smallest coin you steal.   2400
You shall return to Paris or Chartres and leave
Rome that is his inheritance with speed."
The king listens, his head lowered he keeps.
When he looks up, to his knights he appeals:
"My lord barons, listen to what I speak
Guy of Alemagne to disgrace me seeks.
To a hand combat he challenges me
but I am young and very slight in years,
I cannot maintain my honor by deeds.
Is there a Frank who for me will appear?"   2410
They lower their heads when they hear his speech.
The king sees them and grows mad with grief,
beneath his sables pitifully he weeps.
At that moment William Fierebrace appears,
he has led the foragers in the fields.
Still armed he enters the silk tent and sees
the young king sighing and weeping great tears.
When he sees him he grows mad with grief.
Then he shouts for all the barons to hear:
"Ah, poor king, may God give you only grief!   2420
Who has harmed you, dear lord? Why do you weep?"
Louis answered the Count's anxious plea:

"In God's name, sire, I shall nothing conceal.
Guy of Alemagne to disgrace me seeks.
To meet him in combat he orders me;
there is no Frank who for me will appear,
but I am young and very small in years,
I cannot maintain my honor by my deeds."
"King," said William, "God give you only grief,
for your love I have performed twenty-four such feats.   2430
Did you think I would fail you now in need?
No, by God, I shall undertake this deed.
All of your Franks are worthless men and weak."
When he sees the messenger his words are fierce.

lix

"My friend, fair brother," says William the brave,
"go to Guy the Alemand for me and say
that a knight who would his lord sustain
is eager this combat to undertake.
I shall have all the hostages I claim;
as many as he would have, let him take.   2440
Whoever conquers, will make his terms plain."
The palatine Bertrand rose in his place.
"Uncle, he says, "we suffer too much shame.
All battles and combats you quickly claim.
Beside your valiant deeds, ours are in vain.
This combat, sire, I would undertake:
grant me this honor, uncle, by your grace."
The count answers: "This mad speech is in vain.
When Louis wandered about in despair,
there was no one here so mighty or brave   2450
who dared his glove before him to raise.
Do you think that I would now cede my place?
I would not for the fief of Abilant famed.
Messenger, brother, to Guy d'Alemagne say:
let him arm and ride to the field today.
There Count William in arms will await."
Spurring his horse he rode back to the gate;

from the Franks to Rome he did not delay.
Guy the Alemand met him as he came.
"Friend, fair brother, how did the Franks behave?"   2460
"I shall tell you all that, sire, in God's name.
A knight of the host will his lord sustain,
is eager for combat, and he will claim
many hostages; he prepares in haste.
You may have as many as you will take.
Whoever conquers shall his will attain.
As far as I know, William is his name.
A knight, Bertrand, leapt up in his place;
he is his nephew, that I can truly say,
the combat he was anxious to undertake."   2470
"My friend," said Guy d'Alemagne, "brother fair,
when I have finished and William lies slain,
if this nephew of his, this Bertrand, came
he would not seek far a combat to claim.
Have my finest armor before me laid."
And he answered: "It will be as you say."
It was brought before him without delay.
On his back the iron-ringed hauberk was placed,
more red than burning fire was the mail,
the brilliant helmet on his head was laced,   2480
a carbuncle set in the nasal, rare.
His sword girded on his left side he wears.
Then they led forth his noble charger brave,
another sword from the saddle-bow displayed;
onto his steed the knight leaps with sure grace,
stirrups and saddle-bow he disdains.
At his neck a huge, heavy shield he bears.
In his fist a powerful spear he takes,
from five golden nails its standard waves.
Spurring his mount he rode swift through the gate.   2490
He rode on into the Neiron plain.
The count had already chosen the place.
He summoned Guielin and Bertrand to say:
"On the field I see my enemy waits,

he will hold me a coward if I delay.
Have my finest armor before me laid."
And they answered: "It will be as you say."
It was brought before him without delay.
To arm him Louis the valiant came;
he donned the hauberk, the bright helmet laced,   2500
and girds Joyeuse on the left at his waist,
which Charles the warrior to William gave.
They lead forth Alion the charger brave,
and he mounts with agility and grace.
At his neck a huge heavy shield he bears,
in his fist a powerful spear he takes,
from five golden nails its standard waves.
Through the encampment he makes his way
riding hard to the hill, he will not stay.

lx

Unto the hill William the marquis climbs.   2510
Guy of Alemagne addresses the knight:
"Who are you there, and take care not to lie,
whose heart is so bold that he dare defy
me in combat? Who possesses such pride?"
"Truly," says William, "I shall soon reply.
I am William, son of a noble knight,
Aimeri of Narbonne, defiant and wise.
With a sword of polished steel I shall fight
against you, who are so agile in strife,
by the terms which have been devised.   2520
The king of Saint Denis holds Rome by right.
I fought to keep it when he was denied,
with Corsolt the Arab on this hillside,
the strongest man who of mother took life.
He struck the nose from my face in that fight."
When Guy hears him, he almost loses his mind.
He would not be there for Paris' fiefs wide.
He sees William and addresses the knight:
"If you are that William the marquis wise

of Count Aimeri of Narbonne's noble line,   2530
let us make peace and as good friends retire;
you and I will hold Rome with equal right."
"Wretch," says William, "may just God curse your life!
I did not come to listen to your guile.
To betray my lord is not my desire;
I could not do so were my limbs the price."
When Guy hears him he almost loses his mind.
He swears by the apostle in Rome's shrine:
"To ask something of you was base and vile.
I defy you by God in paradise."   2540
"I accept your challenge," William replied.
Further than a bow shoots, apart they ride,
they face each other, defiant their eyes.
Before their breasts the mighty shields held high.
They are well equipped for a furious fight,
with polished spurs their chargers they incite,
lances lowered, they are ready to ride.
Mighty blows on their broad curved shields they strike,
the bucklers are broken and bent behind,
but they cannot tear the strong hauberks white.   2550
The lances shatter, they are too light,
high into the air the splinters fly.
They strike fierce blows on their chests and their sides,
their mighty arched shields join in violent strife,
their hauberks and their chargers of high price.
On their heads crash and roar the helmets bright,
blood and sweat pour down from both sides
until all four have fallen, mounts and knights.
The good steeds motionless on the ground lie
but the vassals swiftly on their feet rise,   2560
swords drawn, they hold their shields before them high;
they will show they are not friends in this fight.

lxi

Count William has leapt swiftly to his feet,
to God our righteous father he appeals:

"Holy Mary, virgin and maid, help me!
No man has ever thrown me from my steed."
Guy of Alemagne shouted an answer fierce:
"By God, William, He won't stay your defeat.
I am claiming Rome, her walls and her fief.
This heritage will not pass to Louis."　　　　　　　2570
"Wretch," says William, "may God bring you to grief!
For by the apostle whom pilgrims seek,
before the sun sets or the evening nears,
your body I shall so savagely treat
that you will not be worth a byzantine piece."
He holds Joyeuse, its blade was of fine steel.
He sees Guy, and attacks him in fury.
Such a blow on his bright helmet he deals
that its flowers and stones fall at his feet.
Had the hood of his hauberk not been beneath,　　　　2580
after that blow it would have served no need.
Above his hip, the sword's blade had cut deep,
through more than a foot of the flesh it pierced.
Above the belt, the bare bone appeared.
"Truly," says William, "I have made you bleed.
Now you know well that my blade is keen."
Guy of Alemagne shouted an answer fierce:
"Ahi! William, may God bring you to grief!
Did you think for so little to rouse my fear?
Our poor flesh can oppress a man's body.　　　　　2590
But, by the holy cross that palmers seek,
before the sun sets or the evening nears,
for my flesh with your own you will pay dear."
He holds his sword, its blade was of fine steel,
he sees William, attacks him in fury.
Such a blow on his bright helmet he deals
that its flowers and stones fall at his feet.
Had the hood of his hauberk not been beneath,
there would have been no heir of Count Aimeri.
But God would not suffer such a defeat.　　　　　2600
By this blow Guy does not gain what he seeks,

up to its hilt the sword is split deep.
He draws the other swiftly from its sheath.
William sees him and laughs heartily.
He holds Joyeuse, its rich blade was of steel,
he sees Guy and attacks him in fury.
A fierce blow on his bright helmet he deals,
down through the shoulder its force he feels.
Even his chest is cut through and pierced,
stunned by the blow he falls dead at his feet.   2610
Into the Tiber he threw the enemy.
The iron he was wearing carried him deep,
his body was never by men retrieved.
William sees it and cries out in relief:
"Montjoie," he cries, "God and Saint Denis, hear—
on this wretch I have avenged King Louis."
He mounts Alion, his noble steed,
and leads Clinevent, which he will not leave.
Back to the army they ride with all speed.
Count Bertrand, his nephew, goes out to meet   2620
him with Louis, rejoicing in his deed.
Guielin and Walter did little but weep;
never under heaven had they known such fear
except when Corsolt met him in combat fierce:
"Uncle William, are you safe, how do you feel?"
"I am well," he says, "by God's kind decree!
Fair nephew Bertrand, I will not conceal,
I have brought for you this excellent steed
for the combat you would have fought for me."
Bertrand answers: "My thanks, uncle, for this deed!"   2630
Among the Romans there was terror and fear.
One said to another: "We are deceived.
Our lord has been killed and crushed in defeat.
We must humble ourselves at William's feet;
let us go quickly to him to entreat."
One said to the other: "That is agreed."
With crosses of great richness and beauty,
censers and psalters and phylacteries,

and holy bodies from the church they proceed.
They open the gates in welcome, and greet   2640
their rightful lord, whom in joy they receive.

lxii

William the noble count has entered Rome.
With his lord swiftly to the church he goes,
and there sets him firmly upon the throne
and crowns him before all the Frankish host.
All the baronage then swore him an oath.
Some swore an oath that they would uphold,
others swore one that they easily broke.
As you shall hear before the sun is low.   (a)

lxiii

William the brave is in Rome to defend
King Louis and set the crown on his head.   2650
His empire is secure, the traitors dead.
William prepares to set out with his men,
they wander through many plains and forests
before they reach France where their travels end.
The king to the city of Paris went,
William to Montreuil-sur-mer returned then.
The noble count now thinks only of rest,
of sport in the woods and river torrents,
but it will not last as the count intends,
for the Franks again begin to rebel;   2660
some make war and others are oppressed.
Cities are burnt, lands ravaged with death,
by their king Louis they will not be checked.
A messenger to tell William was sent.
The count hears him and goes wild in distress,
he calls Bertrand: "Sir nephew, listen well.
For the love of God what do you suggest?
My lord king has lost his inheritance."
Bertrand answers shortly: "Let him be then.
Let us leave him and France to the devil to tend,   2670

this king is such a fool, with all your help
not a foot of his lands can he defend."
William answers: "All this we must forget.
In his service I vowed my youth to spend."
The count summons all his men and his friends.
They have ridden hard through land and forest,
in Paris their journey is at an end.
There William brought King Louis his help.
They began to wage war on the rebels.
But William of the Short Nose was compelled   2680
to leave the land with dangers so beset,
where too many enemies seek his death.
He took the child whom he strove to protect
to Laon where he could safely be kept;
within it he set up a strong defence,
outside the pillage and fire was intense.
The count began to have huge bars hewn then,
to pierce high walls and destroy their strength.
Within a year he had had such success
that fifteen counts to the royal court were sent   2690
to swear that they held their inheritance
from King Louis by whom all France was held.
To William's sister the king was wed.
Into great honor Louis ascends—
but when he was rich he forgot his friend.

The Conquest of Orange

i

Listen my lords, and may God give you grace,
the glorious son of Holy Mary,
to a good song that I would offer you.
It is not a tale of pride or folly,
or deception plotted and carried out
but of brave men who conquered in Spain.
They know it well, who have been to St. Gilles,
who have seen the relics kept at Brioude,
the shield of William and the white buckler,
and Bertrand's too, his noble nephew.   10
I think that no clerk will belie me,
nor any writing that's found in a book.
They have all sung of the city of Nîmes,
which William holds among his possessions,
the great high walls and the rooms built of stone,
and the palace and the many castles
and by God, he had not yet won Orange!
There are few men who have told it truly,
but I shall tell what I learned long ago,
how Orange was destroyed and undone.   20
This William did, of the bold countenance.
He expelled the pagans from Almeria,
and the Saracens of Eusce and Pincernie,
those of Baudas and of Tabarie.
he took as his wife Orable the queen—
she had been born of a pagan race—
the wife of Tiebaut, king of Africa.
Then she turned to God, blessed Mary's son,

and founded churches and monasteries.
There are not many who could tell you of them.   30

ii

Hear me, my lords, noble knights and worthy,
if it please you to hear a good deed sung,
how Count William took and destroyed Orange
and took to wife the wise Lady Orable,
who had been Tiebaut of Persia's queen.
Before he was able to win her love,
he had, in truth, to suffer great pains,
many days he fasted, and waked many nights.

iii

It was in May, in the early summer,
the woods blossoming, and the meadows green,   40
the sweet waters withdrawing into streams
and the birds singing sweetly and soft.
One morning Count William arises,
and goes to the church to hear the service.
He comes out when the service is over
and mounts the palace of the heathen Otran,
whom he had conquered by his fierce courage.
He goes to look from the great windows
and gazes far out across the kingdom.
He sees the fresh grass and the rose gardens,   50
he hears the song-thrush and the blackbird sing,
then he remembers the joy and pleasure
that he used to feel when he was in France.
He calls Bertrand: "Sir nephew, come here.
We came out of France in great poverty,
we brought with us no harpers or minstrels,
or'young ladies to delight our bodies.
We have our share of fine well-groomed horses,
and strong chain-mail and gilded helmets,
sharp, cutting swords and fine buckled shields,   60
and splendid spears fashioned of heavy iron,

and bread and wine and salted meat and grain;
but God confound the Saracens and Slavs
who leave us to sleep and rest here so long
for they have not yet crossed the sea in force,
to give us the chance to prove ourselves.
It tires me to stay so quiet here,
shut up so tight inside these walls,
as if we were all held as prisoners."
His mind is led astray in this folly, 70
but before the sun is hid or vespers sung,
he will be brought news of such a nature
that he'll be filled with anger and fury.

iv

William stands at the windows in the wind,
sixty of his Franks in attendance,
not one of them without new white ermine,
stockings of silk and cordovan sandals.
Most of them loose their falcons in the wind.
Count William, feeling great joy in his heart,
looks into the valley through the steep mountains; 80
he sees the green grass, the roses in bloom,
and the oriole and the blackbird in song.
He calls Guielin and Bertrand to his side,
his two nephews, whom he loves so well:
"Listen to me, worthy and valiant knights,
we came from France not very long ago;
if only we now had a thousand girls,
maidens from France, with graceful charming forms,
so that our barons might be entertained,
and I too might delight in making love; 90
that would be greatly to my liking.
We have enough fine chargers, swift and strong,
sturdy chain-mail and good shining helmets,
sharp, cutting spears and splendid heavy shields,
good swords whose hilts are fashioned of silver,
and bread and wine, cheeses and salted meat.

God confound the Saracens and Persians
who do not cross the sea to do battle.
Our stay inside here starts to weary me,
for I have no chance to test my courage."   100
He wanders distracted in his folly,
but the sun won't set nor will evening come,
before he is brought such a piece of news,
that it will make him both angry and sad.

V

William is at the windows on the wall,
with him there are a hundred Franks and more;
there is not one who is not clothed in ermine.
He looks below where the Rhone river roars
and to the East, where the roadway runs;
he sees some wretch emerge from the water;   110
it is Gilbert, from the city, Lenu.
He was captured on a bridge of the Rhone,
the Turks, shouting, brought him back to Orange.
Three years they held him in prison there,
until one morning as the day appeared,
when it was God's will that he should escape,
a Saracen untied him by the gate
and then began to beat and insult him.
When the knight had as much as he could bear,
he seized him by the hair and pulled him down;   120
with his huge fist, he struck him such a blow,
that it shattered both his chest and his spine.
Dead at his feet, he has thrown down his foe.
Down from the window, now, he throws himself,
he can no longer be restrained or held.
From there to Nîmes he comes without a stop,
he will report such tidings here today
to our barons, who talk now of trifles,
that will relieve William of his boredom
and bring delight with ladies in the nude.   130

vi

William the noble is at the window.
The fleeing captive has crossed the Rhone,
climbed the hills and gone down the valleys,
from there to Nîmes, he has not made a stop.
He enters the gates of the good city
and finds William beneath the full pine,
and, in his train, many excellent knights.
Beneath the pine, a minstrel is singing
an ancient song, of venerable age.
It is quite good and it pleases the count.   140
And now Gilbert begins to climb the steps;
William sees him and looks at him closely,
he is black and dirty and yet he's pale,
sickly and pallid, tired and thin.
He thinks he must be Saracen or Slav
who has been sent from across the sea
to bring him a message and take one back.
But then the poor wretch begins to greet him:
"May the Lord God who made both wine and grain,
and gives us light and brightness from heaven,   150
who made man and woman to walk and speak,
preserve William, the marquis of the short nose,
the flower of France and his noble knights,
the fighters whom I see assembled here!"
"My good friend and brother, may God bless you!
But tell us now, do not keep it hidden,
who taught you to call this William by name?"
"Sire," he answers, "you will hear the truth now;
inside Orange I have been a long time,
and could not find any way to escape,   160
until one morning as day was breaking,
it was Jesus' will that I be set free."
And William says: "God be praised for that!
But tell me now, do not hide it from me,

what is your name, in what land were you born?"
"Sire," he says, "you will soon hear the truth,
but I have suffered so much torment and pain,
I have waked through the nights and fasted all day,
it is four days since I have eaten at all."
And William says: "You will have all you wish."   170
The count then summons his chamberlains:
"Bring this man plenty of food to eat,
with bread and wine, mixed with spices and honey,
cranes and geese, and peacocks with pepper."
And this was done, as he had commanded.
When he has been richly entertained,
he sits willingly at the feet of the count
and begins to relate the news he brought.

vii

Count William has seen the strange messenger,
he summons him and then asks this question: 180
"Where were you born, friend, and in what country?
What is your name, where in France have you been?"
Gilbert replies, a most valiant knight:
"I am Guion's son, the Duke of Ardennes,
and of Vermendois, which he also holds.
Through Burgundy I came from Alemaigne,
I set sail on the waters of Lausanne,
but a wind caught me and a great tempest
and carried me to the port of Geneva.
Pagans captured me at Lyons on the Rhone   190
and led me off to the port at Orange.
There's no fortress like it from here to the Jordan;
the walls are high, the tower large and wide,
the courtyards, too, and the whole enclosure.
Twenty thousand pagans armed with lances,
seven score Turks, bearing standards—
the city of Orange is guarded well,
for they're afraid that Louis will take it,
and you, sweet lord, and the barons of France.

There's Aragon, a rich Saracen king,   200
the son of Tiebaut, of the land of Spain,
and lady Orable, a noble queen;
there is none so lovely from here to the East,
a beautiful body, slender and fine;
her skin is white, like a flower on the stem.
God, what good is her body or her youth,
she doesn't know God, our father almighty!"
"It's true," says William, "their power is great,
but by Him, in whom I have placed my faith,
I shall not bear shield or lance any more   210
if I do not manage to meet them soon."

viii

Count William has listened to the baron
who is sitting beside him on the step;
he addresses him and speaks with affection:
"Fair brother, friend, you have told quite a tale.
Did the Saracens keep you long in prison?"
"Yes, they did, sire, three years and fifteen days,
and there was no way for me to escape
until one morning when God gave us day,
a Saracen, evil and arrogant,   220
wanted to beat me, as he had each day.
I seized him by the hair on his forehead,
struck him so hard on the neck with my fist,
that I shattered all the bones of his throat.
Then I escaped through the window, alone,
so that not one of the enemy saw.
To Beaucaire, the port at Oriflor, came
Turks and Persians, the king of Aragon,
the elder son of King Tiebaut the Slav;
he is large and heavy and strong and tall,   230
his head is broad and his brow bound with iron,
his nails are long and pointed and sharp,
there is no tyrant like him under the world's cloak.
He murders our Christians and destroys them.

Whoever could win that city and tower
and put to death the treacherous villain,
he would have spent his labor very well."

ix

"Good brother, friend," says Count William the brave,
"Is Orange really as you have described?"
Gilbert answers: "It is even better.   240
If you could see the principal palace,
how high it is and enclosed all around,
as you look at it from any view;
if you were there the first day of summer,
you would hear the birds as they sing there then,
the falcons' cry and the moulting goshawks,
the horses' whinny and the braying mules
that entertain and delight the Saracens.
The sweet herbs smell most fragrant there,
spices and cinammon which he had planted.   250
There you might see the fair Lady Orable
who is the wife of Sir Tiebaut the Slav;
there is no one so fair in all Christendom,
nor in pagan lands wherever you seek.
Her body is lovely, slender and soft,
and her eyes change color like a moulting falcon,
but of what use is all her beauty
when she does not know God and his goodness?
A noble man could be well pleased with her,
she could be saved if she wished to believe."   260
Then William says: "By the faith of St. Omer,
good brother, friend, you sing her praises well.
But by Him who has all mankind to save,
I will not carry lance or shield again
if I don't win the lady and the city."

x

"Good brother, friend, is Orange then so rich?"
The fugitive answers: "God help me, my lord,

if you could see the palace of the city
with its many vaults and its palisades,
as it was built by Grifon of Almeria,   270
a Saracen of most marvelous vice.
No flower grows from here to Pavia
that is not painted there in gold artfully.
Within is Lady Orable, the queen,
the wife of King Tiebaut of Africa.
There is none so lovely in all pagandom,
her body is beautiful, slender and fine,
her skin is as white as the flower of the thorn,
her eyes bright and hazel and always laughing;
But what good is her gay spirit to her   280
when she doesn't know God, blessed Mary's son."
"You have set," William says, "great worth on her,
and by the faith that I owe to my love,
I shall eat no more bread made from flour,
no salted meat, I shall drink no more wine,
until I have seen how Orange is set.
And I must see that tower of marble,
and Lady Orable, the gracious queen.
Love of her has me so in its power,
that I could not describe or conceive it.   290
If I can't have her soon, I shall lose my life."
The fugitive says: "This idea is insane,
if you were now inside that palace
and could see the vast Saracen array,
God confound me, if I thought I should live
long enough to see such a thing achieved.
Best let it be, the whole idea is mad."

XI

Count William listens to the troubled words
that the fugitive has spoken to him.
He summons the people of his country: 300
"Give me advice, noble men of honor.
This poor wretch has praised a city to me,

I was never there, I don't know the land.
But the Rhone runs here, a swift, moving stream,
except for it I should have gone by now."
The fugitive says: "This whole plan is mad.
If you had a hundred thousand with swords,
with beautiful weapons and golden shields,
and you wished to engage the enemy,
if there'd been no water or obstacle   310
before you could even enter the gates,
a thousand blows of the sword would be struck
and belts would be torn and many shields pierced
and many fine men struck down in the streets.
Let it all be, it is madness to try."

xii

"Look here," William says, "You have disturbed me,
you have just told me about this city
that no count or king possesses its like
and you would prevent me from going there.
By St. Maurice, who is sought at Amiens,   320
I tell you, you shall accompany me,
and we shall not take horses or palfreys
or white chain-mail or helmets from Amiens,
no shield or lance or Poitevin spears—
but javelins, like greedy fugitives.
You have spoken enough Turkish in that land
and African, Basque and Bedouin tongues."
The wretch hears him, imagine how he feels—
he wishes he were at Chartres or Blois
or at Paris in the land of the king,   330
for he does not know how to get out of this.

xiii

Now William is angry and filled with wrath,
his nephew Bertrand undertakes to speak:
"Uncle," he says, "give up this madness,
if you were now in that city's palace

and you could look at those Saracen hordes,
you would be known by your bump and your laugh,
they would quickly suspect that you were a spy.
Then, I'm afraid, you'd be brought to Persia,
they would not feed you on bread or flour,   340
nor would they wait long before they killed you;
they would throw you into a stone prison,
and you wouldn't come out again in your lives
until King Tiebaut of Africa came
and Desramé and Golias of Bile,
they would sentence you however they wished.
If, because of love, you come to judgment,
the people of your kingdom will say
that you were cursed for the sight of Orable the queen."
"Look," says William, "I have no fear of that   350
for, by the apostle sought in Galicia,
I would far rather die and lose my life
than go on eating bread made from flour
or salted flesh or fermented wine.
Instead I shall see how Orange is set
and Gloriete with its marble tower
and lady Orable, the gracious queen.
The love of her torments and governs me—
a man in love is reckless and a fool."

xiv

Now William is troubled about Orange,   360
his nephew Bertrand begins to chide him:
"Uncle," he says, "you'll bring shame on yourself
and dishonor, and have your limbs torn off."
"Look," says the count, "that is not what I fear,
a man who's in love is completely mad.
I would not give up, though I lose my limbs,
not for any man who might beg me to,
going to see how Orange is set,
and Lady Orable, so worthy of praise.
Love for her has so taken hold of me   370

I can't sleep in the night or take any rest,
I am unable to drink or to eat
or carry arms or to mount on my horse
or go to mass, or to enter a church."
He orders ink ground up in a mortar
and other herbs that the baron knew of;
he and Gilbert, who does not dare leave him,
paint their bodies in front and behind,
their faces and their chests, even their feet,
so they resemble devils and demons.   380
Guielin says: "By St. Riquier's body,
you have both been transformed by a miracle,
now you could wander throughout the world,
you wouldn't be recognized anywhere.
But, by the apostle who's sought in Rome,
I would not give up, though I lose my limbs,
going with you to see how it will be."
With the ointment he too is painted and swabbed;
there are the three all prepared to set forth,
they take their leave and depart the city.   390
"God," says Bertrand, "good and righteous father,
how we have been deceived and betrayed!
In what madness was this affair begun
which will bring us all dishonor and shame,
if God does not help, who must judge us all."

XV

William goes forth, the marquis of the fierce look,
with brave Gilbert and the proud Guielin.
Count Bertrand has already turned back
but these go on without further delay.
Below Beaucaire they have found the Rhone   400
and at Dourance they've crossed over it.
Thereabouts they begin to swim quietly,
they cross the Sorgues without barge or ship.
By Aragon, they have gotten across;
straight towards the walls and moats of Orange

the high halls and the fortified palace
adorned with golden pommels and eagles.
Inside they can hear the little birds sing,
the falcons cry and the moulting goshawks,
the horses whinny and the braying mules,   410
and the Saracens entertained in the tower,
the soft fragrance of spices and cinammon,
all the sweet herbs they have in plenty.
"God," says William, "who gave me life and breath,
what wealth there is in this wondrous city!
How rich he must be who possesses it."
They do not stop until they reach the gate
and then Gilbert addresses the porter
in his own tongue, he speaks courteously:
"Open these gates, porter, let us come in,   420
we are interpreters from Africa
and men of King Tiebaut the Slav."
The porter says: "I have not heard of you.
What people are you who call me out there?
King Aragon is not yet awake,
and I do not dare to open the gate,
so much do we fear William of the short nose,
who captured Nîmes with such violent force.
You remain here, I shall go to the king;
if he commands, then I'll let you enter."   430
"Go right away," says the baron William,
"quickly so that we lose no more time."
The porter leaves without any delay,
he climbs the marble steps of the palace.
He finds Aragon seated by a pillar,
surrounded by his Saracens and Slavs.
Courteously he begins to address him:
"Sire," he says, "listen to this report:
at the gate there are three honorable Turks
who claim to be from Africa beyond the seas."   440
"Then go, good brother, and let them come in;
there are many things I should like to ask

about my lord who has waited so long."
And so he runs back to open the gate.
Now William has gotten inside Orange,
with him Gilbert and the worthy Guielin.
They will not get out once the gates are shut
before they have suffered distress and pain.

XVI

Now William has gotten inside Orange
with Guielin and the noble Gilbert.   450
They are disguised by alum and black dye,
so that they look like Saracen tyrants.
In the palace they find two Saracens,
they call to them and speak their idiom,
one tells the other: "They're from Africa,
today we shall hear some good news from there."
But Count William keeps walking straight ahead,
towards the palace of the Persian Tiebaut.
The columns and the walls are built of marble
and the windows sculpted of fine silver;   460
a gold eagle sparkles and shines.
The sun doesn't enter, nor a breath of wind.
"God," says William, "redeemer and father—
who ever saw such a splendid palace!
How rich he must be, the lord of this hall,
would it were God's will, who formed all mankind,
that I had with me my palatine Bertrand,
and all the ten thousand Frank warriors!
We would bury the unlucky Saracens.
I would kill a good hundred before noon."   470
He finds Aragon beside a column
and around him fifteen thousand Persians.
William is dead, if he can't deceive them.
Now you shall hear how he speaks to them:
"Emir and lord, noble and valiant knight,
Mohammed greets you and the God Tervagant."
Says the emir: "Baron, you may approach.

Where are you from?" "The African kingdom
of your father, the mighty king Tiebaut.
Yesterday morning as nones was sounded,   480
we got to Nîmes, the strong and rich city,
where we expected to find King Otran
and Sinagon and the tyrant Harpin.
But William had killed him, with his Frank troops;
our men were murdered, bleeding and torn.
He put the three of us in his prison, too,
but he is so rich in family and friends
that somehow we were allowed to escape.
We don't know how—may the devil take him!"
Aragon says: "How sad this makes me.   490
By Mohammed, in whom I believe,
if I had William in my power now,
he would be dead and suffering torment,
his bones and ashes scattered to the winds."
William hears him and he lowers his head.
He wishes that he were at Paris or Sens;
he calls on God, his merciful father:
"Glorious sire, who has formed all mankind,
who was born of the Virgin in Bethlehem,
if the three kings came in search of you   500
and if you were hung on the cross by tyrants,
and by the lance, you were pierced in the side—
Longinus did it, who could not see—
and blood and water ran down from the point;
he rubbed his eyes and the light was restored.
If this is true, just as I have told it,
guard our bodies against death and torment.
Don't let Saracens or Persians kill us!"

xvii

William is in the palace at the tower.
He calls his other companions to him   510
quietly, so the pagans cannot hear:
"My lords," he says, "we shall be in prison

if God does not help by His most holy name."
"Uncle William," Guielin answers him,
"Noble lord, sire, you came here seeking love,
you see Gloriete, the palace and tower,
why don't you ask where the ladies are kept.
You might well find a way to deceive them."
And the count says: "You are right, my young squire."
Now King Aragon begins to question him: 520
"Baron, when were you in Africa?"
"My dear lord, no more than two months ago."
"Did you see King Tiebaut of Aragon?"
"Yes, my good lord, when he was at Vaudon.
He embraced us and sent you this message,
that you maintain his honor and city.
Where is his wife? Will you show her to us?"
"Of course, my lords," says the king Aragon.
"There is none lovelier up to the clouds.
But barons," he adds, "I have need of my father;   530
the Franks are taking our castles and towers.
William is the one, with his two nephews.
But, by Mohammed's and Tervagant's faith,
if I now held William in my prison,
he would soon be burned in fire and coals,
his bones and ashes scattered through the air."
William hears him, he holds his head down
and wishes he could be at Reims or Laon.
He calls on God and His glorious name:
"Glorious father, who made Lazarus,   540
and became incarnate in the Virgin,
preserve my body from death and prison.
Don't let these evil Saracens kill us!"

XVIII

Now William is in the noble palace;
pagans and Saracens call for water,
the tables are placed, they sit down to eat.
William sits too and his nephew Guielin;

they speak softly and hold their heads down,
they're in great fear that they will be captured.
King Aragon has them served splendidly.   550
They have plenty of bread and wine at the meal,
cranes and geese and well-roasted peacocks,
and other foods I cannot describe.
There is as much as anyone could wish.
When they have eaten and drunk to their pleasure,
the cup-bearers come to take up the cloths.
Pagan and Saracens start to play chess.
William hears all the palace resound,
which is sculpted of green marble and dark,
he sees the birds and lions depicted: 560
"God," says the count, "who was hung on the cross,
who ever saw so splendid a palace!
If it pleased God, who never deceives us,
that we had the palatine Bertrand here,
and the twenty thousand Franks with their arms,
the pagans would meet a bad end today.
By my head, I would kill eighty myself."

XIX

King Aragon has summoned Count William
to sit beside him beneath a pillar
and in his ear he questions him softly: 570
"Noble Turk," he asks, "now tell me the truth,
what sort of man is William of the short nose,
who captured Nîmes with his powerful force
and murdered King Harpin and his brother?
He had you thrown into his prison, too."
And William answers: "You will hear the truth now.
He is so rich, in pride of possessions,
that he has no care for gold or silver;
instead he let us escape for nothing
except that he made us swear by our laws.   580
He sent you a message we cannot hide,
that you flee over seas to Africa,

you will not see the month of May go by
before he attacks with twenty thousand men;
your towers and columns will not save you,
your magnificent halls, nor your deep moats.
With iron clubs they will all be destroyed.
If he captures you, you will suffer torture.
You will hang from the gallows in the wind."
Aragon says: "What madness is this—   590
I shall send overseas to Africa,
my father will come with his mighty nobles,
with Golias and the king Desramé,
Corsolt of Mables, his brother Aceré,
and Clariau and the king Atriblez
and Quinzepaumes and the king Sorgalez,
the king of Egypt and King Codroez,
and King Moranz and the king Anublez,
and the prince of Sorgremont on the sea,
my uncle Borreaus and all his sons,   600
and the thirty kings who were born in Spain.
Each one will bring twenty thousand armed men
and we will fight at the walls and the moats;
William will be dead and go to his end
and his nephews will be hung from the gallows."
William hears him and almost loses his mind;
between his teeth, he answers him softly:
"By God," he says, "you pig, you are lying,
instead three thousand Turks will be killed,
before you conquer or hold Nîmes in fief."   610
If he had arms to equip himself now,
he would hold all the palace in terror
for he can no longer control his rage.

XX

Now William is in the great stone hall:
"King Aragon," he begins his address,
"Sire," he says, "will you show me the queen
whom Africa's emperor seems to love so?"

Aragon says: "It is madness in him,
for he is old and his beard is snow-white,
and she is a young and beautiful girl,   620
there is none so fair in all pagandom.
In Gloriete he enjoys his loves—
better if he loved Soribant of Venice,
a young bachelor who still has his first beard,
who knows how to live with arms and pleasure
better than Tiebaut of Slavonia.
An old man is mad to love a young girl,
he is soon cuckolded and driven mad."
When William hears him he begins to laugh.
"Tell me," asks William, "you don't love her at all?"   630
"Not I, certainly, God curse the woman!
I only wish she were in Africa
or at Baudas, in Almeria."

XXI

In the palace is William the noble,
and Gilbert too and the mighty Guielin;
they go out through the center of the hall,
led by an unsuspecting pagan,
to the queen who is so loved by the king.
Better for them if they would return
beyond the Rhone and go back to Nîmes;   640
before evening comes or the sun can set,
unless God acts with his noble power,
they will suffer what will cause them sorrow.
At Gloriete, they have now arrived,
of marble are its pillars and walls,
and the windows sculpted in fine silver,
the golden eagle, resplendent and bright,
the sun cannot enter, nor does the wind blow;
it is beautifully done, pleasant and charming.
In one part of the chamber, inside,   650
there is a pine grown in such a way,
as you shall hear, if that is your wish:

the branches are long and the leaves are large,
the flower it bears wond'rously fair;
it is white and blue, and even red.
There's an abundance of carob-trees there,
spices, cinnamon, galingale, and incense,
sweet fragrances, of hyssop and allspice.
There sits Orable, the African lady,
dressed in a gown of marvelous stuff,   660
tightly laced on her noble body,
and sewn along the sides with rich silks,
and Rosiane, the niece of Rubiant,
makes a gentle breeze with a silver fan.
She is more white than snow in the sunlight,
she is more red than the most fragrant rose.
William sees her and his blood turns cold,
he greets her nobly and courteously.
"May that God save you, in whom we believe!"
The queen answers: "Baron, please approach me.   670
Mohammed save you, on whom the world depends."
Beside her, she has them sit on a bench,
that is sculpted in silver and gold.
Now they can speak somewhat of their wishes.
"God," says William, "this is paradise here!"
Says Guielin: "I've seen nothing finer,
I would like to spend all my life here.
There would never be a reason to leave."

XXII

Now William is seated in Gloriete,
and Gilbert and the worthy Guielin,   680
near the ladies in the shade of the pine.
There sits Orable, of the bright face,
wearing a piece of ermine fur
and underneath a samite tunic,
tightened with laces on her lovely body.
William sees her, all his body trembles.
"God," says William, "it is Paradise here!"

If God would help me," Guielin responds,
"I would remain here most willingly.
I would not seek either food or sleep." 690
Then the noble lady begins to ask:
"Where are you from, noble and gentle knight?"
"Lady we are from the Persian kingdom,
from the land of your husband, Tiebaut.
Yesterday morning, when day was breaking,
we were at Nîmes, that marvelous city,
we expected to find people of our race,
King Sinagon and Otran and Harpin,
but Fierebrace had killed all three of them.
The Franks captured us at the gates of the city 700
and led us before the palatine,
but he is so rich and supported by friends
that he does not care for silver or gold.
Instead he let us escape in this way:
first we had to swear an oath by our laws
and carry this message which I bring to you,
that you must flee to the Persian kingdom,
for you will not see the month of April pass
before he comes with twenty thousand men.
The palace and the walls will not save you, 710
nor the broad halls, nor the strong palisades,
with iron clubs they will all be destroyed.
If he captures Aragon the Arab,
your stepson, the prince that you love so much,
he will make him die an unpleasant death,
by hanging or burning in fire and flame."
The lady hears him and sighs tenderly.

XXIII

The lady listens to the strange message,
then she asks them, she is anxious to know:
"My lord barons, I am versed in your tongue. 720
What sort of a man is William Fierebrace,
who captured Nîmes, the palace and the halls

and killed my men, and is still threatening me?"
"Indeed," says the count, "he has a fierce heart,
his fists are huge and his arm is mighty.
There is no man from here to Arabia
who, if William strikes him with his sharp sword,
would not be hacked apart, body and arms,
straight to the ground drives that sword as it cuts."
"Indeed," says the lady, "this is distressing.   730
By Mohammed, he will hold great domains.
Happy the lady who possesses his heart."
Then the villainous pagans come in a crowd;
today William will find more trouble
than he has encountered in all his life.
May God protect him against loss and harm!

XXIV

Now William has climbed inside the tower,
and Gilbert and the worthy Guielin;
beside the ladies under the pine,
he sits chatting softly with the queen.   740
The treacherous pagans are massed outside
to watch the barons and look at them.
Unless God helps, who was hung on the cross,
today William will be badly abused,
for there is a pagan, Salatré—
may He confound him who must save us all—
one whom the count had captured at Nîmes,
but one evening the scoundrel had escaped
and had fled through the moats and found his way,
so that he could not be recaptured or found.   750
He causes terrible trouble for William,
as you are about to hear recounted.
To Aragon, the scoundrel now comes,
into his ear he pours out a whole tale:
"By Mohammed, sire, arouse your barons.
We can avenge now the fierce cruelty
that would have struck me at the city of Nîmes.
You see that strong figure in the tower?

That is William, the marquis of the short nose,
and his nephew is the other young knight,   760
the third one, who carries the heavy club,
is the marquis who escaped from here.
To deceive you, they have donned this disguise,
for they hope to capture this good city."
Aragon asks: "Do you tell me the truth?"
"Sire," he answers, "you'll be sorry if you doubt me.
That is William who had me imprisoned,
he would have had me hanging in the wind
if Mohammed had not protected me.
This is the day that he'll be rewarded."   770
Now hear me tell, noble barons and good,
for the love of God who hung on the cross,
of that villain, what evil he worked.
He takes a tunic, made of pure gold,
and hurls it straight into William's face,
it strikes William just above the nose,
he is discovered, his color comes off;
his skin is white like a summer flower.
When William sees this, he almost goes mad,
throughout his body the blood runs cold.   780
He calls on God, the king in majesty:
"Glorious father, who must save us all,
who deigned to become flesh in the Virgin,
all for the people whom You wished to save,
You gave up Your body to pain and torment,
to be wounded and injured upon the cross,
as this is all true, lord, in Your goodness,
guard my body from death and destruction.
Don't let the Slavs and Saracens kill us!"

XXV

When Aragon hears what the Slav tells him,   790
that he recognizes the three companions,
he rises to his feet and begins to speak:
"Sir William, your name is well known here,
you'll be sorry you crossed the Rhone, by Mohammed!

You will all be put to a dreadful death,
your bones and ashes scattered in the wind.
I would not, for a dungeon filled with gold,
rescue you from death and burning to coals."
William hears him, his color like ashes;
he wishes he were at Reims or Laon;   800
Guielin sees that they can't hide any longer,
he wrings his hands and tears at his hair.
"God," says William, "by Your most holy name,
glorious Father who made Lazarus
and in the Virgin took on human form,
who saved Jonah in the belly of the whale
and Daniel the prophet in the lion's den,
who granted pardon to Mary Magdalene,
brought the body of St. Peter to Rome,
and converted his companion, St. Paul,   810
who was, at that time, a very cruel man,
but then became one of the believers,
together with them he walked in processions,
as this is true, sire, and we believe it,
protect us against death and foul prison.
Don't let treacherous Saracens kill us!"
He has a stick, large and sturdy and long;
with his two hands, he raises it high
and brings it down on the false Salatré,
who had denounced him to King Aragon.   820
Right through his head comes the blow of the club,
so that his brains pour out on the ground.
"Montjoy!" he cries, "strike ahead, barons!"

XXVI

William has all the palace in terror.
Before the king he has killed a pagan.
Count William has found himself a club
that had been brought there to make a fire.
He runs over to it, swiftly and sweating,
grabs it in his fists and lifts it high.
He strikes Baitaime, the reckless pagan,   830

a vigorous blow of the club on his skull,
which causes his brains to fly from his head.
Before the king he has struck him dead.
And Gilbert, too, goes to strike Quarré,
he shoves his club into his stomach
and forces a good part of it out the side.
He throws him down before the pillar, dead.
"Montjoy!" he cries, "barons, come, strike ahead!
Since we are certainly destined to die,
let's sell ourselves high as long as we last!"   840
Aragon hears; he thinks he will go mad.
Aloud he cries: "Barons, capture these men!
By Mohammed, they will be killed straightway
and tossed and thrown into the Rhone,
or burned in fire and scattered to the wind."
Guielin shouts at them "Barons stand aside,
for by the apostle we seek at Rome,
you won't take me without paying for it."
In fierce anger, he brandishes his stick.
Count William begins to strike with his club   850
and Gilbert with his iron-bound cudgel,
mighty blows the noble barons strike;
fourteen Turks they have thrown to their deaths
and so terrified all the others
that, striking, they chase them out through the gates.
Then the towers are bolted and shut,
and by the great chains, the bridge is hauled up.
May God now help, who was hung on the cross!
For William is in a dangerous spot,
and Gilbert and the worthy Guielin,   860
In Gloriete where they have been trapped,
and the Saracens, the raging cowards,
attack them from outside with no respite.

XXVII

The Saracens are fierce and arrogant,
they attack them by hundreds and thousands,
throwing their lances and piercing steel darts.

The Franks defend themselves like noble knights,
casting those pigs into moats and channels,
more than fourteen have already fallen.
The most fortunate has his neck splintered.   870
Aragon sees it and begins to rage,
from sorrow and anger he is nearly mad.
With a loud, clear voice, he begins to shout:
"Are you up there, William of the fierce look?"
The count answers: "Certainly I am here.
By my prowess I have found good lodging,
may God help me, who was raised on the cross!"

xxviii

Now William has entered Gloriete
and begun to speak to the Saracens:
"Damned be he who thinks he can hide!   880
I entered this city in order to spy
and I have deceived and tricked you so well
that I have chased you out of Gloriete.
Henceforth you will be guardians of this tower,
protect it well, your reward will be high!"
Aragon hears him and begins to rage.
He summons the Saracens and pagans:
"Quickly to arms, now, my noble knights.
The assault must now be begun in force.
Whoever captures this William for me   890
will bear the standard for all my kingdom;
all my treasures will be open to him."
When his men hear this they are pleased and encouraged,
the craven flatterers run for their arms
and attack William in front and behind.
The count sees them and nearly goes mad.
He invokes God, the true and righteous judge.

xxix

Now William is angered and sorrowful,
and brave Guielin and the noble Gilbert.

At Gloriete, where they are trapped inside,   900
they are sought by all of that pagan race,
they throw their lances and piercing steel darts.
William sees them and nearly loses his mind.
"Nephew Guielin, what is holding us back?
Never can we hope to return to France,
if God does not help us, with his power,
we shall not see cousins or family."
But Guielin of the graceful body:
"Uncle William, you're speaking to no end.
Because of your love you made your way here;   910
there is Orable, the African lady,
and none so fair alive in this world.
Go now and sit beside her on the bench,
put both your arms around her lovely form
and don't be slow to embrace and kiss her,
for by the apostle penitents seek,
we shall not have the value of that kiss
unless it costs twenty thousand silver marks
and great suffering to all our people."
"God," says William, "your words so incite me   920
that I can barely keep my reason."

XXX

Count William is now angry and enraged,
and Gilbert and the worthy Guielin;
inside Gloriete where they have been trapped
with the Saracen pagans pressing hard;
they defend themselves like skillful knights,
throwing down clubs and huge heavy cudgels.
Now the queen begins to counsel them:
"Barons," she says, "Franks, give yourselves up.
The villainous pagans hate you fiercely,   930
you will soon see them climbing the steps,
you'll all be dead, murdered, and dismembered."
William hears her, his mind is distraught.
He runs to the chamber beneath the pine

and wildly begins to beg the queen:
"My lady," he says, "please give me armor,
for the love of God who was hung on the cross!
For, by St. Peter, if I live through this,
you will be richly rewarded for it."
The lady hears him and weeps with pity.   940
She runs to the chamber without delay,
to a coffer, which she quickly opens.
She takes from it a good golden shirt of mail
and a bright golden helmet, set with jewels;
William runs to take the things from her,
and to receive what he has so desired.
He dons the hauberk and laces the helm,
and Lady Orable girds on the sword
which belonged to her lord, Tiebaut the Slav.
She had not wished any man to have it,   950
not even Aragon, who wanted it so,
and was the son of her wedded husband.
At his neck she hangs a strong polished shield,
on it a lion wearing a gold crown.
In his fist he holds a good, heavy lance,
its standard held by five golden nails.
"God," says William, "how well armed I am now.
For God, I beg you to think of the others!"

XXXI

When Guielin sees that his uncle is armed,
he too runs into the lady's chamber   960
and calls to her, sweetly begging her aid:
"Lady," he asks, "by St. Peter of Rome,
please give me arms, we have such great need."
"My child," she says, "you are so very young,
if you live long you will be a brave man.
But the Vavars and Hongars hate you to death."
In her chamber she takes out a mail-shirt
which Isaac of Barcelone had forged—
there was no sword that could pierce that mail.

He puts it on and his uncle is glad;   970
he laces the Alfar of Babylon's helm,
the first king who had held that city.
There is no sword that can destroy it
or knock off a stone or ruby flower.
She girds the sword of Tornemont of Valsone
which was stolen from him by thieves at Valdonne,
and then sold to Tiebaut at Voirconbe;
he gave a thousand besants for it
for he hoped to pass it on to his son.
She girds it at his side, the straps are long,   980
at his neck she hangs a large, round shield,
and hands him a lance, my lady of Valronne,
the handle is large and the blade is long.
He is well armed and Gilbert as well.
Today Gloriete will be contested.

XXXII

William and his nephew are now well armed,
and Gilbert, too, and they all rejoice.
On his back a strong, double shirt of mail,
on his head they lace a green barred helmet,
then they gird a sword of steel at his side,   990
and they hang a quartered shield from his neck.
But before he takes the good sharp spear,
the evil pagans have advanced so far
that they are beginning to mount the steps.
Count William goes to strike down Haucebier
and Gilbert, the gate-keeper, Maretant,
and Guielin goes to attack Turfier.
These three pagans do not escape death;
they smash the tips of the pointed spears
so that the splinters shoot up toward the sky.   1000
They are now forced to rely on their swords
which they are anxious to try out and prove.
Count William has drawn his sword of steel,
he strikes a pagan across the back

and cuts him down like an olive branch.
Down into the palace the two halves fall.
And Gilbert goes to strike Gaifier
and sends his head flying into the palace.
Guielin too is not at all frightened.
He holds his sword and grasps his good shield;   1010
whoever he meets is destined to die.
Pagans see him and begin to retreat,
the craven flatterers take to flight.
The Franks chase them, the noble warriors,
more than fourteen they've already destroyed,
and terrified all the others so
that they drive them back out through the gates.
The Franks run to shut them and bolt them;
by the great chains they have pulled up the bridge
and attached it fast against the tower.   1020
Now let God think of them who judges all!
Aragon sees it and his mind rages.

xxxiii

Now William is sorrowful and angry
and Gilbert and the worthy Guielin;
they are pressed hard by the pagan masses
who throw their lances and well-turned darts
and beat down the walls with clubs of iron.
William sees it, he is consumed by rage.
"Nephew Guielin," he asks, "what shall we do?
Never, it seems, will we return to France.   1030
Nor will we kiss nephews and relatives again."
"Uncle William, this is useless talk,
for by the apostle who's sought at Rome,
I'll sell myself high before we give up."
They climb down the steps of the tower
and strike the pagans on their rounded helmets;
they cut straight through their chests and their chins
until seventeen lie dead in the sand.
The most fortunate has his lungs cut out.

When the pagans see this, their hearts tremble, 1040
they cry aloud to mighty Aragon:
"Make a truce with them, we'll never get in."
Aragon hears them, nearly dissolved in rage,
he swears by Mohammed he will make them pay.

XXXIV

Aragon sees the pagans hesitate,
he calls them graciously and then he says:
"Sons of bitches, pigs, you'll be sorry you came.
You'll never hold fiefs or marches from me,
you can look for them in fiercer fighting."
And so they do, the miscreant swine, 1050
they throw their darts and miserable lances,
with iron clubs they beat down the walls.
William sees it, nearly mad with fury:
"Nephew Guielin, now what can we do?
We are all dead, and doomed to destruction."
"Uncle William, you're talking like a fool,
for by the apostle we seek in the ark,
I'll make them pay before pagans get me."
The points of their spears have all been shattered,
but each of the three picks up an axe 1060
which the noble Lady Orable gave them.
They go out again, bearing new weapons
and strike the pagans on their red targes,
cutting straight through to their faces and chests.
More than fourteen now lie on the marble, 14 ?
some of them dead, the others unconscious.
Never did three men do so much damage.
Aragon sees it and nearly goes mad.

XXXV

When Aragon sees his people so pressed,
then he grieves and almost bursts with anger. 1070
In a clear voice, he cries out to the Franks:
"Are you up there, William of the fine body,

the son of Aimeri of Narbonne the great?
Do something for me that I greatly desire,
leave Gloriete, the palace, right now
and go away healthy, safe and alive,
before you lose all your limbs and your blood.
If you refuse, you will suffer for it.
By Mohammed, in whom I believe,
here in this place, a great pyre will be built,   1080
you will all be burned and roasted in there."
William answers: "Your talk is for nothing.
We have plenty of bread and wine and cheese
and salted meat and wines, honeyed and spiced,
and white hauberks and green shining helmets,
excellent swords with hilts of silver,
sharp piercing spears and good heavy shields
and lovely ladies to entertain us.
I shall not leave while I am yet alive,
and soon the noble king Louis will know,   1090
my brother Bernard, who is hoary and white,
and the warrior, Garin of Anseune,
and the mighty duke Bueves of Commarch,
my nephew Bertrand, who is brave and valiant,
whom we just left behind us at Nîmes.
Each one of them, whenever he wishes,
can well send twenty thousand warriors.
When they find out what is happening here,
how we are established here within,
they will come to our aid most graciously   1100
with as many men as they can gather.
I tell you, these walls will be no defense,
nor this palace, where gold shines in splendor;
you will see it shattered in a thousand parts.
If they capture you, it will not go easy,
you will be hooked and hung in the wind."
Aragon says: "We shall grieve all the more."
Pharaon speaks, the king of Bonivent,
"Emir, sire, you are not worth a glove.

By Mohammed, you have very little sense. 1110
Your father was worthy and valiant,
and he left this city to you to defend,
and the palace, Gloriete, as well.
These three scoundrels who are challenging you
have been killing your men and your people;
by Mohammed, you are not worth much
if you can't burn them in stinking Greek fire."

xxxvi

"Pharaon, sir," says the king Aragon,
give me better counsel, for Mohammed's sake,
you see Gloriete, the palace and tower, 1120
whose foundation is set so deep and strong.
All the people from here to Moncontor
could not make any opening in it.
Where the devil would we get the coals?
We have no wooden branches or sticks.
Those three pigs got in there by their arrogance.
but they won't get out in seven years."

xxxvii

"Pharaon, sir," says the king Aragon,
"for Mohammed, whose laws we uphold,
you must advise me immediately. 1130
Behold Gloriete, the splendid palace
the foundation is laid in solid rock.
All the men from here to the port of Vauquois
could not make a hole in its walls in a month.
From what devils could we get the coals
when we haven't a twig of wood or laurel?
In their arrogance those three got inside,
but in seven years, they will not get out."
Now a pagan, Orquenois steps forward,
his beard is black, but his hair white with age, 1140
his eyebrows white, if I judge them rightly.
In a loud voice, he cries out three times:

"Emir, sire, will you listen to me,
and tell me if it would be worth my while
to deliver William the Frank to you
so that you might hold him in your prison?"
Aragon answers: "Yes, by my faith.
Ten mules laden with the best Spanish gold
I would give to one who could tell me that."
Orquenois says: "Then listen to me.   1150
If you will give me your promise straightway,
I shall do it, whatever may happen."
Aragon says: "I swear this to you,
and I pledge faithfully here and now
that when you wish you shall have those riches."
The pagan replies: "I give you my word."

xxxviii

Orquenois says: "By Mohammed, sweet lord,
I shall tell you how to take him with guile:
there is Gloriete, the marble tower,
its foundation set well in the stone.   1160
It was built by Grifaigne of Almeria,
a Saracen of great cleverness.
You never knew what tricks they had designed:
Beneath the earth, a solitary vault,
a portcullis into your palace.
Take a thousand Turks and go there yourself
to lay a siege at the front of the tower
and attack at the same time from behind.
William will soon be dead and in torment."
Aragon says: "By Mohammed, that's true.   1170
You'll be rich for this, by my lord Apollo!"

xxxix

When Aragon has learned of this secret,
that there is a cave in the earth beneath him,
his joy is such that it makes his heart leap.
He takes a thousand Turks, their helmets laced,

and another thousand he leaves in front
to keep up the siege of Guielin and William;
the others turn round and go quickly
not stopping until they reach the entrance,
carrying candles and lanterns along.   1180
They enter the cave, that foul hostile race.
The honorable knights know nothing of them
until they're already inside the palace.
William is the first to find out they are there.
"God," says the count, "glorious in heaven,
we are all dead and delivered to pain."
Guielin says: "By St. Hilaire's body,
as God helps me, Orable has betrayed us.
May God confound the whole Saracen race!"

xl

Count William sees the palace being filled   1190
with Saracens who come there in anger;
he sees the hauberks and the helmets shine.
"God," says the count, "who never deceives us,
we are all dead and doomed to destruction."
"In faith, my good lord," answers Guielin,
"we were betrayed by Orable the fair.
May God confound pagans and Saracens!
This is the day that we must meet our end.
Let us help ourselves, as long as we can,
for we have no friends or relatives here."   1200
Count William brandishes the sword of steel,
in fury he moves to strike a pagan
back-handed and cuts him straight through the middle.
The pagans are terrified by this blow.
They rush at him enraged and distressed.
They defend themselves like emboldened knights;
he strikes great blows, the count palatine.
The assault is fierce and the slaughter great,
but it won't end until they're defeated.
No battle was ever fought so well.   1210

In their defense they have killed thirty Turks.
Who cares, if they can never finish them!
The pagans and Saracens lay hold of him,
Turks and Persians and the Almoravi,
Acoperts, Esclamors and Bedouins;
by Mohammed they swear vengeance will be had.
They will avenge the death of their friends.

xli

William is captured by deadly treason
and with him Gilbert and the brave Guielin.
The Saracen villains have them in their hands   1220
and swear by Mohammed to take revenge.
They send twenty boys into the city
to dig a ditch that will be wide and deep,
and to fill it with kindling wood and twigs
for they intend to grill our barons.
Orable comes, she is fair of visage,
and addresses her stepson Aragon:
"My friend," she says, "give these prisoners to me,
I shall place them in my deepest dungeon,
where toads and adders will feed on them   1230
and small serpents will devour them."
"My lady, queen," says the king Aragon,
"you were the cause of this trouble
when you armed these treacherous swine up there.
Damned be the man who would give them to you!"
The lady hears him and trembles with rage.
"You'll be sorry for that, you bastard pig!
By Mohammed, whom I praise and adore,
if it were not for these other barons,
I would strike you on the nose with my fist.   1240
Get yourself out of my tower quickly,
if you stay longer you will regret it."
She addresses the treacherous villains:
"Vile thieves," she says, "put them in your prison
until Tiebaut returns from Valdon,

and Desramé and Golias the blond.
They will take the vengeance they desire."
"I swear it, lady," says King Aragon,
William is cast into the deep dungeon,
and Guielin and the valiant Gilbert.
For a while we must let our barons be;   1250
when it is time we will come back to them.
Now we must sing of the pagan people.

xlii

King Aragon does not rest with his deed,
he sends his messengers over the seas
and they depart, without pause or halt,
from here to the Rhone they don't rest or stop,
and there they embark on a galley,
on the ship of Maudoine of Nubie.
It is artfully covered with silk,   1260
and does not fear a storm or tempest.
They lift their anchor and hoist their sails,
they take to sea, leave the city behind,
they glide and skim and they steer and they sail,
they have a good wind to carry them straight.
When they reach the port beneath Almeria,
they drop anchor and lower their sails.
Mounting their horses, they still do not stop.
They do not pause or rest from their ride
until they reach the African city.   1270
They dismount in the shade of an olive
and begin to climb to the great stone hall.
They find Tiebaut and his pagan nation
and greet him as Saracen custom bids:
"That Mohammed, who holds all in his power,
preserve King Tiebaut of Esclavonie!
Your son, of the bold look, sends you this plea,
that you come to his aid with all your knights.
He has captured William, I'll hide nothing,
the son of Aimeri, from Narbonne the rich,   1280

inside Orange, the well-protected city;
in disguise he had entered the town,
intending to take it as he had Nîmes
and make love to Lady Orable.
But their devilish scheme did not succeed.
They gave us a hard time from Gloriete
which he managed to hold for seven days;
if it hadn't been for the underground cave
whose stones are set beneath the palace,
you would no longer possess Orable,   1290
your wife, who is such a noble lady.
But Mohammed sent you aid in your need,
we have him now in a lonely prison
from which he will never escape alive.
Vengeance will be taken as you will it."
When Tiebaut hears this he begins to laugh,
he summons the people of his empire.
"Now quickly to arms, noble knights and free!"
and they obey without any delay,
mounting horses from Russia and Puglia.   1300
When Tiebaut leaves the African city,
he takes with him pagans of Almeria
and others from Suite and Esclavonie.
At the head, before him, are sixty thousand.
They don't pause or rest till they reach the sea.
In little time the ships are prepared
with wine and meat and biscuits and grain.
They embark quickly, that Saracen race,
raise their anchors and hoist their sails.
The wind blows hard and drives them straight on,   1310
they reach the sea; they are on their way.
Then might you hear such horns and trumpets,
horses neighing and greyhounds barking,
braying of mules and whinnying chargers,
sparrow-hawks crying out on their perches.
You might hear those sounds from a great distance.

Eight days they sail, on the ninth they arrive,
but before they reach Orange the rich,
Tiebaut will know such sorrow and anger,
as he has not felt in his life before.   1320
For he will lose his fortified city
and his wife, the elegant Orable.

xliii

William is deep inside the prison,
Gilbert too and the noble Guielin.
"God," says the count, "Father and redeemer,
we are dead and abandoned to torment!
God, if only King Louis knew of it,
and my brother Bernard, hoary and white,
and Garin the mighty, of Anseune,
and Bueves the great warrior of Commarch,   1330
and my nephew, Bertrand, valiant and brave,
whom we left behind at the city of Nîmes,
and all twenty thousand fighting Franks.
We could derive great comfort from their aid."
Guielin says, the knight of gracious bearing:
"Uncle William, there's no point to such words.
Send for Orable, the African's lady,
to help, for the love she bears her lover!"
"God," says William, "you have taunted me so,
it will not take much for my heart to burst."   1340

xliv

Now William is angry and depressed
and Gilbert too, and the worthy Guielin,
inside the prison where they await death.
But while they are lamenting their lot,
Orable suddenly appears at their cell.
When she sees the counts, she begins to speak:
"Listen to me, noble, valiant knights,
pagans and Saracens hate you unto death.

They intend to hang you tonight or tomorrow."
"We can do nothing, lady," says Guielin,   1350
"but consider, noble, gentle lady,
if we could be let out of this dungeon,
I would become your man by oath and vow
and happily I would render service
whenever you, noble lady, might wish."
"But," says William, "it is she who betrayed us,
because of her we are in this dungeon."
The lady hears him and breathes a sigh.

xlv

"My lord baron," says the gracious Orable,
"by Mohammed, you accuse me wrongly.   1360
It was I who armed you in that tower;
if you could keep fighting in the palace
until word reaches Louis, the son of King Charles,
and Sir Bernard of Brabant and the others,
and Aimeri and all your magnificent line,
the treacherous swine would not know of it
until they had reached the marvelous tower,
and then they'd be able to free this land,
its narrow passes, its fords and gorges."
Guielin replies: "Lady, you've spoken well.   1370
If we were now let out of this prison,
I should be your man the rest of my life."
"By my faith," Orable the queen answers,
"if I thought that my pains would thus be repaid,
if William Fierebrace promised to take me,
I would set all three of you free
and would swiftly become a Christian."
William hears her, his spirit's restored.
"Lady," he says, "I shall give you my gage,
I swear this to you by God and St. James,   1380
and by the apostle we seek in the ark."
"Then," says the lady, "I require no more."
She unlocks all the doors of the prison

and they leave it, those brave valiant men;
each of them rejoices in his heart.

xlvi

Now the lady has received the counts' oaths,
and set them free from their prison;
she leads and guides them into Gloriete.
Up in the palace, they sit down to dine.
When they have all been richly feasted,   1390
the noble lady addresses them thus:
"My lords, barons, listen to me now.
I have taken you out of your prison,
I have led you into my palace,
but I do not know how you will escape.
What I have in mind, I had best tell you:
beneath us here, there is a secret cave
which no man yet born of woman knows,
except my ancestor who had it dug;
from here to the Rhone a tunnel was carved.   1400
If you manage to send a messenger
to Count Bertrand and the other barons,
they might come to speak to you underground,
and the infidel pagans would not know
until they had entered the tiled palace
and begun to strike with their broad swords.
In this way they could set the city free
and all its passes, its gorges and moats."
And William says: "My lady, that is so.
But where can we find a messenger."   1410

xlvii

"Nephew Guielin," Count William then says,
from here to Nîmes do not stop or pause,
you must tell your brother Bertrand of us
and bring him to our aid with all his men."
"Uncle William," says Guielin, "what the devil—
may God help me, this must be a joke.

For by the faith I owe to St. Stephen,
I would rather die in this lovely tower
than in sweet France or at Aix-la-chapelle."

xlviii

"Nephew Guielin," says the noble William,   1420
"you must find your way through the cave below,
not stop for a moment from here to Nîmes,
and tell the palatine Bertrand for me
to bring me help immediately."
"Uncle William, there is no point to all this;
I would not desert you, to save my limbs.
I would rather die inside this tower
than in sweet France among my relatives.
Send Gilbert of Flanders instead."
"Will you go, brother?" asks the good William.   1430
And the baron replies: "I shall go, indeed,
and carry your message faithfully."
"Go then, good brother, I commend you to Jesus,
and tell the palatine Bertrand for me,
that he must help without any delay.
If he does not, by God the redeemer,
he will never see his uncle again."

xlix

When the messenger hears that he must go,
then he begins to rage and wonder
how he can ever escape from there.   1440
"I've never been there, I don't know where to go."
But the lady says: "I shall guide you there.
You need not fear any man born of woman,
except Jesus Christ, the almighty lord."
Next to a pillar she has a stone moved,
which measures a fathom in length and width.
"My brother," she says, "you can enter here.
At its head, you will find three pillars,
formed and designed with vaulted archways."

He leaves them and begins to wander,   1450
not knowing where, underneath the city.
Count William accompanies him quite far
with lady Orable and baron Guielin.
They do not stop until the three pillars;
through their midst, he reaches the outside
and comes to the Rhone where he finds a boat;
then he moves softly across the water.
Count William has already turned back
with Guielin and Orable of the bright face;
All three of them have entered Gloriete.   1460
It would have been better if they had gone on
and descended to the dungeon below,
for not a thing have they done and plotted
that was not overheard by a pagan
who goes to tell it to King Aragon.

l

This Saracen is evil and deceitful,
he goes to denounce them to King Aragon;
as soon as he sees him, he starts to speak:
"Emir and lord, grant me peace and listen
to what your stepmother has been plotting   1470
with the captives whom you held in your prison.
She has taken them all out of the dungeon
and conducted them up to the palace;
in Gloriete they sat down to a meal."
Aragon asks: "Is this true, messenger?"
"Sire," he answers, "I am not a liar,
I have seen them taking secret counsel
and kissing and embracing one another.
She loves them more, and William in bed,
than your father or the king Haucebier."   1480
Aragon hears and almost loses his mind;
he summons his Saracens and Slavs.
"Barons," he says, "give me counsel on this,
tell me in what way I ought to proceed

against my stepmother who has shamed me,
disgraced me and dishonored my father."

li

Aragon says: "Good and powerful knights,
by Mohammed, gather up all your arms.
Whoever now takes armor and weapons
will pay for it before we capture them."   1490
His men answer: "Just as you command."
Fifteen thousand men rush to arm.
God, what trouble when William finds out,
and Lady Orable and brave Guielin.
In Gloriete where they are hidden,
they play at chess, in all confidence;
they suspect nothing, the noble counts,
when the Slavs and Saracens fall on them.

lii

Aragon finds William beneath the pine,
and Lady Orable and bold Guielin;   1500
the palatine counts know nothing of it
until they are taken by Saracens,
Turks and Persians and evil Bedouins.
By Mohammed they swear they'll have revenge;
Pharaon says, he lays claim to finesse,
"Emir and lord, listen to what I say.
Tiebaut your father is brave and noble,
who left this city to you to protect,
and Gloriete the royal palace.
These swine have dared to challenge you for it,   1510
they have murdered your men, hacked and killed them.
By Mohammed, I am not worth a cent,
if I do not have all their limbs torn off;
and your stepmother, who has shamed you so,
I shall see burn and roast in a fire."
But Escanors, who is white-haired and old:
"King Pharaon, you have not spoken well."

liii

Says Escanors, who is hoary and old:
"King Pharaon, you have not judged this well.
You ought never engage in such folly.   1520
If it once starts, you cannot control it.
Emir, my lord, grant me peace and hear me:
Tiebaut your father is a noble man,
he left this city to you to protect,
and Gloriete, the palace and the fief.
If you were really to burn his lady,
he would only be furious with you.
But have these counts thrown back into prison
and put Lady Orable in with them.
Then send a messenger over the seas;   1530
your father will come, with King Haucebier,
and let them decide how they'll be avenged."
Aragon says: "You have spoken well.
You'll be rewarded, you will lack nothing.
But I have already sent a messenger
to my father, the king who rules Africa.
Within eight days he should have returned."
They throw William into prison again
with Guielin, who is bold and skillful,
and Lady Orable is cast in with them.   1540
God save them now, who is judge of us all!

liv

Now William has been cast into prison
with Guielin and the gracious Orable;
the unhappy lady cries in despair.
"God," she says, "our good, heavenly father,
this poor creature has not been baptized yet.
I hoped to become one of God's faithful.
Sir William, your valor has brought me harm,
your noble body and knightly honor,
for you I've been thrown into this dungeon,   1550

in anguish as if I had been a whore."
Guielin says: "What nonsense is this,
you and my uncle are not badly off;
through your great love, you should bear this trouble."
William hears him and rages with anger,
in his fury, he swears by St. James:
"If it were not to my shame and disgrace,
I would give you a good blow on the neck."
Guielin says: "That would only be madness.
From now on I shall say, no matter who hears,   1560
you used to be called William the strong-armed,
but now you will be William the lover.
It was for love that you entered this town."
The count hears him, he looks down at the ground.

lv

Now William is furious and distressed,
and Lady Orable and Guielin his nephew,
inside the dungeon where they have been thrown.
"God," says the count, "glorious king of heaven.
We are all dead, betrayed and deceived!"
"What folly it was to start this affair,   1570
by which we are all dishonored and shamed,
unless He, who judges all, rescues us.
Alas, if King Louis the fierce only knew,
my brother Bernard, the white-haired and old,
and valiant Sir Garin of Anseune,
and within Nîmes, the powerful Bertrand.
We certainly have great need of their aid."
"Uncle William," says the fierce Guielin,
let that be, we have no need of them here.
Here is Orable, the gracious lady,   1580
for you to kiss and embrace as you wish,
I can think of no lovelier lady."
"God," says the count, "now I shall go mad."
The pagans hear them quarrel in the prison,
more than forty, they rush in and seize them

and throw the two men out of their dungeon.
They leave Orable, the gracious lady,
but lead uncle and nephew to the palace.
Pharaon speaks, who is fiercest of all:
"Emir, sire, grant me peace and hear me.
Your father, Tiebaut, must be respected.   1590
He left this city to you to protect
and Gloriete, the palace and the fief.
You see this pig, this young bachelor,
nothing you say does he hold worth a cent.
By Mohammed, you're no more than a clown
if you do not have him torn limb from limb,
him and his uncle, William, the warrior."
Guielin hears him, his sense begins to stray,
he grinds his teeth, his eyes roll in his head;   1600
he steps forward, he has pulled his sleeves back;
with his left fist, he grabs him by the hair,
raises the right and plants it on his neck.
The bone in his throat is almost shattered.
He lets the pagan fall, dead, at his feet.
William watches and rejoices in it.
"God," says the count, "who are judge of us all,
now we are dead and abandoned in pain!"

lvi

William sees Pharaon who has fallen:
"God," says the count, "good king of paradise,   1610
now we are dead, and given up to pain."
"Do not despair, uncle," says Guielin,
"in this palace you are not without friends."
"Indeed," says William, "there are few of those."
Then the young Guielin looks around.
He notices a huge axe near a pillar,
moves forward and seizes it with both hands,
and goes to strike a barbarous pagan.
He cuts through him all the way to the chest.
Aragon looks, almost loses his mind,   1620

he cries aloud: "Seize him, Saracens!
By Mohammed, they shall be abused,
they will be swung and dropped into the Rhone."
Guielin says: "You swine, get away from here.
You have had us led out of your prison
and conducted up here to the palace,
but by the apostle who is blessed at Rome,
you have thus acquired such companions,
they'll make you angry and very sad."
At these words two Saracens appear,   1630
bearing in their hands a serving of wine,
which they intend to serve in the palace,
but when they see such mighty blows struck,
they run away and let everything fall.
Count William runs to seize the huge tray.
Swiftly, he takes it in both his hands
and strikes great blows at pagan Saracens.
Anyone he reaches does not rejoice.

lvii

Now William is inside the tiled palace,
and Guielin his renowned nephew.   1640
One has an axe, the other the tray;
the noble vassals strike great blows with them.
Fourteen Turks have already been killed,
and the others are so terrified,
that they chase them out through the doors,
which they run to bolt and lock after them.
By its great chains, they have pulled up the bridge.
Aragon sees it and his mind rages.
He calls on all his Saracens and Slavs:
"Give me counsel, by Mohammed, my God.   1650
This William has badly abused me,
he has seized my principal palace,
I don't see how we can enter again."
Let us leave the Saracens here for a while,

for we must sing once more of Gilbert,
the messenger who has crossed the Rhone.
He mounts the peaks and descends the valleys,
from here to Nîmes, he has never paused.
It is morning, Count Bertrand has arisen,
he climbs the palace of the heathen Otran   1660
whom he had conquered by his fierce courage.
The count stands at the great windows
and looks down across the kingdom.
He sees the green grass and the rose gardens
and hears the oriole and blackbird sing.
He remembers William of the short nose
and his brother, the highly praised Guielin,
and tenderly then he begins to weep,
grieving for them as you will now hear:
"Uncle William, what madness it was   1670
to go to Orange just to look at it,
disguised in rags like some poor beggar.
Brother Guielin, how worthy you were!
Now you've been killed by Saracens and Slavs,
and I am left all alone in this land.
I see no man here of all my great race
to whom I can go for good counsel.
The Slavs will soon return to this place,
Golias and the king Desramé,
Clareaus and his brother Aceré,   1680
Aguisant and the king Giboé,
and the royal prince of Reaumont by the sea,
the kings Eubron, Borreaus and Lorré,
and Quinzepaumes and his brother Gondrez,
the thirty kings who were born here in Spain.
Each one will have thirty thousand armed men
and they will attack the city of Nîmes;
they will capture me by powerful force,
I shall be dead, murdered or killed.
But there is one thing I have determined: 1690

I would not fail, for the gold of ten cities,
to return to the land where I was born,
and bring back with me all my barons,
whom William of the short nose once led here.
And when I come to the city, Paris,
I will descend on the enameled stones;
sergeants and squires will come to greet me
and they will certainly ask for William,
and for Guielin my worthy brother.
Alas, I will not know what to tell them,   1700
except that the pagans killed them at Orange!"
Twice he falls in a faint on the marble step,
and his barons run to lift him up.

lviii

Count Bertrand is saddened and desolate,
for Guielin and the noble William.
He grieves with fine and courteous words:
"Uncle William, how madly you acted
when you decided to go to Orange
as a poor beggar, disguised in rags.
Brother Guielin, what a good man you were!   1710
Now Persians have killed you and Saracens
and I am alone in this pagan land,
I have no cousin or brother with me.
Now King Tiebaut will return from Africa
and Desramé and the huge Golias,
the thirty kings with their vast forces,
and they will lay siege to me here at Nîmes.
I shall be dead and doomed to torments,
but by the apostle penitents seek,
I shall not, even if I lose my limbs,   1720
give up until I reach Orange the great
to avenge the sorrow and the torment
that Saracens made our people suffer.
Alas, poor wretch, why do I hesitate
to go and present myself before them!"

lix

Count Bertrand is sad and filled with anger,
but just when he is weeping and sighing,
Gilbert arrives and enters the city.
He climbs the steps of the great stone chamber.
Bertrand sees him and he begins to laugh,   1730
in a loud, clear voice he cries out to him:
"You are most welcome, here, good, noble knight!
Where is my uncle of the bold countenance,
and Guielin? Don't hide it from me!"
And Gilbert answers as a noble knight:
"Within Orange, the fortified city,
in Gloriete, the tower of marble;
evil pagans hold them in their power.
It won't be long before they are both killed.
William sent me, I hide nothing from you,   1740
to ask you to help with all of your knights,
immediately, without any delay."
Bertrand hears him, then he begins to laugh.
He calls on everyone who can hear him:
"To arms, now, quickly, my good, noble knights!"
And they obey, without any delay,
mounting their Spanish and Sulian horses.
When Bertrand leaves the city of Nîmes,
he brings every man in his command,
at the head are more than fifteen thousand.   1750
From here to the Rhone they don't pause or stop,
they all embark on ships and galleys.
The Franks put to sea, they sail and steer.
Beneath Orange, there in the vast plains,
the proud companies disembark,
they pitch their tents and raise their pavilions.
Count Bertrand has allowed no delay,
he looks at the messenger and says:
"Now, Sir Gilbert, do not lie to me.
Should we attack this city of Orange,   1760

can we break down the walls and the stone halls?"
Gilbert answers: "Your idea is mad.
She does not fear the whole kingdom of France—
you couldn't take her any day of your life."
Bertrand hears him and nearly goes mad.

lx

"Gilbert, brother," Count Bertrand demands,
"shall we attack the mighty Orange,
could we break down these walls, these high buildings?"
Gilbert answers: "There is no sense in this.
You could not take her in all your lifetime."   1770
Bertrand is enraged by that answer
and the messenger tries to comfort him:
"Sire," he says, "listen to my plan:
I shall get you into the city
without the Persians or Saracens' knowledge."
"Go ahead, good brother, with Jesus' aid!"
He goes, because he knows what is needed,
with thirteen thousand Frankish fighting men,
leaving the others behind at the tents.
They do not stop before they reach the cave,   1780
through the pillars they make their way in—
they are without candles or burning lights—
one after the other in deep darkness.
Bertrand begins to lose heart at this,
he calls the messenger and asks aloud:
"Gilbert, my brother, don't conceal the truth,
my uncle is dead, I'm beginning to see,
and you've sold us to the infidel race."
Gilbert answers: "You're talking nonsense—
I could not do that to save my own limbs.   1790
You will arrive soon inside Gloriete,
by God, I beg you, do it quietly."
"Go on, good brother, with God's protection."
And as they move along, speaking thus,
they suddenly find themselves in Gloriete.

Count William has seen them as they arrive:
"God," says the count, "good father, redeemer,
now I see what I have needed so long."
The valiant fighters unlace their helmets,
they embrace and kiss, weeping in their joy.
Count Bertrand is the first to address him: 1800
"How are you, uncle? Hide nothing from me."
"I'm fine, good nephew, by the grace of God,
though I have suffered great pain and distress.
I didn't expect to see you while I lived,
for the torments of Saracens and Persians."
"Uncle William, you will soon be avenged."
Up in the palace an olifant sounds,
outside in tents and pavilions, men arm.
Count William is bold and valiant.   1810
They approach the gates of the fine city,
the bridge is lowered, they quickly descend
to open the gates as fast as they can,
and the men outside begin to pour in,
shouting "Montjoy!" in the front and the rear.
At their joy, the pagans are terrified,
they run to arm, the treacherous cowards;
from their lodgings they begin to come forth,
running to equip themselves for defense.
But all their armor is not worth a glove,   1820
for there are too many Franks by then;
Bertrand has taken over the city.
To win that strong and valiant fortress,
you might have seen such a furious combat,
so many lances broken and shields crashing,
so many hauberks of Moorish chain pierced,
so many Saracens bleeding and dead.
When Aragon sees his people killed,
his grief is such, he almost goes mad.
He leaps in the saddle of a spirited horse,   1830
grabbing a shield he had taken from a Frank,
he looks on the ground and sees a sharp spear,

he leans down to take it with both his hands
and urges the horse with his sharpened spurs.
He thrusts himself in the thick of the fight.
First he kills our Folquer of Meliant
and then another and a third after him.
Bertrand sees him and almost goes mad,
he draws his sword, whose blade cuts so well,
and strikes Aragon, he does not spare him.   1840
The blow he strikes with such vicious intent,
he cuts through him all the way to his chest.
He knocks him dead from his spirited horse.
Pagans begin to lose force and courage.
But why should I extend this tale further?
Cursed be he who would have escaped it!
Over the earth flows a river of blood.
Count William does not wait any longer,
he runs immediately to the dungeon
and frees Orable of the graceful form.   1850
He calls Bertrand and says this before all:
"Good nephew," he says, "hear what I intend:
this lady of the noble, charming form,
who rescued me, certainly, from death,
I made her a most faithful promise
that I would indeed take her as my wife."
And Bertrand says: "Then why do you delay?
Keep the covenant you have made with her,
and marry her in happiness and joy."
"Nephew," says William, "just as you command."   1860

lxi

Count William is most noble and worthy.
When he has conquered the city by force,
he has a great vessel prepared
and clear water is poured into it.
Then comes the bishop of the city, Nîmes;
they have Orable take off her robes,
and baptize her to the honor of God,

divesting her of her pagan name.
The barons, Bertrand and Guielin, sponsor her
and Gilbert, the worthy and wise.   1870
By Christian law, they call her Guiborc.
To a church consecrated by them,
where Mohammed had once been invoked,
Count William goes to make her his wife.
The mass is sung by the bishop Guimer.
After the mass they return from the church
and the lady is led into Gloriete,
in the paved halls the wedding is splendid.
Count Bertrand serves them as is fitting,
and Gilbert and the worthy Guielin.   1880
Eight days they feast in joy together;
there are harpers and minstrels in plenty,
and robes of silk and delicate ermine,
and mules of Spain and well-groomed horses.

lxii

Count William has married his lady;
now he remains thirty years in Orange,
and no day goes by without a challenge.

Aliscans

i

There, on that day, when the sorrow was great ⌉ -
and the battle raging at Aliscans, ⌋
Count William suffered heavy distress.
They all fought well, the Palatine Bertrand,
Gaudin the dark and Guichard the mighty,
and Guielin and the bold Guinemans,   (a)
Girard of Blaye and Walter of Toulouse,
Hunaus of Saintes and Huon of Melans.
But Vivien's help surpassed the others.
In thirty places his hauberk is torn,
he had suffered seven wounds on his body,   10
from the least of which an emir would have died.
He has killed many Turks and Persians,
but all that is not worth two besants
for so many come from ships and barges
and from dromonds and swift-moving craft,
no man alive ever saw so many.
Shields and armor cover the Archant.
Great is the noise the craven traitors make,
the slaughter fierce and the fighting heavy,   (a)
and on the earth, run rivers of blood.   (b)

. . .

iii

Count William sees his men dying;   40
it troubles him that he cannot defend them.
He looks for Vivien, but does not see him.
When he can't find him, he thinks he'll go mad.

In his anger, he attacks a pagan;
down to his shoulders he makes his sword felt.
But now the Saracens begin to come.
All Aliscans seems to be covered.
The noise is such, it makes the earth tremble.
Boldly they come to attack our men.
You might see a fierce, bristling combat,   50
so many shields crushed and lances shattered,
so many hauberks torn and ripped apart,
so many feet and hands and heads cut off,
the dead stumbling over each other;
more than twenty thousand have fallen there.
The cries can be heard two leagues away
and Vivien is fighting furiously
at the Archant, but he is close to death.
Through his wounds, he can see his guts pour out;
May God take his soul that's about to depart!   60

iv

Vivien is in the midst of the Archant
and his guts are slipping out of his body.
With both his hands he tries to hold them in.
He takes the standard from his sharp spear
and pulls it tightly around his sides,
then he sits upright on his mount again
and charges hard into the enemy.
With his steel sword he does a lot of damage;
the boldest among them flees before him.
Striking, he drives them as far as the sea.   70
From a valley appear the men of Gorhant,
a people of curious appearance.
They all have horns both in front and behind
and each one carries a heavy mace,
fashioned of lead and of good, strong iron—
with such weapons of lead, they hunt their beasts.
Ten thousand, the craven infidels number.
They run around, barking so fiercely,
that the whole shore resounds with the noise.

When Vivien sees the Tervagant race   80
with their ugly looks and strange behaviour,
and hears the noise that they are creating,
if he's terrified, it is no wonder.
He turns the head of his charger around.
He has not fled the thrust of a lance
when he sees before him a running stream
but well he knows that he's failed in his vow.
The noble count stops immediately
and begins to confess his sins to God.
With his right hand he beats his chest: 90
"God, forgive me, for fleeing this way.
I have not fled in my life before
but I'll make the pagans pay for it now."
He spurs his horse straight towards that cattle.
May God guard his soul, for his end is near.

[V–XIII   Vivien turns and fights furiously. His cousin Bertrand hesi-
tates to attack the pagan troops—ten thousand, black and horned—until
he sees Vivien in their midst. When they fight together "there is no
need for Roland or Oliver." Vivien wants Bertrand to go for William's
help, but Bertrand will not leave him, a reverse of the *Chanson de Roland*
situation. Alone, they almost succeed in routing the pagans when Aero-
fle appears with ten thousand more. Bertrand and six of his cousins are
captured, but Vivien keeps fighting until he meets Haucebier:]

This Haucebier is of great renown,
through all pagandom, they speak of him.
He has more strength than fourteen Slavs.
Would you like to hear something of his looks?
The nape of his neck is half a lance long,   360
and his sides, about a fathom around.
His shoulders broad, he is surely no boy,
his arms are large, and his fists solid;
his forehead between his eyes measures half a foot,
his head is huge, with masses of hair,
his eyes are red and flaming like coals
and he carries a club of solid lead.

But for Rainoart, there was never a man
who could kill him, as the song tells us.

• • •

He holds the stump of a lance in his hand;
the baron throws it with such great force
that it tears the brilliant hauberk apart
and pierces the padded garment beneath;
it tears through even the red silk tunic
and into his chest as far as his lungs.
Vivien falls, deserving or not,
Haucebier says: "We'll have peace from him now.   380
Let's go after William at Aliscans
and lead him off to prison on our ships
to present him to his enemy, Tiebaut,
so that he may take what vengeance he likes."
Now they turn around, spurring their horses
and leave Vivien lying on the sand.
The baron sits up, when he comes to,
looks around him and sees a Gascon steed.
He seizes it without any delay,   (a)
with great effort, he mounts in the saddle,
and comes to Archant, beneath a round tree   390
where there's a pond and a lot of water.
There he dismounts and begins to pray
that God will pardon him for his sins.

[XIV–XVII   Vivien prays that he may see William before he dies, but
an angel appears to tell him that William is surrounded by the enemy
and cannot get through in time. William keeps fighting although only
fourteen men are left of the twenty thousand he had brought into battle.
As the fifteen Christians try to make their way back to Orange, they
meet tens of thousands of pagans who continue to pour out of the ships.]

"God," says William, "who hung on the cross,
what living devils brought so many here?
I think the world is flooded with Turks.
I see no hill or valley that's not filled with them,
no plain or stream that hasn't been glutted.

Damned be the whores who brought so many forth, 500
and worse to the swine who engendered them!
My sweet lord, God, give some thought to my life!
Lady Guiborc, you won't see me again.
My horse," he says, "you are really tired.
If only you could have rested four days,
I would take on the Saracens again
and avenge myself; I'm not justly wounded.
But I know well you cannot help me.
May God defend me, you cannot be blamed
for you have always served me well. 510
Few the moments you were not galloping
and running hard, pricked on and spurred;
for your service I am grateful to you.
If you could only be brought back to Orange,
you would not be saddled for three months;
you'd eat no barley that hadn't been ground
two or three times, from your neck-feeder,
and the forage would be noble meadow-grass,
all selected and sifted in season.
You would drink only from a golden cup, 520
four times a day you would be groomed
and wrapped completely in expensive cloths.
If the pagans carry you off to Spain,
so help me God, I shall be very angry."
Baucent hears him and wrinkles his nose,
listening like a man of wisdom.
He shakes his head, paws the ground with his hoof,
his breath returns, he's completely revived.
He whinnies as if he had just been let 530
out of the stable and was newly shod.
When William sees that his horse is revived,
that brings him more joy than fourteen cities.

xviii

Count William can sense that his horse is fresh,
he cuts across a valley towards Orange,
at his back the infidel pagans pursue.

Suddenly, on his right, Brodual springs out,
with ten thousand of that craven race.
There's not one who doesn't brandish a lance
with a rich standard of wool and silk cloth.
They raise a racket, the treacherous swine.   540
They cut William off from the hill and valley.
Toward Orange there's no place to defend himself;
when the count sees he can do nothing else,
he turns back to Archant through a thicket.
The pagans chase him with terrible noise.
"God," says William, "good father of our spirit,
who took lodging in the Virgin's womb,
and were brought forth on the holy Noel,
and then suffered pain for our mortal sins;
you broke down the awful gates of hell,   550
you led out those who knew no more pain
and now rejoice in eternal glory.
As this is true, give help to your vassal
so he may see the loyal Guiborc again,
and King Louis, the royal emperor,
and Aimeri, the dear father of my flesh,
and Ermengard, my natural mother,
and my dear brothers who are mighty lords.
There was no battle like this at Ronceval—
if God save me and snatch me from this day—   560
as I shall fight before the nativity
against this people whom God will punish."
• • •

XXI

Count William is a man of strong action,
but he is wise, for he knows how to flee,   620
and when one should change one's way and detour.
"It is true valor," he says, "to protect oneself;
it's a bad joust that sees many men die.
When one sees that there can be no advance
and that his force will not get him through,

if he remains, you may hold him a fool
when, for one blow, he would gather a hundred."
I can tell you, without lying, in truth,
that no man could endure such feats of arms
as William has, may God bless him for it. 630
He took great pains to serve God always,
to sing his psalms and to keep his law;
he didn't let pagans rest for a day.
When he captured them, they did not languish,
he never let them lie in his prison,
he never set a ransom for them,
but quickly parted their souls from their bodies,
for which no Saracen will cherish him.
But our lord wishes to preserve him now
and send a holy angel when he dies, 640
and so it is good that you hear this song;
for he is holy, God has blessed him
and in glory has placed and set him
with his angels, to serve and adore.
There's no need to pad the tale of his valor,
and men should listen to it willingly;
it should be loved and cherished by them—
a good example can be gleaned from it.
It is fitting that the singer be given
goblets and robes and tunics to wear,
who preserves the memory of William's deeds.

XXII

. . .

William's jeweled helmet hangs down behind him,
the laces are torn, he has knotted them; 670
his shield is gouged in thirty places,
broken on all sides and in pieces;
his white hauberk is ripped and ragged.
There are fifteen wounds over his body,
Beneath his hauberk the blood is congealed;
on his head the helmet is battered,

his steel blade is dirty and stained with blood,
his arms and his fists are all bloody.   (a)
It's not hard to see he comes from a battle.
A fog and a wind have arisen,
the atmosphere is dark with the dust.
Count William cannot carry out his wish.   680
He comes to Archant angry and distressed;
the field is littered with dead pagans,
but he catches sight of Vivien's shield—
he knows it well—and his mind is troubled.
The count begins to look towards the right
and sees Vivien lying at a ford
beneath a tree full of leaves and branches.
Over his body there are fifteen wounds,
the least of them would have killed an emir.   690
His arms and his legs are all cut up.
The count looks at him, he is badly shaken;
he spurs his horse like a man enraged
and makes his way through the midst of the dead.
The count finally stops in front of the child,
he cannot speak, for the sorrow he feels.

[XXIII–XXVIII Vivien lies near a pond, his sword beside him; his
body is torn by wounds, but his arms are crossed on his chest and his
face is turned to the east. William grieves over his nephew's body, alter-
nately weeping, lamenting his loss, and fainting, a ritual mourning (cf.
Charlemagne's grief for Roland in the *Chanson de Roland*). Vivien revives
long enough to confess himself to William and to receive the eucharist
from him.]

XXIX

William weeps, he will not be comforted.
He holds Vivien resting in his lap
and gently begins to caress him.
On his bosom, he lets his head rest   (a)
and laments softly over him.   (b)
Then he begins to confess the child

who tells everything, leaving nothing out,
that he knows or can remember.
Vivien says: "I am troubled, now;
on the day that I was first to bear arms,
I vowed to God, and all my peers heard me,   850
that I would not flee before Turk or Slav,
the length of a lance, as I could judge it,
nor would they see me turn from a battle,
dead or alive, they would find me there.
But one group made me turn around today,
I don't know how far, I could not judge it;
I'm afraid they made me betray my vow."
"Nephew," says William, "there's no need to fear."
With these words, he has him take the bread
for the honor of God, and bow his head.
Then he beats his chest and stops speaking,   860
except to send a farewell to Guiborc.
His eyes are darkened, the struggle begins.
The noble count is watching him closely,
so that he can lay him down gently.
His soul departs, it can no longer stay.
In Paradise, God gives him dwelling,
He places him besides His angels.
When William sees it, he begins to weep.
Now he knows well, that there is no remedy.
He lays the child in his buckled shield   870
for he knows that he cannot carry him,
and with another shield he covers him.
Then when he tries to mount his horse,
his heart fails him and he faints again.
When he recovers, he berates himself:
"By God, William, you used to be praised
throughout the land, you were called Fierebrace.
But now I have proved myself a coward,
by deserting him whom I ought to carry
to see that he's buried in Orange   880
and do him honor as well as I can.

Better for me to let myself be hurt
and my body be wounded and destroyed."
Then he goes and lifts the child from the shield
and quickly returns to mount Baucent.
He has seized the child by his bright hauberk
but before he can set him on the horse,
he will have to sweat in anguish.
Finally he departs, he will not delay,   (a)
but before he sees the sun disappear,   (b)
he will have to sing of other torments.   (c)

[XXX–XXXII Saracens appear and William cannot move the body.
He covers it with a second shield and tries to flee, but even alone he can-
not make it, so he returns to watch over the body through the night. At
dawn he rides off quietly, and almost immediately he meets fifteen
pagan kings. He appeals to his horse for support:]

"Baucent," he says, "if you can get me through,   990
to the other side of that mountain,
I will make my escape, if God permits.
But first I must strike down these fifteen,
for I will have to make my way through them.
Now I must embolden my spirit;
if I have the support of my steel sword
I think that, with God's help, I'll defeat them,
and then we can proceed at our leisure.
If I can get you back to Orange,
I shall have you served with great honor."   1000
Baucent listens and begins to whinny.
"God," says William, "now I have my desire,
for I know that my steed will not give up."
He grasps his shield like a man of fury,
straight at the kings he directs Baucent.
Now you will hear of the fierce battle waged;
may Jesus support and preserve him there!

[XXXIII In the first assault, William kills seven kings and the eighth
flees, but the other seven attack. One is Esmeré, son of the Tiebaut who
was married to Orable (Guiborc), now William's wife.]

"Sir step-father," cries the king Esmeré,   1050
why did you wrongfully disinherit me,
throw me out of Orange by treachery   (a)
and take my mother against my will,
and unjustly behead my two brothers?
You beat them so, with all your men watching,
on a marble in the ornately paved hall,   (a)
that their blood ran down in great streams;
then you hanged them from a wide-branching tree.   (a)
Sir William, I have not forgotten it.   (b)
By Mohammed! it has brought me great shame.   (c)
I am no good, if they are not avenged;   (d)
on your head this must be put right."
William answers: "You talk like a fool.
When a man does not love Christianity,
when he hates God and scorns charity,
he has no right to live, I speak the truth.   1060
Whoever kills him has destroyed evil.
I avenged God, He is grateful to me.
You are all dogs and rightly so-called,
for you have neither faith nor loyalty."

[XXXIII–XXXVII William kills all but two of these kings, but soon
he meets others. One is Aerofle, Tiebaut's uncle, who carries a sword a
fathom long and rides a charger big enough to carry two fully armed
men at full speed for a day, without sweating. William covets the horse
and tries to make peace:]

The count addresses the pagan king:
"Saracen, brother, tell me by your faith,
what I have done for you to hate me so.
If I have seized or stolen anything
I shall make it good, as you require;
it will be set right quite honorably."
Aerofle says: "This is very foolish.   1190
By Mohammed, it does not please me   (a)
that men believe in the holy Trinity
or your baptism or your Christianity

or that Jesus wields any power.
If you believe as I set it forth—
that in the Virgin He was not made man—
I shall let you make your way in safety
back to Orange the marvelous city.
I'll give it back to my brother Desramé
and your lady to King Tiebaut the Slav.
In this manner we can make our peace.   1200
But otherwise, things cannot be set right."
"Indeed," says William, "you're asking too much.
I would not agree for a valley of gold.
I would much rather let my head be cut off
and my body dismembered piece by piece,
than abandon the King of majesty.
You are mad, you have no humility,   (a)
blaspheming wretch, may your body be damned!   (b)
I don't value you more than a dead dog   (c)
and none of your gods is worth a cent.   (d)
Whatever you have said and described
I deny in honor of almighty God
and I will uphold this with my steel sword."
With these words, the two challenge each other.   1210

XXXVIII

Aerofle says: "Listen to me, William,
I shall fight with you and do you know why?
Christianity is not worth anything.
Who takes it on his head makes a mistake,
and I defy baptism the same way,
for it is not worth a breath of wind.
All your masses and your God's sacraments,
your marriages and your betrothals,
your litanies and your nuptial service,
and the law by which your people live,   1220
are not the truth but a deception.
Beliefs like yours are formed by enchantment.
God is above in his firmament;

there is not an acre of earth down here,
but it is all at Mohammed's command.
He bestows on us the storms and the wind,
the fruit of trees, the wine and the grain;   (a)
one must believe in him and do his will."
"Pig," says William, "this is all a mad lie."
The count bends down and reaches towards the ground,
he sees a lance and takes it, from his horse.   1230
Then the two come together furiously,
but William's horse moves very slowly,
the pagan's as though he were shot from a bow.
Each strikes the other with such violence
that the shields are pierced through the silver,
the hauberks offer them no protection.
The iron touches the flesh along their sides;
they are not badly injured but they are wounded.
They hurl themselves hard against each other   (a)
so that one will fall while the other stands,   (b)
and both of them are covered with blood.

[XXXIX–XLVI William's sword is Joyeuse, given to him by Charle-
magne; when it fails, he curses it; when it cuts off Aerofle's leg, he
blesses it. He refuses Aerofle's offer of ransom and cuts off his head; then
he arms himself in the pagan's armor, sets Baucent free, and rides off on
Aerofle's horse, Folatil. Since he knows the Saracen tongue, as well as
Latin and Greek, he intends to get through the enemy lines disguised as
Aerofle. He succeeds at first, but his ermine and his blood-spattered legs
give him away. The pagans kill Baucent, who is following William, and
wound his master. William unseats one pagan and tries to keep his
horse, but when others attack he cuts off the animal's head rather than
leave him to the enemy. When William finally reaches Orange, how-
ever, his disguise works against him.]

xlvii

William rides on, the marquis of the fierce look,
spurring hard, he doesn't want to delay.
Pagans pursue him, more than thirty thousand,   1550

but the marquis sits on his good charger;
unless he falls, he needn't fear them for a cent.
By two full leagues, with the hardest riding,
he has outstripped the pagan enemy.
He enters a valley and climbs a cliff;
he sees Orange, its tower and belfrey
and Gloriete, the good, rich palace,
with walls of brass, that he had once attacked.
"God," says the count, "who watches over all,
with how much joy I left the other day,   1560
but I have since lost many valiant knights
for whom I could never be repaid.
Ah, Guiborc, noble and honored lady,
when you learn of the mortal anguish
of my nephews, whom you cherished so,
I think the sorrow will drive you mad."
The count faints on the neck of his charger;
he'd have fallen, were it not for the stirrups.
Then he goes back, riding along a path,
straight to Orange, he does not draw rein,   1570
he comes to the gate and calls the keeper,
in a loud voice he begins to halloo:
"Open the gate, let the bridge be lowered;
hurry, brother, I am in great danger."
When the gate-keeper hears him entreating,
he goes to look, leaning from the turret;
he doesn't recognize the Arab's horse
nor the standard that he sees billowing,
nor the green helmet and the quartered shield.
He thinks this is one of the enemy   1580
who intends to betray and deceive them.
He says to William: "Go back aways there,
for, by St. James, to whom I must pray,
if I see you approach any closer,
I shall strike you on that barred helmet so hard
it will make you fall right off your horse.
Get away from here, you lying traitor,

William should be coming back from Archant.
Did you think that we inside are all hicks?"
The count answers: "My friend, don't be afraid;   1590
I am William, the marquis of the fierce look,
who went to Archant to avenge his grief
and to bring help and support to Vivien.
But there I received a sorrowful pay—
my men are dead, I have nothing for them,
and I myself did not escape whole."
The keeper hears him and begins to wonder;   (a)
by the God of glory, he crosses himself.   (b)

xlviii

Count William is in terrible straits;
he tells the porter: "Friend, open the gate!
I am William, you must believe me."
The keeper says "Sire, be patient for a while,   1600
I must go up there, but I'll come right back."   (a)
From the turret he descends quickly,
he comes to Guiborc and cries out to her:
"Nobel countess, for God's sake, hurry,
outside our walls, there is an armed knight
on such a horse, I've never seen the like.   (a)
His body is covered with pagan arms,
his fierceness is great, in a strange manner,
he looks like a man just come from battle,
for I saw his arms were covered with blood.
He seems awfully large, armed on his charger,
and he says that he is William of the short nose.   1610
Come, lady, for God's sake, so you'll see him."
Guiborc hears him, her blood turns cold.
She comes down from the noble palace
to the battlements over the moats
and asks William: "Vassal what do you want?"
The count answers: "Lady, open the gate,
quickly, and lower the bridge for me,
for Baudus and Desramé are after me

and twenty thousand Turks in jeweled helmets.
If they catch me, I am as good as dead.   1620
Noble countess, for God's sake, hurry.
And Guiborc says: "Vassal, you will not enter.
I am alone, I have no man with me,
but this gate-keeper and an ordained priest
and a child not more than fifteen years old,
only ladies whose hearts are in anguish
for their husbands, whom my lord has led to fight
at Aliscans against pagan infidels.
No gate or doorway will be unlocked   1630
until William returns here to us,
the noble count, whom I love so well.
May God, who hung on the cross, protect him!"
The count hears her and bows his head for pity,
The marquis of the short nose weeps.
The water runs in a stream down his nose.
He calls Guiborc again, when he looks up,
"It is I, lady, you're terribly wrong;
I'm amazed that you don't recognize me.
I am William—you will regret your doubts."   1640
Guiborc answers: "Pagan, you are lying.
By the apostle we seek in Noiron,
I would have to see the bump on your nose
that King Ysorez gave you before Rome.   (a)
That is a mark which I know well enough;   (b)
and a wound which you have on your side   (c)
that Tiebaut the Slav gave you in battle,   (d)
before gate or doorway is unlocked for you.

xlix

Count William wants to get inside quickly.
It is no wonder, he has reason to fear
for behind him all the road resounds
with that people that he can never love.
"Noble countess," says the baron William,
"you have made me wait outside too long.   1650

You see all the hills covered with pagans;
if they reach me, I tell you without lie,   (a)
all the gold in the world will not save me   (b)
from being torn apart before your eyes."   (c)
"Indeed," says Guiborc, "The more I hear you speak,
the less you seem to resemble William.
I never saw him afraid of the Turks.
But, by St. Peter, whom I must adore,
I shall not have gate or postern opened
until I have seen your head uncovered
and looked at the bump on your nose with my eyes,
for many men are alike in their speech.
I am alone here, no one can blame me."   1660
The count hears her and lets his visor drop.
"Lady," he says, "now you can look at me."
But as Guiborc is studying him,
she sees a hundred pagans cross the fields
from Toledo, which they had been looting.
Corsu of Urastes made them leave the camp,
with their help he presented to Desramé
two hundred captives, young knights all of them
and thirty ladies with fair complexions   1670
who were bound together with heavy chains.
Pagans beat them—may God destroy them all—
they make the blood spurt through their flesh.   (a)
Lady Guiborc hears them crying out
and calling upon almighty God.
She says to William: "Now I am certain
that if you were the worthy Sir William
of the strong arm, who is praised everywhere,
you would not let pagans take our people
or beat and abuse them in such disgrace.
You would not let them pass so close to you!"   1680
"God," says the count, "now I will prove myself!
But, by Him, who holds all in His keeping,
I will not stop, if my head is cut off,
if I must be cut apart while I live,

without fighting them now in front of her.
For her love, I must endanger myself;
in order to exalt and lift high God's law,
I must endure pain and toil with my body."
He laces his helmet and lets the horse go,
as fast as he can race under him,   1690
he rides to meet and attack the pagans.
In the shield of the first he makes a hole
and tears his hauberk and rips off the edge;
he thrusts iron and wood right through his body,
the standard comes out on the other side.
He throws him over, dead, his legs in the air.
Then he draws the sword that he took from a Slav
and sends the head of a pagan flying;
he cuts deep into another's brain,
and then he knocks a third over dead   1700
and strikes the fourth so he has no time to speak.
Pagans see him, they can't help fearing him;
one begins to explain to another:
"That is Aerofle, Cadroe's uncle,
who has just ravished and laid waste Orange;
he is angry, we made him furious
because we were not at Aliscans.
I think he will make us pay well for it."
They all take to flight to save their own lives,
leaving their prisoners standing there still.   1710
Baron William follows to cut them apart
and they flee him, they don't dare stay longer.
Guiborc sees it and begins to weep;
in a loud voice she cries out to the knight:
"Come back, sweet lord, now you may enter."
William hears her and turns back again,
he gallops first towards the prisoners,
looses their chains, one after another,
and orders them to go into Orange.
They go but they won't be able to enter.   (a)

{L The entire pagan troop, still thinking that William is Aerofle, allow themselves to be captured and bound by William, who kills them all and rides into Orange with their supplies. But more pagans arrive.}

li

Now the pagans have surrounded Orange,
they have burnt and laid waste the land around.
William has taken the armor from his head,
Lady Guiborc has ungirded his sword;
she takes off the helmet, sad and in tears
and then she takes the great gilded hauberk;
beneath the chain-mail his flesh has been torn
in fifteen places, wounded and injured;
his whole arm is covered with blood.   1800
Water rises from his heart to his eyes
and begins to run warm down his face.
Guiborc sees it and changes color.
"My lord," she says, "I am your sworn lady,
married to you faithfully by God's law;
for your sake I became a Christian,
baptized and raised in the holy font,
given new life in God with sacred oil.
Your words should not be denied to me.
There is one thing that will drive me mad,   1810
that I had the gate locked against you,
but if you had had in your company
Bertrand, the count of the handsome face,
the child Guichard, who strikes well with the sword,
and Guielin, Gaudin of Pierelee,
and Vivien, for whom I am anxious,
and all the barons of this land, safe,
minstrels would have been at the gathering;
many violas would have been tuned there.
All around there would have been rejoicing.   1820
But it wasn't so—William, that frightens me."
"God," says the count, "holy, honored Virgin,

all that she says is certainly true.
My life must be lived from now on in sorrow.
Noble countess, there's no use hiding it;
all my companions are now dead,
at Aliscans they were all destroyed.
There is not one whose head was not cut off.
I fled from it, I could not remain;
the Turks pursued me almost the whole day."   1830
Guiborc listens and falls, faint, to the ground;
when she comes to, she begins to rave.
"Aiee!" she cries, "how I have been cursed!
I may well say I am miserable,
so much youth is destroyed because of me.
What a bad time it was that gave me life!   (a)
Holy Mary, crowned queen of heaven,
if only I had been dead and buried!
My great sorrow cannot be forgotten,
until my body is thrown in the earth."
And then she weeps many sad tears.   (a)

lii

The sorrow in Orange is heavy.   1840
Guiborc weeps, I know not how many others.

[LII–LIV   William recounts the battle and Vivien's death. Guiborc urges him to send to France for aid from his brother-in-law, King Louis, and from his own father and brothers. He is afraid that such a message will not be well received, so he must carry it himself.]

lv

"My lord, William," says Guiborc weeping,
"you must go there, in your own cause.
I shall remain in Orange, the great,
with the ladies, there are so many here.
Each one will have a Moorish coat of mail   1950
and on her head a green shining helmet,
at her side she will gird a good sword,

at her neck a shield, a sharp spear in her hand.
There are also I don't know how many knights,
whom you set free from the infidels.
We shall climb up on these walls in the front
and defend them well, if the Turks attack.
I shall be armed like any warrior.
By St. Denis, whom I take as surety,
there is no pagan, Saracen or Persian,   1960
if I can reach him by throwing a stone,
who will not be knocked off his charger."
William listens, and embraces Guiborc,
with great love they kiss each other,
one weeping for the other's sorrow.
And Guiborc goes on begging William
to go to France as is necessary
for the support he so badly needs.

lvi

"My lord, William," says Guiborc, the prudent,
"Now you must go to France, the renowned;   1970
you will leave me grieving and distracted
among people who have no love for me
and you will ride off to that rich country.
There you will see many lovely maidens
and many ladies, noble and adorned.
I know how quickly you will forget me;
then your love will be directed there.
What would you want to seek in this country,
where you were made to suffer such pain,
such hunger and thirst and so much sorrow?"   1980
The count hears her, he looks at Guiborc;
the water from his heart mounts to his eyes,
then it begins to run down his face,
along his chin and onto his tunic.
He embraces Guiborc and comforts her;
he kisses her often and caresses her.
Then the count says: "Lady, don't be upset.

You have my word, which I have sworn to you,
that I shall not take this shirt off,
or my pants or hose either, or have my head washed,   1990
I shall not eat meat or taste pepper,
I shall not drink wine nor any spiced drink
from a wooden cup or a golden goblet,
except water, that must be allowed me.
I shall not eat kneaded hearth-cakes,
only coarse bread that is made from the chaff;
I shall not rest on a feathered mattress
under linen sheets and embroidered covers,
only on the felt that covers my saddle
and whatever garments I am wearing.   2000
My lips will not touch any other mouth
until they have kissed and tasted yours
in this palace, where the hallway is paved."
The count kisses and embraces her again
and they shed many tears together.

[LVI–LXIV Disguised again as Aerofle, William makes his way through the pagan lines but when he reaches Orleans, the Franks are wary of him, riding alone and armed. Their chatelain tries to find out who he is, but William will not stop to answer. When the chatelain persists, William kills him. The townspeople raise the alarm and attack William with arrows, but he charges and routs them, killing fifty. As he leaves, his brother Hernaut rides in at the head of a company of knights. Hernaut is told of the unknown attacker and pursues him. They fight and Hernaut is unseated. William, exulting, identifies himself, and there is a moving reunion between the brothers. They sit beneath a tree and William tells of his losses at Aliscans. Hernaut agrees to help. They kiss, William avoiding Hernaut's mouth, and William leaves for Laon where the king is holding court. As he rides through the town, he is ridiculed for his huge horse, his torn armor and shabby clothes. At court, the squires are afraid of his size and fierce look. Louis sends the squire Sanson to find out who he is and what he wants. When the king learns it is William,]

Louis hears him and bows his head low.
He tells Sanson: "Go and make it known
that he will never be received by me.
May his body be given to the devils;
he will have brought us such trouble and pain,
he's not a man but a living devil.
May he be cursed in his neck and his nose.
Whatever has happened to him is good!"   2400
The king sits there sad and lost in his thoughts,
the young men of the court descend the steps
and the knights of whom there are so many,
to whom the count has made many fine gifts,
pelts of sable and ermine collars,
and hauberks and jewel-adorned helmets,
and swords and many buckled shields,
gold and silver, coined pieces of money,
and palfreys and well-groomed chargers,
but when they see how he is reduced,   2410
they do not go to kiss or embrace him.
The count is very poorly greeted
and addressed as though he were an enemy,
scorned and despised by one and the other.
Again and again they insult the count.
So it happens when a man becomes poor,
he's no longer cherished, served or honored!
And William says: "My lords, you do me great wrong.
I have nourished and advanced all of you
and many times bestowed fine gifts on you;   2420
I've presented money and robes and horses;
if I can't give now, I should not be blamed,
for at Archant I was badly beaten.
My men are dead, I have very little left.
• • •
Lady Guiborc, who showed you so much love,
sends me to you to plead for your help.
For God's sake, my lords, take pity on her!

Give us your help, it will be charity."
After they hear him, not a word is spoken.
They leave William and return whence they came;   2440
• • •

lxv

Now William's alone beneath the olive.
• • •
The count sits down, he feels nothing but rage;
across his knees he places his steel blade
and sadly he thinks about his wife.
The other knights go back into the palace.
King Louis begins to question them:
"Where is William, the marquis of the fierce look,
who has given us so much pain and trouble?"
"He stays alone, sire, beneath the olive."
Louis picks up a sprig of mustard,
he goes to the window and leans over it,   2470
he sees William weeping and grieving
and calls to him and begins to shout:
"Sir William, go and find yourself lodging
and see that your horse is taken care of,
then come back to the court to take your meal.
You have come too shabbily to pay court.
Why have you not brought a page or squire
to serve you and to take off your boots?"
"God," says the count, "I could easily go mad,
when he takes such pains to make me angry,   2480
who should be giving me honor and praise,
who should cherish and love me of all men.
But, by Him who must be the judge of all,
if I can make my way into the palace,
before night has fallen tomorrow,
with that sword whose handle is of pure gold,
I intend to cut off his head
and bathe many others in their own blood.
They'll be sorry they showed me pride and scorn.

Before I leave, I will take counsel with them,   2490
in such a way, if I can manage it,
that I shall have made my feelings quite clear."
Then he begins to roll his eyes,
to gnash his teeth and shake his head.

[LXVI   Louis sets a guard at his gate to keep William out, but a
burgher, Guimar, offers him shelter and food. William takes only dry
bread and water, because of his vow to Guiborc. In the morning, he re-
turns to court where the king is supposed to crown his wife, Blanche-
flor, William's sister.]

lxvii

Count William has come out of his lodging;
beneath his tunic he wears a hauberk
and keeps his sword hidden under his cloak.
The count has come up to the palace;
there is no gate that can stand against him.   2570
To the midst of the hall comes the angry count,
where he finds many counts, princes and dukes,
and knights of all ages, young men and old,
and noble ladies dressed in fine gowns,
in robes of silk and cloth of beaten gold.
Count William is recognized by all there,
but he is not well received among them.
Because he is so shabbily clothed,
there is not one who will give him greeting,
not even the queen, who sees him well enough.   2580
She is his sister and should love him most.
He is completely ignored by them all.
William sees it and is fiercely angry;
he sits down on a bench without a word,
beneath his cloak he holds his sword bared.
Little is needed for him to attack,
but before the count moves from his place,
Aimeri has dismounted on the step,
accompanied by seven score shields.

The noise is enormous, the cries and shouts,   2590
the Franks are excited, they rise at once.
The king, too, gets up to meet Aimeri.
Now William's power and strength increase;
if Ermengard can, she will get him help.

lxviii

Onto the step Aimeri has dismounted,
and Ermengard, the noble countess;
with them have come four of their sons:
Hernaut the brave, Bueves of Commarchis,
there is Guibert, and Bernard the white-haired,   2600
but the wretched Aimer is not there.
He is in Spain among the Saracens
where he is fighting by night and by day.
Before Aimeri reaches the vaulted palace,
his son-in-law Louis comes to meet him,
and the queen, she has such a bright face.
The count is received with kisses and joy
and Ermengard, the noble countess,
the good lady, who has known such trouble.
In an armchair, they have placed Aimeri,   2610
beside him sits the king of St. Denis
and the countess sits beside the empress
who is her daughter, so it is written.
Each of the knights has taken his own seat,
down through the hall, they needn't ask for rugs.
There is a soft fragrance of rose and lily,
the incense is lit in the censers;
the minstrels have taken up their viols.
Great is the joy in the royal palace;
there's abundance of fur, varied and gray,   2620
but before the evening that ends this day,
fear will be felt by the most courageous.
The emperor will wish he were at Paris,
and the queen in her chamber at Senlis,
for Sir William of the short nose, the marquis,

still sits all alone, disturbed and angry,
enraged and fierce, with violent thoughts.
"God," says the count, "I've been too cowardly,
I see before me my father and friends,
my noble mother who gave birth to me,   2630
whom I have not seen for seven years.
I have taken too much, I am shamed and disgraced,
if I don't have revenge, I must go mad."
With these words, the count leaps to his feet,
his fist has never abandoned his sword;
down through the hall, he approaches Louis,
speaking in a loud voice that's heard by all:
"Jesus of glory, king of paradise,
preserve her who brought me to life,   2640
and my dear father who begot me
and all my brothers and my other friends,
and destroy this evil and useless king
and my sister, the whore, the courtesan,
by whom I was so shamefully received,
in whose court I was ridiculed and scorned.
When I dismounted beneath the olive,
not one of his men, not big or little
came forward to hold my Arabian steed.
By all the saints whom God has blessed,
were it not for my father who sits beside him,   2650
I would cut through to his brain with my sword."
The king hears him and his blood deserts him;
the queen wishes she were at Senlis,
or Estampes or the town of St. Denis.
There is no Frank who is not terrified.
One says to the other: "William is mad!
We will be sorry that he entered this land."

lxix

When Ermengard sees her child before her,
and Aimeri, they are filled with joy.
They rise immediately from their armchairs   2660

and embrace William on every side.
His four brothers come to embrace him,
they want to kiss him but he withdraws
his mouth to avoid meeting theirs.
They go through the palace rejoicing;
some are happy, the others are sad.

[LXIX   William tells his father of his losses at Aliscans, of Guiborc
holding Orange with food running out, and of Louis' unfriendly recep-
tion.]

Louis hears him, he hangs his head low,   2690
wishing he were at Hui or Dinan,
and the other Franks are silent and mute.
Not one is prepared to come to his aid;
one says softly to the other:
"What living devils could endure so much?
Never did so many valiant knights go,
who were never to return to France.
For our harm we met William and his pride;
he left Orange; let the infidel have it.
May he take Vermendois to the port of Vuisart."   2700
Through the palace, they are silent and mute,
there is not one whose heart is so valiant
that he dares to come forward to help him.
They are all mute, the little and the great.
Sir Bernard of Brubant weeps for Bertrand
and Bueves weeps for his son Gerard.
Lady Ermengard stands in her place
and in a clear voice shouts at them all:
"By God, you Franks, you are all cowards.
Sir Aimeri, your courage is failing.   2710
Sweet son, William, you needn't be distressed,
for by the apostle penitents seek,
I still possess a treasure so large
that twenty oxen could not carry it.
I shall give it all, to the last besant,

to the soldiers who are willing to fight
and I myself shall ride into combat,
my hauberk on and my bright helmet laced,
the shield at my neck, the sword at my side,
a lance in my fist, in the first ranks. 2720
Even if my hair is hoary and white,
my heart is nonetheless bold, and rejoices
that I can help, if it please God, my child.
For, by the apostle penitents seek,
when I am armed and seated on my horse,
there's no pagan, Persian or Saracen,
if I can reach him with my cutting sword,
who will be able to keep his seat."
Aimeri hears her and softly he laughs,
he gently sighs in his heart with pity, 2730
and all their sons weep from their eyes.
The heart of Aimeri begins to expand.
Count William does not hesitate further,
in a little while he will speak aloud
to the men of France in his fierce anger.

lxx

Now William is in the great, paved hall,
beneath his cloak he holds his sword bared,
his clothing is torn and hanging in shreds,
his hose are black, his shirt is not washed,
but his head is still held erect, 2740
his nostrils wide, his nose high, his face raised,
with huge strong fists and a powerful arm.
His body is long and his chest is broad,
his feet arched and his legs well-formed,
between his two eyes, there is a wide span
that measures more than a palm across.
There's no man more fierce to the Frozen Sea.
He looks severely at his sister
who bears on her head a crown of gold
and sits beside the king who had wed her. 2750

The count looks at her with furious rage,
his face enflamed by violent wrath,
his words resound through the golden hall:
"Louis, sire, you pay your debts badly.
When the court was assembled at Paris,
just after Charlemagne had left this life,
all the men of the country despised you.
You would have lost your inheritance in France,
the crown would never have been given you,
but I took on such fighting for your sake   2760
that in spite of them, was placed on your head
the great crown, fashioned of the purest gold.
They feared me so, they dared not prevent it,
but you've shown me today poor love in return."
"Indeed," says the king, "this truth is well known.
Now the honor will be repaid you
for all France will be abandoned to you."   (a)
Blancheflor hears him and cries out, very loud:
"Truly," she says, "you'll be disinherited,
devils must have made this arrangement.
A bad end to him who agreed to it!"   2770
William hears her and looks straight at her.
"Shut up," he says, "you well-known bitch,
Tiebaut of Arabia had you at his will,
and many times, like a well-trampled whore.
Your word is certainly not to be heard.
Since you enjoy your meat and your pepper
and drink your wine from a golden cup,
wine with honey or mixed with spices,
you eat hearth-cakes kneaded four times over;
since you hold your covered goblet   2780
near the fire, alongside the chimney,
until you are warmed and roasted
and enflamed and set afire with lust
by the gluttony which consumes you;
when lechery has so fired you,

and Louis has taken care of you well,
ridden you beneath him, two or three times,
when you are satisfied in your lust
and sated with the eating and drinking,
you don't remember the snow or the ice   2790
or the great battles, or the privation
that we suffer in a strange country
within Orange, from the infidel race.
What do you care if the wheat is ruined!
Evil woman, you well-known stinking bitch,
you have often attacked my words today
and dishonored me before the king.
Living devils have set that crown on you!"
He comes forward and lifts it from her head.
Before all the Franks, he throws it down;   2800
quickly he puts his hand to his sword,
the marquis had hidden it in his folds;
he would have cut her head off right there—
he would not be stopped by any man—
but Ermengard takes the sword from his hands,
embracing William and his sword and hilt,
and the queen flees, all disheveled,
so distressed, she seems a mad woman.
She rushes, fleeing, back to her chamber
and falls to the ground in a faint, from fear.   2810

• • •

[LXX Her daughter, Aelis, comforts the queen but reminds her that
she owes her crown to William and should not abuse him. The queen
repents and Aelis goes to ask her uncle to forgive her mother.]

She goes through the halls with her head bowed
and hears the great noise in the paved hall.
The Franks are whispering secretly: 2860
"William has brought shame on the queen;
if he hadn't been stopped, he would have killed her.

Louis did not protect her very well,
he would have bought Orange rather high.
Cursed be the hour that it was founded,
so much of our youth has met its end there.
Look at the devil, what a large head he has!
An evil spirit has entered his body,
see how it has set fire to his face!
Before the court is disbanded today   2870
that sword, I believe, will be well paid for,
covered with our flesh and stained with our blood.
If only God, who made heaven and the dew,
would will him now beyond the Frozen Sea,
or in Egypt in a deserted land,
or at sea inside the salted ocean
with a huge stone tied to his neck.
Then France would be saved from his evils."

[LXXI–LXXIII   Though everyone else is afraid to approach William,
Aelis kneels before him and offers herself as a hostage should her mother
ever oppose him again. He forgives his sister and apologizes for his harsh
words. The court celebrates their reconciliation with a banquet to which
William invites the burgher who had housed him; he attends himself
but takes only bread and water.]

Squires and pages take away the cloths
and then count William addresses the king:
"What did you decide," he asks, "son of Charles?
Will you help me against Mohammed's race?
The army should be at Chalon by now!"
And Louis says: "We shall talk about it
and in the morning we will let you know
what is my will, whether to go or not."
William hears him and turns red as coal;   3050
in his anger he twists his moustache.
"What the devil!" he says, "we'll talk about it!
Is this the tale of the crow and the sheep?
I can see that you take me for a fool."

He bends over and picks up a club
and says to the king: "We give back your fief;
I won't hold as much as a spur from you,
I shall not be your friend or your vassal
and you will come, whether you like it or not!"
Hernaut stands up, his moustache is red,   3060
and says to William: "Don't get angry!
The king will say what he wishes and wants.
Retain your fief, for we'll all support you.
My brothers and I will accompany you
and take two thousand men to Aliscans.
The pagans are dead if we find them there."
Aimeri says: "These are weak words.
We must help him with what power we have.
All France should be at his disposal,
he is a seneschal, with the standard;   3070
by rights everyone should come to his aid
and vengeance be taken on any who refuse.
My son is too high a lord to be scorned.
But by the apostle we seek at Rome,
if my heirs would not be punished for it,   (a)
if it were not considered mortal treason,
from the highest princes of the French realm
I would put seven score in my prison.
Who's a lord now would then seem a mere boy.
Proud men and villains should be chastised!"
Aelis hears and answers her grandfather: 3080
"Aimeri, sire, may your words have success;
whoever fails you should not be ransomed,
but be hanged from on high like a thief."
The queen of the bright visage speaks:
"Aimeri, sire, by Saint Simon's body,
I shall have nothing in France worth a spur
that will not be at William's disposal.
But it will be felt on the nose and the chin."
Louis hears and raises his moustache;
he will soon speak for the good of them all.   3090

[LXXIV Louis will not go himself but he promises to send a hundred
thousand men with William, and summons them immediately.]

Inside the palace is the valiant William.
He begins to look all around the hall,
from the kitchen he sees Rainoart return
and enter the palace through a doorway;
his body is large, his look of a boar.   3150
In all France there is no finer young man,
nor any so strong, to carry great weights,
or better skilled at throwing a stone.
The load he can carry, without a lie,
would be difficult for a cart to bear;
in swiftness, he has no equal in France,
bold and courageous when it comes to a fight.
The chief cook had him shorn during the night,
blackened and soiled with the fire-shovel,
his whole face had been smeared with charcoal.   3160
The squires begin to make fun of him,
with huge brooms they turn him around
and push and shove him against one another.
Rainoart says: "If you don't leave me alone,
by the faith that I must bear to God,
if you get me angry at you,
I'll make whoever I catch pay for it.
Am I a fool that you tease me this way?
You play your tricks in a vicious way.
Damned be the man who cares for your games!   3170
Leave me in peace! I don't want to touch you."
And one of them says: "You speak valiantly,
brother Rainoart, teach me to fight!"
And with these words he lets his hand go,
on the nape of his neck, he strikes a blow
so that the whole hall resounds with it.
Rainoart says: "Now I have taken enough.
He seizes the other swiftly in his arms,
spins him around twice, at the third lets him go.

He hits a pillar with such violence   3180
that his sides break and his heart is shattered
and both his eyes fly out of his head
and his brain pours out and scatters.   (a)
Now you might see the squires enraged,
more than fifty attempt to kill him;
they want to beat him with huge clubs,
when Aimeri begins to swear
by St. Nicholas, whom we should adore:
"There is none so valiant, if I see him
touching that man, I won't pierce both his eyes!"
They immediately leave him in peace.   3190
Count William quickly demands of the king:
"Sire," he asks, "who is this bachelor
that I saw fighting with the squires?
I've just seen him hurl one against that pillar
in such a way that he broke all his limbs.
By St. Denis, he's to be respected."
Louis answers: "I bought him at sea
from merchants; I gave them a hundred marks,
and had him brought here in my company;
they told me he was the son of a Slav.   3200
I have had him asked often enough
who his father is, but he won't name him.
Because of his size I cannot love him,
so I have him living in my kitchen.
I cannot give him any other work
and I don't want him raised and baptized.
I have seen him carry four hogsheads of water
on one club and raise it to his neck—
no man has ever seen his equal in force."

[LXXV–LXXIX   William is impressed with Rainoart's size and beauty,
despite the soot that covers him and the unpredictable nature of his be-
havior, and asks Louis to give him Rainoart. Louis is happy to get rid of
him and Rainoart is anxious to join the assembling army. To replace his
old club, which had been burned and split, Rainoart cuts down the

king's favorite tree, a spruce that could give shade to a hundred knights. When the king's forester tries to stop him, Rainoart rips out his shoulder and tosses the rest of him up into the trees. He brings the spruce to a smith to be hooped and waxed. When it is ready, Rainoart swings it around in delight, accidentally catching and demolishing the smith's mule. That night, he gets drunk and four squires steal his club while he sleeps, and bury it under dung in the stable. Rainoart departs with the army the next morning, forgetting his club as he will do many times again. On his way back for it, he passes an abbey where the smells and sounds from the kitchen arouse his hunger. The porter tries to keep him out, but Rainoart forces his way into the kitchen. The cook scolds the porter and Rainoart throws the cook into the fire and then fills himself on geese torn from the spit and rolled in garlic, a thousand rissoles, and a barrel of wine. Then he looks for the monks.]

He asks the porter: "Where have the monks gone?
Have they finished their services yet?"
The porter replies: "I'll tell you the truth;
they have entered the refectory,
where the noble men of the order eat.   3670
You have done wrong with the cook, whom you killed,
and with the rissoles, which you have eaten."
Rainoart asks: "Hadn't he wounded you so
that a hundred devils would have been angry?
Come and point out the prior or abbot."
And the porter answers: "As you wish."
They make their way to the refectory,
and Rainoart cries in a very loud voice:
May the God who gives us all light
preserve the monks who are assembled here!"   3680
They look at him, not one says a word,
and Rainoart finds himself a tub
filled with newly fermented wine.
He takes a pot and dips it in,
puts it to his lips and pours it down;
in a single gulp he's drunk the whole vat
that holds easily a full hogshead.

A knight is badly disturbed at the sight;
he has a loaf of well-kneaded bread,
he strikes Rainoart such a hard blow   3690
that the bread is split into four pieces.
Rainoart says: "You have attacked me,
you'll be sorry, by the faith I bear God."
He grabs the monk and draws him close,
then hurls him so violently at a pillar
that both his eyes fly out of his head.
The other monks have taken to flight.
Now Rainoart goes over to the claret
and drinks as much of it as he likes.
He tells the porter: "I've been here long enough.   3700
Let's go now, I've done what I came for."
They go out the gate and find the poor there,
who are waiting for alms to be given them.
They all shout: "Sir porter, for God's sake,
have your monks taken their dinner yet?
Give us some charity!"

lxxx

When Rainoart hears the poor people
begging for bread, by God omnipotent,
he is moved by pity as his law decrees.
He tells them: "Be quiet, good children.   3710
You will have some, if God gives his consent."
He runs back to the refectory
where he finds an enormous basket;
he fills it with more than a hundred loaves
and as many quarters as it can hold.
He comes immediately back to the poor
and distributes the bread generously,
leaving what remains with the porter.
The poor people shout in his praise:
"May the lord God who watches over us,   3720
preserve this alms-giver for a long time!
There has never been such a good man."

[LXXXI–LXXXIII   Back at Laons he forces the squires to lead him to
his club. Before he can leave with it, the cook appears, insults him and
threatens to cut up the club for firewood. Rainoart crushes him with it,
saying he must go to help his sister Orable and William. He returns to
the army, leaping for delight and kissing his club; he washes it and
wipes it with his coat. While others make fun of him, William defends
him and the princess begins to love him. As the army passes through
Orleans, William makes amends to the town for the chatelain he had
killed. Louis and the ladies turn back and William's father and brothers
go home to gather their forces.]

lxxxiv

Count William is hastening on his way
straight to Orange he goes with his army;
they have ridden every day the whole day,   3970
not even by storms have they been delayed,
they are not stopped by snow or by frost
until they see the smoke of Orange,
the lands which the pagans have laid waste
and the city they have fired and burned.
They had attacked this very morning.
In the great palace with the paved hall,
Lady Guiborc had donned her shirt of mail,
laced on a helmet and girded a sword;
there was no woman who was not armed that day,   3980
and at the windows of the great square tower.
The knights guarded the gate below,
the assault was fierce and the combat rough,
the ladies threw down quantities of stones;
many Saracens had their heads crushed
and lay dead and bloody, their mouths open.
The tower of Orange is set in such a place
that they don't fear attack worth an apple.
The pagan army has sounded the charge;
they leave Orange, they have fired the city,   3990
back to Archant the host has returned
to make an engine that will crush the tower
and a great chariot enclosed in iron   (a)

by which the stone will be torn to pieces (b)
and the great tower brought to the ground.
King Desramé has sworn by his beard
that Guiborc will be drawn by horses
and drowned and overwhelmed by the sea.
But I think that his beard will be forsworn.
Count William has caught sight of the smoke,
he says to his men: "Orange is in flames!
Holy Mary, crowned queen of heaven, 4000
Guiborc's been captured by those rotten madmen.
Quickly to arms, noble men of honor!"
A trumpet sounds, the army sets out,
Count William closes his visor,
leaps on his horse with the golden saddle,
at his left side, his sword suits him well;
his shield at his neck, his oriflamme raised,
he comes to Orange riding furiously,
and Rainoart carries his heavy rod,
he follows William with great energy. 4010
The host spreads out over the countryside;
Lady Guiborc has mounted the tower,
towards the left side she has turned her face,
she sees so many flags wave in the sky,
so many green helmets and banded shields,
so many lances and dark gold mail shirts,
so many triangular silk pennants;
the good chargers show their great valor,
the horns are sounded with furious strength,
all the land glitters with the armor, 4020
they ride ranged in their battle order.
Lady Guiborc is terrified,
she thinks they are of the infidel race
already returning from the Archant.
The noble lady rages in her mind,
"Holy Mary!" she implores with fervor;
"Alas, William, you have forgotten me!
Noble count, sire, you stay away too long,
it was a sin to abandon me here.

I know now that I shall be put to death,   4030
you will not see your wedded wife again.
Because I loved you, I will lose my head,
my body will be burnt, the ashes scattered,
or I shall be drowned in the sea
with a huge stone attached to my neck.
However it happens, I cannot escape,
I must be crushed by sorrow and torment."
And with these words she falls down in a faint;
the priest, Stephen, raises her again
and then she sheds a great many tears.   4040

[LXXXV–XCIII William must show Guiborc his nose before she will
let the army enter. Terrified at Rainoart's appearance when she first saw
him, Guiborc later admires his looks and says he must come of a fine
race. As William's family begins to assemble with their troops, William
stands at a window and points them out to Guiborc. That night there is
a banquet in the hall and Rainoart again gets drunk. The more others
ridicule him, however, the more William defends him. He sends Guiborc
to take him in hand.]

Rainoart, holding his club of spruce,
enters the chamber along with the queen
and they seat themselves on the bed rugs.
The chamber is rich, marble and painted,
the sun shines into the room through glass panes.
Guiborc is wise in the Saracen laws,
"Rainoart, brother," she says, "now think if ever
you had a sister, brother or cousin."
Rainoart answers: "Yes, near the shores,
I have a king and a sister, a queen.   4470
There is none so wise to the port of Cabrine,
and lovelier than fairy or siren."
'Then he is silent and bows his head down
and Guiborc opens her purple mantle
and wraps it round him, for her heart tells her
that he is her brother, but she says nothing.

[XCIV–XCV   Rainoart will not tell her who he is until he has distinguished himself in the battle. She arms him with weapons and armor that belonged to her family, though he is scornful of the sword which seems too light to him. He promises to guard William for her with his club, and from this time on, Rainoart's devotion to Guiborc never wavers. At Aliscans, the poet assures us,]

The men of William would not have succeeded	(4579f)
were it not for God and the worthy Rainoart;	(g)
all alone he brought the war to an end	(h)
as you will hear tell and relate,	(i)
if it please you to remain in this place.	(k)
But I can tell you and affirm the truth,	(l)
that a good man should not hear a minstrel,	(m)
unless he pays him for the love of God	(n)
for that is the only work he can do.	(o)

. . .

Minstrels should be properly loved;	(u)
they seek after joy and they love to sing,	(v)
they used to be greatly honored once,	(w)
but the evil, the wicked, the miserly,	(x)
whose only care is to pile up riches,	(y)
to take deposits and to lend money,	(z)
who practice usury day and night,	(aa)
they have disinherited many good men.	(bb)
That's their pleasure, they like no other song.	(cc)
These are the ones who make honor decline;	(dd)
may God damn them, I cannot love them!	(ee)
I shall not give up my fiddling for them,	(ff)
if it bothers them, then let them scream.	(gg)
I keep to good men, let the bad ones be.	(hh)

[When Rainoart leaves Guiborc, he returns to the kitchen.]

xcvi

Rainoart is all alone in the kitchen
where he finds a lot of cranes and mallards,

venison, fish, salmon and sea-wolves.
He takes some of the fattest to eat
and drinks a whole vatful of the sauce.   4620
He takes the neck of a swan that is stuffed
with eggs and pepper, with fish and meat.
He picks up his club, under his right arm,
and comes out of the kitchen with a quick step,
licking himself like a cat, for the sauce.
He is more fierce than lion or leopard;
he approaches the table, no coward,
and sits on the ground in front of William.
The Franks see him and begin to make jokes,
from fifteen sides they extend their goblets   4630
and make him drink in great swallows and draughts.
In the midst of the well-measured hall,
he puts his club, when he's weary from drink.
Aimer and Bernard get up from the table,
Hernaut the red and Guibert of Andernas.
They approach the club to try out their arms
but they can't move it, not for Damascus,
nor could anyone else, for the gold of Baudas.   (a)
But he lifts it as a cat does a mouse.
The Franks say: "You're some kind of Satan!
If you so wish, you will conquer the world."   4640
"By St. Denis, my lords," says Rainoart,
"I don't know if you come from Paris or Arras,
but by the faith that I bear Saint Thomas,
if God preserves me, my club and my arms,
I will defeat the Saracens for you."

[XCVII–XCIX   When the army sets out, Rainoart, once again, forgets
his club. A messenger is sent back for it but it takes fourteen men to lift
it and four horses to pull it in a cart. Rainoart is so anxious to get it,
when he sees it arriving, that he overturns the cart, which breaks the
neck of the shaft-horse. Meanwhile, more than ten thousand Franks,
"the cowards," have deserted the army. William let them go, but Rai-
noart kills fifty of them, drives the rest back and takes command of
them.]

The Franks begin to make fun of the cowards,
but Rainoart says: "Good people, let them be.   4870
For, by the faith that I keep with Guiborc,
the woman I must love most in the world,
who girded this bright sword on me in her rooms,
if you make me angry at you,
I shall begin to strike with my club.
The most valiant that I have heard taunt
will not be able to keep it from singing.
As the son of a king, I must be fierce.
From now on I shall make my power known.
I have let myself be a fool too long.   4880
He deserves poor fruits who will not mature,
and disgrace, who takes no care to amend.
I am a king's son, as I must remember;
the good man proves himself, I have heard said."
When the Franks hear Rainoart speaking this way,
not one is so valiant he dares say a word.
They begin to murmur to one another:
"Bone of the devil, he knows how to talk!"
• • •

[C–CXI The squadrons are named and described. The pagans, alerted
by a messenger, arm and order their troops under the command of
Rainoart's father, Desramé. The armies meet, "the earth trembles, the
grass is stained with blood." In hand-to-hand combats, William's father
and brothers aid each other. Rainoart fights at the head of the company
of cowards, but is cut off from the rest of the army. Plowing through
the Saracen troops,]

He doesn't stop until he reaches their ships;
there the fighting is fierce and hard,   5340
but Rainoart never forgets himself.
He breaks up the ships and shatters the masts
and completely destroys their barges.
He leans on his club, which is stuck in the sea,
Rainoart is light, he takes a good start,
and leaps twenty-five feet in the air

onto a barge whose mast has been smashed.
There the count Bertrand is imprisoned,
and Guielin and Guichard, the renowned,
Gaudin the dark and Hunaus the hardened,   5350
Walter of Termes, the brave and the wise,
Gerard the well-armed from Commarchis.
Rainoart has gotten himself onto that barge
and he finds fifty Turks inside it.
With his club he confesses them so well,
that the most fortunate is badly used;
his whole body and all his limbs are crushed.
Rainoart climbs over an enclosure
and finds Bertrand, where he is imprisoned,
held fast by chains around his legs;   5360
his hands and fists are tightly bound together,
both his eyes are covered with a cloth.
Rainoart comes towards him with his arm raised,
ready to kill him, but suddenly stops,
for he has never touched a prisoner.
In front of Bertrand the worthy knight stops
and asks him: "Friend, where were you born?"
Bertrand answers, he is terrified:
"Sire, in France, a nephew of William short-nose,
pagans captured me four months ago.   5370
In great anguish I am kept chained here,
I have fasted until I'm swollen with hunger.
Now I am to be taken to Arabia;
there is the prison where I'm to be kept.   (a)
Alas! if I am imprisoned there
I shall not leave for the rest of my life.
I'll have no help from any man born
but I shall die in pain and abuse.
God care for my soul, the body is finished.
Noble lord, sire, have compassion for us!"
Rainoart says: "You will soon be set free;   (a)
for William's sake, whom you invoke."   5380

cxii

When Rainoart hears Bertrand say
that he's a nephew of the valiant William,
quickly he goes over to him
and takes the collar off his neck
and breaks the great chains that bind his feet; (a)
he frees his hands behind his back
and quickly uncovers his handsome eyes.
The palatine leaps to his feet,
he sees before him all the armor he wants
and quickly puts on a coat of mail
and then laces a shining green helmet. 5390
Swiftly he has taken up a good sword
which he sees hanging on a stake before him.
Rainoart says: "One can easily see
that you come of a valiant line."
Bertrand says: "Sire, if I had a good mount,
I would be anxious to help my uncle.
By your grace, you've done me great honor—
now if the children could be set free
who languish in prison beside the mast,
I would not trouble you ever again." 5400
Rainoart hears him and immediately goes,
he finds the children weeping tenderly
and lamenting their lot to one another.
They are guarded by fifty Nubians;
God damn them all! how they abuse them,
beating them often with their great flails,
so that the blood flows down their bodies.
Rainoart does not try to speak to them,
but attacks them head-on with his club
and tosses them all into the sea. 5410
Says Rainoart: "Now you can have a good bath;
if only all Tervagant's heirs were there!"
He quickly sets all the children free
and puts everyone off the ship.

. . .

Bertrand says: "Sire if I had a horse now!
My heart is anxious to aid my uncle."
Rainoart answers: "Just be patient;
for all I know you will soon have a mount   5430
and the others, too, each on a dapple."
He sees a pagan running towards him,
well armed with a hauberk of chain mail,
on his head a shining green helmet
and at his neck a shield of ivory;
in his hand he carries a strong sharp spear.
He lets the horse go to attack Elinant;
all his armor is not worth a glove—
he strikes him dead from the spirited charger.
Rainoart lifts the great heavy club   5440
and strikes a fatal blow on his helmet;
he gets no protection from his armor.
He splits him straight through to the saddle
and shatters the whole spine of the horse;
in a moment everything is smashed.
With another blow he has killed Malquidant
and Samuel, Samul and Salmuant.
Not even the horses are safe from death.
"Indeed," says Bertrand, "if you strike this way,
we won't get a horse from you in our lives."   5450
Rainoart answers: "You're in too much hurry;
I can't help it, by my faith, sir Bertrand,
this club is heavy, so the blows are strong.
You will get one, just be patient a while.
Here comes someone astride a black dapple,
he's running quite swiftly; look at him come!"

. . .

[CXII   But each time, he hits too hard and Bertrand gets more impa-
tient with the loss of each horse.]

"God," says Bertrand, "you are taking too long;
I'll never get the horse I am waiting for,

there is no protection against your blows."
Rainoart says: "It disturbs me very much
that there is no way to lighten my blows.   5470
Sir Bertrand, you must not be amazed,
the club is large and it's heavy in front;
when I have raised it to aim a blow,
it comes back down with tremendous force;
and I cannot control it at all."
Bertrand says: "Sire, it's the way you strike,
it would be better to slow down your blows."
Rainoart answers: "I am learning now,
from now on I shall make my blows softer."

[CXIII   But when he attacks Morinde,]

Rainoart strikes him so hard with his club,
in the midst of that helmet of gold and jewels,
that all his armor gives way quickly.
As far as the saddle he cleaves through him
and the horse is split down the middle.
The blow resounds like thunder in a storm,
in a moment he is completely crushed.
On the rebound the club strikes two Turks,
who couldn't have been better killed by four,
and the horses under them are hit too;   5500
they lie crushed in front of him on the field.
"Really," says Bertrand, "these are a devil's blows.
Rainoart, sire, I have begged you
to touch the pagans with that club
in such a way that you control your blows."
Rainoart says: "I had forgotten.
But now I shall do as you advised."

[But then there is Baufumé:]

As far as the saddle he cuts through him
and splits the horse right through the middle;
within a moment, it is all crushed.

"Now," says Bertrand, "I know the truth—
Rainoart, sire, you have no love for us.
We will get no defense or aid from you."
Rainoart says: "I don't do it on purpose,
Sir Bertrand, now you've reminded me,
I have not got used to the proper tap.   5530
Who forgets what he's never done or known
by all rights ought to be forgiven.
Now I'll tap gently, since it pleases you."
He takes his club, grasps and brandishes it;
from beneath, he has grasped the slim part
and turned the larger part to the front.
Now the emir Estiflé appears,
no such villain from here to Dureste,
well armed on a mount with a black star.
He has struck one of our knights,   5540
one of the war-hardened, Rainoart's men,
of those who were rightly called cowards.
Before he can turn his charger around,
Rainoart has struck him so hard with his club
that he has split and shattered his shield,
ripped his hauberk and torn it apart;
he has smashed his sides and crushed his heart
and knocked him dead from his good steed.
That he takes by the rein and presents to Bertrand.
Rainoart asks: "Does this please you better?"   5550
"Indeed, yes, sire, it's worth more than a city."

• • •

[CXIII–CXXI[b]   Once he has mastered the technique, Rainoart quickly
gets horses for Bertrand's six cousins who ride off together and rejoin
William. The pagans outnumber them one hundred to one. Among the
pagans there are many awesome figures: Margot of Bocident, a land
where Lucifer descends and where no wheat grows. Black as ink, like his
horse, Margot is wrapped in a serpent's hide and carries a gold flail. Bor-
rel, wielding a hammer and wearing the hide of a monster, leads four-
teen sons into battle, all carrying flails. Baudus, who normally carries a

mallet, exchanges it for a club made from the mast of a ship, in order to meet his cousin Rainoart. He is fifteen feet tall, with black skin, tightly curled hair, and eyes red as burning coals. Despite their respect for his strength, the pagans are scornful of Rainoart's appearance. When Hauce-bier meets him,]

Rainoart asks: "Saracen, where do you come from?
Stand right there and say what you want!
I guard the Archant, that privilege is mine,
if you want battle, you needn't go further,
I stand here ready to meet your attack.
Come and fight with me on this field!"
Haucebier answers: "Shut up, you ragged fool!
I will never touch a man on foot.   (80)
Your clothes are not worth two coined pennies;
you look like a beggar, who got in the fire
and sat there until you were covered with smoke.
You'd be a real fool if your hair were shaved."
Rainoart says: "Don't you insult me!
What do you care if my clothes are torn,
and if my skin is black and bristled?
The heart is never wrapped in cloth
or bordered in speckled fur or ermine,
but rests comfortably inside the belly;   (90)
he's a fool who despises a man for his clothes.
He might be a noble sunk in poverty.
An evil rich man is not worth two plucked geese;
I wouldn't respect him, I'd call him a fool.
If I am poor, God will give me enough,
I expect to be crowned by him some day
as king and protector of all Spain.
I shall shatter all of Mohammed's walls
and I will have churches and altars built
with the great wealth that is amassed there.   (100)
Then Jesus will be exalted and raised
and his blessed and consecrated body;
holy Christianity will be lifted high."

Haucebier says: "Go your way, you madman!
I would kill you but that would be base.
. . ."

cxxi^e

Great is the battle, they maintain it well,
striking and hacking and raising great cries.
Pagans call on Mohammed and Cahu
and Apollo: "Now show us your power!"
Rainoart has caught sight of his father,
he hears him named and then he knows him.
He goes before him with his bare sword poised
and shouts at him: "Good father, how are you here?
I am your son, whom you lost long ago,
Rainoart, that is, who suffered so much.   (10)
I offer you no greeting or friendship
unless you believe in God and Jesus
and renounce Mohammed and Cahu
and abandon your miserable foolish God
for that Lord who wields power in the sky.
I shall strike you so hard with my sharp blade
that I will sever your head from your trunk."
Desramé hears him, and his blood turns cold;
he says to his son: "Rainoart, what is this?
You have killed and confounded me today,   (20)
it's through you the Franks have taken the field.
I am your father and you have angered me,
you have made me pay well for your begetting.
It distresses me to see you miscreant,
I have searched for you to the bornes of Arthur."
Rainoart answers: "I don't give a straw;
to me Mohammed's no more than a hung dog.
Enter your ships, you have stayed here too long!
It troubles me that I caught up with you;
if I would not be reproached for it,   (30)
I would take your head off from your chest."
Desramé says: "There was never such shame.

Son of a whore, you've made a bad bargain.
If you wait for me, by my hoary head,
I shall make you angry and sorry for it."
He spurs the gelding and, riding swiftly,
strikes Rainoart with his blade of steel;
were it not for the cap on his head,
the blow would have cut through to his teeth.
Rainoart says: "Now you have gone too far.   (40)
If my soul has to burn for this,
I will not leave before you feel my blade."
He runs at him, stretching for a full blow.
Desramé is very much afraid,
he would not stay for a valleyful of gold,
he takes to flight and delays no more.
But Rainoart catches one of his brothers
and sends his head and helmet into the sea.
"Montjoy!" he cries, "William, where are you?
For your sake, I have killed my brother Jambu,   (50)
and I'll do the same to old Desramé."
The pagans are listening, they raise a cry.
More than ten thousand come running at him
to bring their aid to Desramé.

[CXXII–CXXIII   Rainoart moves on to fight others, among them Borrel and his fourteen sons. He seizes their flails and tries to use them, but finally discards them as useless.]

cxxiv

When Rainoart has thrown all the flails,
he takes his club and goes back with it.
He sees a troop of armed Saracens   6050
who are just now coming away from the ships;
they are led by the bearded Agrapars,
the most evil man ever born of woman.   (a)
His hair is black and tightly curled,   (b)
it beats against his thighs behind him,   (c)
and in front he is completely covered   (d)

by his great beard, to the knot of his belt.   (e)
His eyes are red, his teeth jagged,   (f)
he is not more than three feet tall,
but he is fat and his shoulders are broad;
he has a mouth that is terribly swollen,   (a)
hideous is the Turk's appearance.

CXXV

King Agrapars is ugly of feature.
His hair is black and grows down to his heels,
his eyes vermilion like burning coal,
his nose hooked, his teeth like a watchdog's.   (a)
his beard thick just like a Greek's   (b)
his body hairy, on every side,   (c)
nails as sharp as a lion's claws,
and as tenacious as the glue from a fish.   (a)
Anyone he nears has a bad companion.   6060
Through the battle, he rushes wildly,   (a)
crying aloud, "William," in challenge,
"today you will meet a great destruction!"

CXXVI

Agrapars comes, spurring furiously;
he has tormented our people badly,
like a dog he grimaces at our men.   (a)
Whoever sees him feels his blood freeze.   (b)
Rainoart is beneath a tree heavy with leaves.
He has fought so hard in the great battle,   (a)
he's very hot; his helmet is unlaced,
he leans for a short while on his club.   (a)
Just then Agrapars comes rushing at him,
seeing Rainoart resting on the club,   (a)
he leaps at him and tears into him hard,
right to the flesh, leaving no hair at all;
with his rough nails, he has ripped the skin   (a)
so the red blood flows down his face.   6070
When Rainoart sees himself so mutilated,

he says: "You have given me quite a shave,
but you've done too much business with my hair.
By St. Denis, you'll be sorry you did!
If I don't take revenge, I'd be pretty base."

CXXVII

Rainoart is sad, he doesn't know what to do.
He touches his head and finds the wound.
Rainoart says: "This leaves an ugly trace.   (a)
If I don't avenge it, may God never help me!"   (b)
He takes his club, grasping it with both hands,
intending to strike the pagan on the face,
but the other leaps like a savage beast   6080
and when he comes down he tears at his thigh.
Rainoart says: "Pagan, you'd better flee,
or you will feel the sting of my club."
Agrapars leaps and embraces his trunk,
sinking his nails into him with such rage
that he rips a hundred rings from his hauberk;
as he turns, he bites him hard on the face,
so that the clear blood flows down from it.
But Rainoart grabs his arms with such fury,
that he tears one of them from his trunk.   (a)
He throws it on the ground, like it or not,   6090
"Now go," he says, "May God do you no good!
Holy Mary, how my face burns!"

• • •

CXXIX

The Saracen is of foul origin.
He sees Rainoart, looks at him and grimaces,   (a)
he twists his lips and gnashes his teeth.   (b)
Says Rainoart: "You come of a filthy race,
you look like a descendant of monkeys."
And the pagan comes running in fury.
Rainoart lifts his club of spruce,
strikes such a blow on the back of his spine,

that he drops him, dead, beside a hawthorn.
Rainoart says: "Now good luck to you!
You were the one who began the assault,
from now on, I absolve you of hatred."   (a)
And then he leaves, dragging his club.   6110

[CXXX   Rainoart goes on to fight and defeat Crucados, but he spares
his mount.]

He takes the horse because he is so huge.   6140
Rainoart says: "My heart is filled with sorrow
for these pigs who insult and abuse me—
they call me a boy, a beggar on foot—
now I shall mount this noble charger
and I shall be a knight from now on."

cxxxi

Rainoart holds the charger with great joy,
in one hand he has the rein of silk;
the horse whinnies, he is badly upset
by the club which Rainoart still brandishes.   (a)
But Rainoart is afraid of nothing;   (b)
he holds the horse and attempts to mount him.   (c)
Then he reflects and tries another way.   (d)
Rainoart says: "I would mount willingly,
but it seems that my heart is weakening   6150
and how could I then carry my club?
It appears that I am being foolish,   (a)
for all I know, I might even fall."

cxxxii

Rainoart stands in the midst of the sand,
holding the horse by the double reins;
he is not accustomed to riding,
he knows more about the smoke of the kitchen
when it pours forth most fully and strong.   (a)

When he mounts, he doesn't use a stirrup,
but leaps on the saddle, his front to the rear,
his face directed at the mount's tail.
He urges him in back, with his heels,   (a)
and the horse runs away like a hare,   6160
down the valley, straight through a heath.
Rainoart says: "This mare is a fierce beast,
if I had known that she would be like this,
I wouldn't have mounted for Baviere's gold.
Help me, God, true and righteous father,
that I don't fall off and down this cliff!"
In this manner, Rainoart says his prayers
and rides, making ugly expressions.
He doesn't know how, but he falls off the back
and he drops his huge and powerful club.   6170
The baron holds on by the horse's tail
and the animal drags him through the dust,
not stopping until he reaches a stream.
There he leaves Rainoart on the path.

CXXXIII

After Rainoart has fallen to the ground,
he gets to his feet as fast as he can
and grabs the horse, furiously angry.
"Get away from me," he says, "confound you"   (a)
with one of his fists he hits him twice
and the animal falls to the ground.
Then Rainoart starts running back,   6180
"Holy Mary," he says, "where is my club?
If I lose it, William will be conquered!"

[CXXXIV–CXLV   Rainoart's club is found by Walegrape, who usually
fights with a crook. Walegrape is fourteen feet tall, with a red beard,
pointed nose, teeth longer than a boar's and a tongue that hangs out half
a foot. Rainoart gets his club back and they fight, but in the course of
the battle, he loses it again.]

cxlvi

Now the Turk is somewhat reassured,   6350
he holds Rainoart's club which is so heavy,
he cannot manage it well at his sides,
but he is very anxious to move it.
He has told Rainoart what he desires:
"Stop there, vassal, don't be afraid,
something important has occurred to me.
What is your name, in what land were you born?
Who are your father and your relatives?"
Rainoart says: "You will know that very soon,
my name will certainly not be concealed.   (a)
I am Rainoart and I was born in Spain;   6360
my father is the strong king Desramé,
and my uncle, Tiebaut, the fine warrior,
my brothers are Jambu and Persagues,

• • •

and Walegrape, I think is the eldest.
I have fifteen brothers, all crowned kings,
except only myself, I am the youngest.   6370
It seems to me, I am well related,
but I don't value it two cents.
At Palerne I was captured and bought,   (a)
when I was young in my early youth.   (b)
King Louis, who held all France in fief,
bought me there for a hundred silver marks.
I was brought back to Montlaon with him
where I spent more than seven years in the kitchen
and was often very well cared for.
I have been taught to prepare a meal.
Then William of the short nose brought me here.
I would have proved myself well in this battle   6380
but I've met a small obstacle in you;
you have my club and I am unarmed.
It seems to me that you hold the dice now
but if I had thought it through this morning,

I would have guarded myself from this harm.
I would have glued it down inside my fist,
my great club, which you are now holding;
it would not have slipped away so often. (a)
God help me, how unlucky I am!
If you were to give me back my club,
I would redeem it richly from you, 6390
with a hundred silver marks weighed on the scales."
The pagan hears him and shouts aloud:
"Mohammed, sire, may you be adored!
Rainoart, brother, what a joy to find you.
I am your brother, you must believe me. (a)
Come, brother, for Mohammed's sake, embrace me!"
Rainoart says: "Vassal, don't say any more!
If God helps me, I will not love you
until you have been baptized and raised up;
then my suffering will be forgiven you."
Walegrape answers: "The devil with that!" (a)

cxlvii

Walegrape says: "Rainoart, don't be a fool; 6400
believe Mohammed and enter the right path!
You will be crowned today with great rejoicing."
Rainoart says: "Saracen, don't you be a fool,
with your Mohammed; I shall not believe him.
I do not value him more than a dog. (a)
I wouldn't desert, for anything, the law
that God gave us to pursue the right road."
Walegrape says: "He's a fool who scolds you,
for you are a dog of filthy origin. (a)
Your mother certainly wasn't like mine; (b)
a woman of pleasure gave birth to you, (c)
who willingly took money from others. (d)
But I'll do what I wouldn't for anyone else;
if I were to kill you with this club,
it seems to me, I'd be acting badly." 6410
He throws the club out of his way

and Rainoart runs to it with great joy;
he takes his club and swings it around him,
and Rainoart begins to exert himself.   (a)
He seizes Walegrape, strikes him with both hands,   (b)
against his will he turns him four times around   (c)
and Walegrape hits him so hard in return   (d)
that he twists his back between his arms.   (e)
Then the battle begins fiercely again.   (f)

[CXLVII^a–CXLIX^a   After a long battle, in which Walegrape tries to
strangle Rainoart with a looped belt, Rainoart finally kills his brother.]

cl

When the pagans see Walegrape defeated,
the greater part of their barons flee.
It makes Rainoart furious
that he has not destroyed them with his club.   (a)
"Alas," he says, "how unlucky I am!
I have no shoes, my feet are bare,
my blood has run out in thirty places,
I can't run any further on these sharp stones.   (a)
If these infidel pagans escape me now,   (b)
through all of France my praise will be lost."   (c)
The shorn one now plans a great deception: (d)
pretending to be dead, he falls to the ground   6450
and lets out a roar as if fatally wounded,
but all the same he hangs on to the club.
A thousand Saracens come in a rush,
they all look at Rainoart lying there.
The pagans cry: "Don't anyone run—
the one who confounded us has been killed."

cli

The Saracens think that Rainoart is dead;
more than twenty thousand come at a gallop,
and touch Rainoart with lances and crooks.
He leaps up, roaring like a bull,   6460

the pagans see him and turn their backs,
and Rainoart follows them with great strides.
He smashes the pagans' backs with his club,
then he shouts at them a few brief words:
"Sons of whores, you'll be sorry you found me;
I cannot have a single day of rest."

[CLII–CLIV Rainoart fights and kills Grishart, who ate human flesh
and fought with a hatchet. His sister, Flohart, comes to avenge him.]

When Flohart hears all the shouting
and listens to the words that tell
how Rainoart with his heavy club
killed her brother, who now lies, mouth open,   6515
she leaps up, completely dishevelled.
She is fifteen feet tall, the Franks estimate,
and enveloped in a buffalo hide.
Bearing her scythe, she enters the battle,
she is exhausted from killing people,   (a)
any she reaches has used up his life.   (b)
Against her sickle no weapon can last,   (c)
it resounds like bolts of thunder hurled.   (d)
With every blow the mad, dirty, old woman   (e)
kills a whole cart-load of our people.   (f)
William has pointed her out to Rainoart.   6520
"God," says William, "holy, honored virgin,
what beast is this that I see armed over there?
She wreaks great destruction on our people.   (a)
If she lives long, we cannot endure it."
Rainoart says: "This is a foolish worry;
I shall kill her with my heavy club."
Behold Flohart, charging at a gallop,
from her mouth comes a great cloud of smoke,
that pollutes the entire host.
Rainoart goes to meet her as she comes
and shouts to her: "Foul, demented hag,   6530
what living devils have cast you from hell?

By what demons were you engendered
since you are a queen with a crown?
You ought to be in your paved chambers,
with a devil to make love to you.
For a whole mine filled with gold besants,
I wouldn't want to have deflowered you."
When Flohart hears him she almost goes mad.
She shouts at him: "You wretch, you hot bellows!
By Mohammed you'll regret those insults!   6540
With this scythe I'll give you such a blow
that you will never scour pots again,
stir any soups or skim any cauldrons."
She approaches him, her scythe extended,
and Rainoart is really afraid of her.
Against the scythe he throws his club
and the iron that circles it is cut.
The scythe digs into the club a half foot.
Rainoart pulls and the old hag pulls harder,
and her scythe is split into two pieces,   6550
something that gives Rainoart real pleasure.

clv

Rainoart sees that the great scythe is in pieces
and rejoices; the old hag is angry.
With her fist she strikes him over the ear,
so two of his teeth are cracked and shattered.
Rainoart says: "You have repaid me all right."
He jumps forward and embraces the hag
and she grabs him, not the least bit afraid,
with such power, don't doubt for an instant,
that she bends the spine of Rainoart's back.   6560
But Rainoart twists his head away,
for the stench of Flohart is too much for him,   (a)
it stinks more than decomposing flesh.
Flohart seizes him by the front of his hood,
with her teeth she tears it from the hauberk,
she swallows it as if it were cheese.

Rainoart says: "Holy lady, Mary,
I commend to you my body and life.
I am afraid that this one will kill me."

clvi

When Rainoart sees how Flohart rages,
he is very fearful; why should I lie?   6570
He invokes God and prays quietly to him:
"St. Leonard, who releases captives,
St. Julien, I pledge my club to you;
on your altar I'll place it in good faith,
if I can carry the prize from this field."
He strikes the pagan, shattering her body,
she falls dead and lies, her limbs quivering.
Rainoart cries: "Lie there quietly.
Disgusting hag, make sure I don't hear you!"
He takes his club, kissing and fondling it.   6580
Rainoart says: "I would not give you up,
sir club, for the city of Troy,
but the good saint will have you nonetheless."

• • •

clvii

Rainoart comes running through the battle,
he pursues pagans and handles them roughly.   (a)
King Desramé with his rich armor   (b)
spreads great tumult in the combat.   (c)
He finds his son Rainoart before him,
he doesn't know him and I'll tell you why:
he is barefoot and his armor is poor,
he hardly resembles the son of a king.
Desramé says: "Vassal, speak to me!
Who are you? Tell me, by your faith."   (a)
Rainoart answers: "Willingly, by my law.   6590
It would be my shame if I refused you,
you are my father, I know and believe.   (a)
I am Rainoart, I was begotten by you.

I am William's man and love him in good faith.
If you hurt him, I shall hurt you.
The club that I carry defies you,
it has no concern for your laws.
If you don't flee me, I'll give you a blow   (a)
and that helmet will not protect you."   (b)
He seizes him by his embroidered reins,   (c)
King Desramé is in great distress.   (d)

clviii

Desramé says: "Rainoart, gentle friend,
you are my son, I swear in good faith,
I have looked for you all over the world;
believe Mohammed, who is all-powerful.   6600
I do not want to do battle with you;
I don't know how many of my sons are dead.   (a)
If I kill you, it will be against my will;
you'll be in pieces as the writings say."
Rainoart answers: "You needn't worry.
If I escape, you will be in trouble.
I shall not stop before the ports of Lutis;
no castle, city or town or fortress
that I won't destroy, however strong.
A defeated king you will be all your life."   (a)
Desramé hears and grows black with anger.

• • •

clix

"My son, Rainoart," says the King Desramé,
"when I brought you up, I made a mistake,
better for me if you'd been strangled."   6620
Rainoart says: "You have spoken the truth."
He raises the club and moves forward,
but now his intention is changed.   (a)
He looks into his face and shouts aloud:
"Guard yourself now, king, or you will be killed!   (a)
By that lord who was hung on the cross,

I shall strike you if you don't prevent it,
you'll be sorry if you don't believe it."
And with these words, Rainoart's blow descends. (a)
The king evades it, he is not touched,
and the club finally hits the ground
and sinks four feet into it. (a)
And Desramé turns to face his son,
striking two more enormous blows 6630
on top of his helmet; it is so tight
that it is not damaged two cents worth.
But Rainoart is somewhat dazed,
for Desramé is strong and clever.
Now Rainoart is furious;
he strikes at his father on both his sides,
smashing his bones in three places.
No shield or gold hauberk can protect him. (a)
Desramé has fainted from the pain,
he leans slightly over his saddle, (a)
the pagans run and a cry is raised.

[CLIX–CLX   Rainoart is surrounded by pagans; his club is split by his brother Tenebres' sword. He is wounded badly, but William and his brothers come to Rainoart's aid.]

clxi

Great is the combat and strong and hard 6650
and Rainoart has turned away from it.
Beyond the battle he goes to one side (a)
and sits down under a leaf-filled tree.
There he will rest until he gets his breath. (a)
He takes his club and looks long at it,
at the top it is covered with blood,
with the blood of those whom it had killed.
The baron thinks about it for a while, (a)
he remembers the men of his family
whom he has killed and destroyed that day. (a)
"Alas," he says, "I am miserable,

for I have killed all the friends of my blood,
and crushed the body of my father.
This sin will never be forgiven me.   6660
But what did I say? It was my club that did it.
Cursed be the hour that it was made!"
He throws his club down on the field so hard
that one of its ends sticks in the ground.
"There," he cries, "my club, you were cut to do ill.
From now on I must defy you.   (a)
You have received much honor from me,
you could find no man, however well born,   (a)
who would dare to harm you or be disloyal   (b)
and yet you have betrayed and hurt me.   (c)
Now I shall go and you will remain here,
you will never again be carried by me."

[CLXI–CLXIV   A new troop of pagans arrive from the ships and Rain-
oart quickly makes peace with his club. However, the blows he deals
Haucebier shatter the club.]

clxv

When the club of Rainoart is split open,   6760
the pagans run and surround him.
On every side they aim huge blows at him.
Now Rainoart is really afraid,   (a)
he has been hurt in several places;   (b)
without arms, he doesn't know what to do,   (c)
he doesn't remember the sword
which Guiborc girded on at his side.
With both his fists, that are large and sturdy,
he gives the Saracens mighty blows.   (a)
Any he touches is badly treated.
He has knocked out the brains of more than fifty,
but the number of pagans is too vast.
Then Rainoart finally remembers,
when his great fist bangs against the sword.   6770
Now the baron remembers the blade,   (a)

he draws it from its sheath with its brilliant light;
he strikes Golias, who wields Balesgues;
the blade cuts as far as his belt
so that half of it falls on the meadow.   (a)
With another blow he destroys two more.
Rainoart says: "This is a good weapon.
Blessed be the lady who girded it on!
If I had known that blades were like this,
I wouldn't have left one at Montlaon;   (a)
I would have brought them all here with me."

• • •

clxvii

• • •

Rainoart says: "This is a marvel, by God,   6787
that so small a weapon can have such force.
No brave man who has any good in him   (a)
should ever be without four at his side;   (b)
then if one fails, he can use the others.   (c)
Now I can put all the pagans to flight!"

[The pagans flee. Desramé sails away with those who can get to the ships
and the remaining pagans are completely routed. As they flee,]

On the road they encounter Baudus,
who carries the huge mallet at his neck.
He seeks Rainoart but has not found him yet.
The pagans see him and cry out to him:
"Ah, Baudus, sire, take pity on us!
We are all dead, killed and destroyed;
Count William has taken the field.
He chased Desramé into his ship;
he fled by sea and is now in safety.   6830
We're fleeing now, exhausted and confused;
we shall all be dead before it is dark."
Baudus listens and almost goes mad.
He says to the pagans: "Be confident!

Before the night they will feel my great blows.
I will avenge my uncle and his peers."
He departs straightway, taking pagans with him;
they come upon an enormous bean-field,
where there are beans in abundance.
All the pagans go in together,   6840
and that night they take their rest there;
they shake down more than a hogshead of beans
and feast on them, but they have no bread.
They'll be sorry they ate; they'll pay for it—
better for them if they fled to safety.
King Baudus calls the pagans together.

[CLXVII–CLXIX   Baudus leaves to find William and Rainoart. When
he meets Rainoart, his cousin, he tries to make peace with him.]

"Rainoart, brother, listen carefully to me!
Count William has treated you very poorly,
you go nude and barefoot like a beggar.
Act sensibly and come away with me.
I shall share my inheritance with you;
you may have the strong towers of Aire,
and I shall kill the short-nosed marquis
and the Franks he has brought with him here.
Mohammed will be exalted and raised
and their gods dishonored and abused."
Rainoart cries: "You will not say anymore.   6920
I wouldn't do that for a thousand gold marks.
Although I am not yet baptized or raised,   (a)
I believe in God and his blessed goodness,
and the maid who carried him in her womb.
As long as I live, my heart will not change,
for Mohammed is not worth two plucked geese,
except for the gold gathered in him,
he could be thrown into these ditches
like a base dog, when he has been killed."
And Baudus says: "You sound like a madman.

Since I see that you have no faith in Mohammed, 6930
and that you hate and have scorn for our laws,
I shall strike you, if you don't guard yourself."
Rainoart says: "May God be my protection
and my safety be in his hands!
Sir cousin, Baudus, you commit a wrong;
you're my aunt's son and you wish to kill me.
Do you care nothing for humility
or cousins' bonds or love or family?"
Baudus answers: "Not unless you give yourself up
and believe in Mohammed and his powers, 6940
otherwise we will not be reconciled."
Rainoart says: "You shall be disgraced,
for all the words you have ever said
I absolve you, I will not be blamed."
So each of them has made his challenge.

[CLXX–CLXXV They fight, Baudus with a mallet and Rainoart with
his sword. When a blow of the mallet misses Rainoart and strikes a tree,
the mallet splits. Rainoart drops his sword and picks up one of the
pieces, which is more like his club. He says that he has always loved
Baudus and would now if Baudus would accept Christianity. He offers
him friendship and lands, but Baudus angrily refuses. They fight until
both are badly wounded. Rainoart recites a long prayer that he will
conquer and convert Baudus. Eventually he does defeat him, with a
blow on the head that almost knocks his brains out but, miraculously,
does not kill him, and Baudus asks to be baptized, promising to become
Rainoart's vassal.]

When Rainoart has listened to the king
who begs for his mercy, out of love,
and wishes to believe the almighty king,
he couldn't be happier with a valley of gold;
for as a child he had loved him well.
He praises God who had mercy on him
and cannot keep himself from weeping.
He embraces Baudus, holding him tight, 7240

"Cousin," he asks, "have I wounded you much?"
"Yes, indeed, sire, I've bled a long time.
Quickly take off my jeweled green helmet!
Hurry up, sire, or you will see me faint.   (a)
You have so wounded and injured me
that my heart is almost crushed in my chest.
If you have killed me, may you be forgiven,
if I die, it's by my own folly!"   (a)
Rainoart hears him and sighs heavily.
Swiftly he has disarmed Baudus;
he lifts the green jeweled helmet from his head,
he had pushed it all into his skull   7250
and badly damaged the brain in his head.
From the skull he has lifted the cap,   (a)
from his back, he takes the golden-white hauberk.   (b)
When Rainoart has disarmed Baudus,
he sits himself down beside him.   (a)
His body is huge and his chest mighty,   (b)
he measures a whole foot bigger than Rainoart.   (c)
Both of them sit on the grass in the field
and look at each other with great affection.

clxxvi

The battle is over and the field won.
Rainoart sits on the grass in the meadow,
the fierce Baudus next to him side by side.
His body is huge and his limbs solid,
his chest is large and his shoulders broad;
with one of his fists he could kill a bear.   7260
His eyes are red like burning coals,
his hair as black as powdered ink,
his teeth whiter than smooth ivory,
his mouth is big, his nose high and hooked,
his face ample, his eyebrows thick and wide—
in all of Hell, no handsomer devil.

• • •

[CLXXVI–CLXXVII   Baudus faints. When he recovers, he rides off
with Rainoart and the Franks, who have pitched their tents in Aliscans
and prepared a meal with the stores they took from the pagan ships.
Baudus leaves the next day to go home, promising to return and be bap-
tized as soon as he recovers.]

Just at day, when dawn is about to break,
William orders his knights to arm themselves.
Swiftly they all move to mount together.
The count goes to look at Vivien,
beside the pool, where he knows he lies.
The count has him placed between two shields
and beautifully buried beneath a tree.
As he departs, he begins to weep;
you might see many knights fainting there.
Then William has the chief horn sounded;   7370
he does not forget the flail of gold,
the count has it carried along with him,
and Rainoart has his club brought too.   (a)
The army sets out, anxious to make way,   (b)
with great speed, they do not want to stop,   (c)
and Rainoart goes in front, leading them,
his sword in his fist, more fierce than a boar.
A poor man appears before Rainoart
and begins to ask a favor of him.   (a)
"Sire," he says, "let me just speak to you.
I have come to complain of the Saracens.
I saw them enter my lands yesterday,
there was nothing I could do to make them go;
I saw them pillage and lay waste all around,   7380
they shook down more than two hogsheads of beans.   (a)
I was so afraid, I didn't dare stop them.
I had hoped to sell those beans to buy bread
in order to feed myself and my children,
I have nothing else to give them.
Now they must all swell with hunger."

Rainoart says: "They'll be sorry they thought of it.
By St. Denis, I shall make them pay
so not one of them can boast about it.   (a)
Sir peasant, there's no need to worry,   (b)
I'll see that all the damage is repaid,
every shake will cost them a denier."
The peasant says: "May Jesus preserve you!"   7390

• • •

[CLXXVII–CLXXVIII   Rainoart goes to the bean-field and accosts the
pagans, who are terrified of him.]

They all cry out: "Baudus, sire, where are you?"
Rainoart says: "He's not worth a straw to you.   7460
I defeated and conquered him, thanks to God.
You'll regret that you took over this farm;
I owe you a painful greeting for that,   (a)
I want to try my sharp sword out on you.
You will give your horses to the peasant
for I see that his whole harvest is gone."

clxxix

The shouting throughout the bean-field is great,
the pagans flee, they have changed their colors,
I've never seen people in such disorder;
Rainoart pursues them as fast as he can
and shouts to them with enormous force:
"Sons of whores, you'll be sorry you entered these fields, 7470
you didn't come to plow or sow seeds.
The poor man had cultivated them
and taken pains to dig them and plow them.   (a)
He worked very hard until they were hoed;   (b)
he was to sell them for a small profit
but now you have filled your bellies with them;   (a)
by the heart of God, you shouldn't have ruined them.
You've never seen beans bought up in this way,
or any that were so richly paid for."

The pagans say: "Your words are too harsh,
sir vassal, we did not steal them.
There was not one who tried to keep us out."
Rainoart says: "You most certainly stole them, 7480
they were not abandoned to you.
But I'll make you pay for them with this sword." (a)
Then he acquits them, right through the fields,
by hacking away at their chests and hides;
he has killed more than fifteen cart-loads, (a)
they are all dead; they have paid very hard
for the green beans that had not been husked.
Rainoart has shown his generosity,
he has restored his lands to the peasant
and given him all the Saracen arms
and the horses with their golden bridles.

. . .

clxxx

The Franks ride hard, they are anxious to move;
the trumpets are sounded and the horns blown.
The army sets out, intending to advance
with great speed, they've no wish to delay,
they will not stop until they reach Orange.
Great is the tumult as they go through the pass. 7500
You might see many shields disbuckled, (a)
belts broken and saddles overturned, (b)
the hauberks clashing and the jeweled helmets, (c)
you might hear steel strike against iron (d)
and the horses neighing and whinnying. (e)
Great is the noise and the shoving of crowds; (f)
you might see more than fifty succumb.
Before the brave William reaches the palace,
Guiborc has had the dinner prepared. (a)
In Gloriete the horns are sounded for washing,
the knights all go to the water together,
they had disarmed themselves at their lodgings. (a)
That day five hundred bachelors serve,

of whom not one is without his own castle.
But Count William is greatly to be blamed,
for he has forgotten about Rainoart,
he doesn't remember even after supper.
Outside Orange stays the worthy Rainoart,   7510
in his anger he almost goes mad.
He begins to lament to himself:
"Alas," he says, "I might well lose my wits!   (a)
Count William should not have had this thought,
that he would not deign to take me with him,
nor send for me to eat at his table,
and yet I alone ended the battle
and freed his seven nephews from prison.
It was I who killed Saracens and Slavs
and destroyed all my family for him;
if he scorns me, then I should be distressed.   7520
Above all his men, he should honor me,   (a)
love and serve me as it lies in his power.   (b)
But by Him who must redeem us all,   (c)
if I can live one single year longer,   (d)
I shall take all Orange away from him.   (e)
Now I shall go make peace with my father,   (f)
I shall send for Saracens and Turks.   (g)
I shall come to ravage and lay Orange waste,   (h)
to destroy Gloriete and tear it down.   (i)
At St. Denis, I shall be crowned   (k)
and order the head of Louis cut off   (l)
because he made me serve in his kitchen.   (m)
I shall not stop until I reach St. Seigne,   (n)
there'll be no tower that I leave standing.   (o)
I'll kill the people and ravage the land,   (p)
if they refuse to accept my law.   (q)
I shall have Sir William led away in bonds   (r)
so that his family won't dare mention it.   (s)
I know how to treat him like a fool."   (t)
Then he turns back and begins to wander;   (u)

towards Aliscans he starts making his way,   (v)
so filled with grief, he has begun to weep.   (w)

clxxxi

• • •

"My lords," he says, "I might well be enraged.
Count William treats me with little honor   7530
he left me alone like a poor wretch
and did not send for me to eat with him.
Like a beggar he left me at the moats,
he never summoned or called for me.

• • •

I have heard say and I know it is true:
when a thief has been redeemed from the gallows,
he will never be grateful to his lord.
From Sir William, I tell you, of the short nose,
whom I have helped, now I suffer distress.   7550
If I hadn't been there, he'd have been routed,   (a)
not one of his men could have escaped.   (b)
I won't believe in the almighty King,
but in Mohammed who is molded in gold,
and I'll make William sad and angry.
By Mohammed, he'll be sorry he forgot me!
If I don't take revenge, may I be damned.

• • •

Orange will be taken, the country laid waste,
and Gloriete, the palace, destroyed,
and he himself will be caught and bound,
thrown into prison inside Ajete.

• • •

And Aimeri will be raised on the gallows   (d)
and all his sons will have their heads cut off.
In the chapel at Aix I'll be crowned king,
for Louis will be thrown out of France
because of his kitchen where he kept me so long.   (a)
His land will be seized, his country ravaged,   7570

and I shall do what I like with Aelis,
his noble daughter who is so lovely.   (a)
I shall even become her husband, I think.
I have loved her for more than five years,   (a)
she will be queen and I'll be crowned king;   (b)
she needn't complain if I marry her,   (c)
she will be endowed with all of Spain;
Puglia and Venice and Calabria   (a)
I shall give her, before the year is out.   (b)
When you arrive, sir barons, at Orange,
greet the lady Guiborc on my behalf
and challenge the marquis William for me.
Tell him clearly, don't hide anything,
that I'll never be his comrade or friend,
but I shall work to effect his disgrace."   7579

[The knights try to change his mind but he will not listen. They ride
back to William and report Rainoart's threats.]

William hears this and is lost in thought.
"Indeed," says the count, "he should not be blamed.
He has been wise and I've been a fool."
The count summons twenty of his knights
and tells them: "My lords, go to him for me.
By God, I beg, bring him to me in peace,   7630
let him not be insulted or abused."
And they answer: "Just as you command.
We would do much greater service for you."

[CLXXXII–CLXXXIII   But Rainoart will not listen to them; he in-
sults them and William, and renews his threats. When they try to force
him to return, he tears out the iron fret of a hermit's hut, wounds five of
them and chases the rest away. William laughs when he hears the report
and this time he goes himself.]

clxxxiv

Count William is greatly to be praised,
he has gone to bring back Rainoart,

a hundred knights he has ordered to mount,
his brothers go and the brave Aimeri.
The count has Lady Guiborc accompany them,
for the count does not dare ride without her.
Not one of them eases up on his horse
until they see Rainoart going down
into a boat that he wants to use,
with his great club, which he will not forget.
But he doesn't know how to hoist the sail,   7740
how to raise the mast or trim the rigging,
he knows nothing of steering a boat.
Rainoart says: "I could go out of my mind.
I don't know how to turn this ship around,
or how this goes down that I see going up,
I don't know how I have seen them sail."
He takes a pole and begins to push
until the ship goes under on one side,
and keeps pushing until it starts to sink.
If Rainoart had not known how to swim,   7750
he would have drowned before he could escape.
When he gets out, he begins to swear,
"The devils," he says, "get men involved
when they don't know how to handle something.
I must go by land, since I can't by sea."
He takes his club and begins to turn back
towards the shore, he starts to make his way.
Count William begins to call out to him,
very gently without any offense: (a)
"Rainoart, sire, let me just speak to you!
If there's any wrong you accuse me of,   7760
I will make amends however you wish,
to whatever extent you may devise."
Rainoart answers: "Sire, let me alone!
I wouldn't give a fig for your talk.
I won't return until I've crossed the sea.
Then I shall assemble my whole family
and call all the Saracens together.

[He renews his threats until Guiborc kneels before him and asks him to forgive William in return for the arms she had bestowed on him.]

"Lady," he says, "I must love you indeed.
I am your brother, I won't conceal it,
that Rainoart who was stolen from the king,
for whom you heard so much lamenting.
Whatever you wish I cannot refuse.   7800
I shall certainly do as you ask
and forgive William his offense against me.
For love of you, I will call him absolved.   (a)
Never again will you hear about it!
But by Him who has power to save us all,   (a)
if it weren't for you, I won't deny,   (b)
all the gold in the world wouldn't save him!"   (c)

•   •   •

[CLXXXIVᵃ–CLXXXIVᶜ Guiborc asks her brother about his family and he finally tells her his story.]

"Lady," he says, "I am Desramé's son,
who holds Cambie, Pine, and Val Tenebré,
fifty kings are crowned under him.
Now I shall tell you how I have wandered.
My father commended me to a tutor
when he went to fight at Salatré;   (20)
I was a youth of only a few years,
I had gone to a meadow along the shore,
where I played ball for a long while
with the children who came from that kingdom.
That distressed my tutor Giboé,
he beat me so hard, I was covered with blood.
I was upset and my heart was angry;
I took my stick made of tanned leather,
and struck him so hard that his heart burst.
I ran away, when I had killed him,   (30)
fearing my father and his fierce anger.

There were merchants at anchor on the sea;
when they saw me all alone and frightened,
they called to me and took me on their ship,
and I went aboard willing and gladly.
Then, when the weather was right they set sail;
all the way to Palerne they went.
King Louis had gone to visit a saint,
and came that way with his rich retinue.
When he saw me, he bought me quickly,   (40)
and brought me to the city of Laon.
I don't know why, but he began to hate me.
I spent a long time in his kitchen,
I made the fire and skimmed the meat-broth,
I cooked the birds and turned many haunches,
everyone mocked and made fun of me.
In great distress I lived there a long time;
more than seven years, I think, passed by
before William came and asked about me
and then he brought me back here with him.   (50)
• • •
Now I have told you the whole story;
I have a sister, I don't know in what land,   (60)
Orable, and she is beautiful,
there is none so wise from here to Dureste.
I've never seen her, but I've been told.
Tiebaut of Arabia whom I've heard praised,
he married her, that I know is true.
He held this country, the length and breadth,
and Gloriete and the ornate palace.
But a Frank robbed him of his heritage
and took my sister with his rough prowess;
he had her baptized, now she is Christian.   (70)
My heart tells me, I have often thought it,
that you are she; but I have not spoken,
in case it might offend him or you.
But now that I have proved my valor,
and exalted my courage and raised it high,

it will redound to your honor."
Guiborc hears him and weeps tenderly;
she takes Rainoart in her embrace.
"Kiss me, my brother, I have longed for you!
I am your sister, I want it known."   (80)

. . .

clxxxvi

When the barons have eaten at table,
William begins to question Rainoart:
"Tell me, my friend, what we are wondering.
Do you want to be baptized or not,
to believe in God with good intention,
who was incarnate in the Virgin,
and brought back Saint Lazarus from death,   7880
and to bring redemption to our souls
was crucified and guarded like a thief,
and on the third day was resurrected.
If you believe, we shall have you baptized."
Rainoart replies: "We believe it all.
Sir William, you who know the lesson,
you ought to have a fur cape,
trailing all the way down to your heel,
and then the robe and the cowl on your head,
and great boots with fur all around,   7890
and your head crowned with a tonsure,
and you would sit all day on a pallet
and in that church you would say your prayers
and you would be given plenty to eat,
white peas in fat and cheeses in season,
and at times a small portion of fish."
William hears and embraces the baron.
Then you might hear the laughter break out
from the knights who make up the household.
One whispers quietly to another   7900
"Did you hear what Rainoart, the baron, said,
how he told William what he should do?

He is nothing, indeed, if not a fool,
he will never say anything but nonsense.
As God helps me, we have a good minstrel,
who'll make the time pass gaily for us,
almighty God protect him."

clxxxvii

Into a church of canons of the rule,
Rainoart is conducted and led,
accompanied by William and his barons.   7910
Quickly the font is made ready,
in a crypt of polished green marble;
it is huge and wide and extremely deep,
half a lance and fifteen feet in width,
the fountain is filled with cold water,
that is blessed by bishops and abbots.
Rainoart has been stripped of his clothing
and now he is wrapped in a rich silk.
When he has been blessed and consecrated,
and then, with great effort, raised from the font—   7920
he weighs more than several hogsheads of wheat—
to raise him, there is William short nose,
and Aimeri of the hoary beard,
Bernard and Bueves and his brother Aimer,
and Hernaut and the sturdy Guibert,
Count Bertrand and Guichard and Gui,
and the archbishop whose name is Guillemer.
All these hold him, as you have been told,
but Rainoart weighs on them like a pagan.
They do not know when he escapes them,   7930
but Rainoart makes his way to the font,
and drinks the water deeply and long.
When he returns he is quickly seized
on all sides by his arms and his legs
and then Rainoart rages at them:
"My lords, godfathers," says Rainoart, "let go,
you do wrong to conduct me this way.

What I must do, would be better done freely,
it seems to me you're making fun of me.
Sir archbishop, I think you were sleeping;   7940
as God loves me, if I had now escaped,
I would never let myself be caught again."
Then the baron is baptized and raised,
and given new life with the holy oil;
and they clothe him once more in robes of gold;
he is a handsome figure.

[CLXXXVIII–CXCIV   William gives Rainoart the booty from the war
to dispense. Then he makes him a knight. Armed and mounted on a
magnificent horse, Rainoart is expected to joust with a dummy set up in
a field. He sees no point in fighting anything but Saracens, but attacks
the dummy to please Guiborc. His cousin, Baudus, returns with many
knights and is baptized. William sends for his niece, Aelis, to marry
Rainoart. This time Louis receives his messengers well and bestows his
daughter graciously. William holds a great feast for the wedding.]

Minstrels from all over the kingdom   8300
are gathered there; they have heard and been told
that the count is giving Rainoart a bride.
He's expected to give and spend a great deal;
there is much rejoicing when they assemble.
On this day, many instruments are heard,
and many songs sung and played on the viol.
The feast in the palace is magnificent;
there are so many settings, I can't count them.
When they have eaten and drunk their fill,
the minstrels are paid to their delight.   8310
Count William bestows so much on them,
gold and silver he gives in plenty,
they all rejoice and thank him for it,
Then ask leave to depart and go away.

[CXCV–CXCVI   After the wedding, William gives the cities of Torte-
lose and Porpaillart to Rainoart. He will defend them against Desramé

who will come within the year to avenge himself on William. Henceforth William will be well protected. Now Aimeri and his sons can leave Orange and return to their lands.}

cxcvii

• • •

Count William of the short nose, the marquis,
remains in Orange very sad;
the counts Bertrand and Gui stay on with him,
and Walter of Termes and Guichard the bold,
Gaudin the dark, who is not yet recovered
from the wound he had beneath his chest.
In Orange are no more than a hundred good men.
William weeps through the night and in the day (a)
for his brothers, he is sad and depressed, (b)
and for his father and his other friends. (c)
He grieves and thinks often of Vivien,
the water flows down over his face.
The noble Guiborc tries to comfort him 8390
and the children she had brought up tenderly (a)
the counts Bertrand, Gerard and Anseis. (b)

cxcviii

William weeps and Guiborc comforts him:
"Noble count, sire, do not be distressed!
He who has lost will win it again,
and he who is poor will some day be rich.
Who laughs in the morning will weep at night;
a man of good health should not complain.
It is a long time since the world began,
Adam is dead, whom God created first,
and his children, as many as he begot; 8400
in the deluge, all the world was flooded,
when our lord restored the world. (a)
No one but Noah escaped from that death
and his household whom he saved in the ark; (a)
if God wishes, he will renew the world.

It has endured much and will endure more;
many have died and many will die still;   (a)
not one of us can escape from death.
But as long as one remains in this world,
he must carry on as best he can.
If he serves God, his end will be good.
A man who has a good wife should rejoice;
and if he is worthy, love her with good heart.   8410
Good counsel, when given, should be followed,
and I am one who will give some to you:
Rebuild Orange. It will regain its glory,
with the great wealth you have from Archant,
send for masons, many of them will come.
If you do that, you need have no more care,
I am the one who will take charge of it."
"God," says William, "what a countess this is!
Another will not be born in this age."
Count William does not waste any time,   8420
immediately he sends for the masons
and carpenters, as many as he can find.
As best he can, he rebuilds Orange
and closes it in with great moats and walls.

• • •

[CXCIX   Rainoart finally departs with his wife.]

When Rainoart has mounted the horse,   8470
he seems exceedingly fierce and proud.
He leads his knights away with him
and his wife who is very lovely.
Now William goes off with Rainoart
because of the castles he bestowed on him,
Tortelose and Porpaillart on the sea.
When he has made certain of the castles,
the count returns and Rainoart stays there;
good people inhabit Porpaillart,
it's furnished well with riches and goods.   8480

The tribute is a thousand marks of weighed gold,
twenty hogsheads of pepper, a hundred silk cloths.
Rainoart lies down inside the paved palace
with his wife who loves him well.
She is a maiden and he a bachelor,
who has never spent time with a woman,
but that night he gives up his innocence.
Together they lie in a bed side by side,
he and his wife fulfill their desires.
That night Maillefer is engendered,   8490
the strongest man ever born of woman,
but he will burst the heart of his mother,
and must be taken from the side of her body.
Because he is torn from his mother with iron,
he is named, at his baptism, Maillefer.
William of the short nose sorrows for her
and Rainoart is so stricken with grief,
that he does not live seven years after.
Most people say that it drove him mad,
but he killed a thousand Saracens still,   8500
and his father Desramé was killed.
Now begins a song of great valor,
never in your life will you hear better:
how Rainoart killed that great devil
King Loquifer, who was without faith,
and how he killed Isabras on his ship,
and how his son Maillefer was stolen,
and brought up and raised in Odierne.
Then he was proclaimed king and emir
and won his heritage as far as Montnuble.   8510

William in the Monastery

Listen to a verse that's widely praised,
about William, the marquis of the short nose,
and Guiborc, the lady of the bright face,
who held Orange and the city of Nîmes
and Tourtelose and Porpaillart on the sea.
To Sir William she had brought much wealth;
they were together a hundred years and a summer
before the lady of the bright face died.
She had known her share of pain and suffering
and many joys; that is truly so.   10
Sir William accomplished his desires
when he made peace with King Tiebaut.
From then on he held his lands in peace
on this side of the sea, that is the truth.
And the pagans were so in fear of him
that they trembled at the sound of his name.
In peace he held the forests and the fields
and all the country.

ii

Lady Guiborc, so worthy of praise,
is struck ill and cannot be cured.   20
She lies at Nîmes, I tell you what is true.
William is distressed and upset about her,
as are many ladies and his family, too.
The lady Guiborc sends for Sir William
and he comes to her—he will not refuse.
"What would please you, lady, for holy charity?"
"I'll tell you," says the lady, "in God's name.

I am very sick, I cannot escape.
We have often joked and laughed together,
now I beg you, for holy charity,   30
if I've offended you in word or thought,
by God I pray that you will forgive me."
And William answers: "Just as you wish.
By God and by me let all be forgiven.
I shall have little joy when you leave me,
it troubles me to lose you so soon."
"William, sire," Guiborc says, "listen to me:
let my jewels be given to my handmaids
and my treasures to the nuns and abbots,
to the clerks and priests who do God's work.   40
And now let the last rites be given me."
And the count says: "I consent willingly."
All the clergy is summoned by William
but they come there of their own desire.
They administer the last rites in full
and when they're finished the lady sighs;
she commends William to Jesus
and afterwards speaks no other word.
Count William weeps with tender pity;
he is parted from his lady in this world.   50
They carry the lady straight to the church,
solemnly the priests sing the service—
great are the offerings William has made—
after the mass the lady is buried.
Count William mourns in great sorrow
all through that day until evening comes.
Then he goes to rest in his splendid bed.
But God does not wish him to be forgotten,
he sends an angel to make his will known
that William should go to Genevois on the sea. 60
When the good count has heard God's words,
he will not transgress the command;
commending to God the people of his land,
he leaves the kingdom in his godson's care,

to whom they must swear homage and faith.
When this is done, he will not be delayed;
quickly he has his charger made ready,
and girds his sword at his left side,
his good buckler he does not forget;
all his armor he carries with him.   70
He leaves the city, he will not remain,
he takes with him no companion or peer
and straight to Brides he follows the way.
He comes to the city and rides through it,
to the church of the worthy St. Julien
and there says his prayers.

iii

William Fierebrace enters the church,
he lifts his hand to make the sign of the cross,
then he kneels down and bows before the saint.
"St. Julien, I am now in your care;   80
for God, I have left my castles and marches
and my cities and all my kingdom.
St. Julien, I commend my shield to you
by this accord: I put it in your care,
but if Louis, the son of Charles, has need,
or my godson, who holds my heritage,
against pagans, the foul savage race,
I shall take it again. And in its place,
three gold besants, at Christmas and Easter,
I shall give you for the rest of my life."   90
The count takes hold of it by the silk strap
and carries it to the marble altar.
There it is seen still by fools and wise men,
all those who go as pilgrims to St. Gilles.
There too is the club of the noble Rainoart,
with which he killed many fierce Saracens.
The marquis remounts his good battle-horse,
he leaves the city and resumes his journey,
towards Genevois he rides.

iv

Count William makes his way to Genevois,   100
to the abbey which the angel had shown him.
His good charger he has brought with him;
he wears his good hauberk and his helmet,
his sword of steel and the spear that cut well;
all day long, every day, the count rides hard
until he reaches Genevois. He doesn't stop then,
but makes his way directly to the church.
He approaches the altar and presents his arms;
he has no desire to fight anymore,
unless Louis has great need of him   110
against Saracens whom he'll never love.
He reaches the cloister, afraid of nothing,
finds the abbot and greets him courteously.
The abbot sees William—he knows him well—
he sits beside him and begins to ask:
"Sir William, what are you seeking here?"
The count answers: "I won't hide that from you;
an angel came, God had sent him to me,
so that I would come here and become a monk.
Do this for me, it will be great charity."   120
"Willingly, sir," the abbot responds;
"you'll be a monk, you won't be turned away;
the chapter will not object to you,
so it seems to me."

v

"Sir William," says the abbot, "good, sweet lord,
you have caused the death of many men;
penance for that I cannot keep from you
for your sins, there have been twenty thousand.
You will be a monk and accept suffering,
but tell me, do you know how to chant and read?"   130
"Yes, lord abbot, without using a book.
You are a master, you know how to write

on parchment or on tablets of wax."
The abbot listens and begins to laugh
and all the monks who are in the chapter.
"Sir William, you are a noble man and a lord;
if God helps me, we will teach you to read
in your psalter and to sing matins too,
and terce and nones and vespers and complines.
When you're a priest you will read the gospel   140
and you will sing mass."

vi

Count William makes his request of the abbot:
"For the love of God, sweet lord, make me a monk,
let me take orders and have me tonsured!"
The abbot says: "By St. Peter of Rome,
it will be done before nones are sung,
and the chapter will not oppose me in this."
He takes scissors and cuts the tonsure.
When William is shaved, he seems a fine man.
The abbot summons a monk by name,   150
"Go quickly and find a black robe for me,
take the stole that befits a nobleman,
a cape and hood, a wool tunic and cowl,
and the fur-piece that is rich and fine—
there is none better from here to Barcelona;
a cousin of mine born in Perone
brought it to me from beyond Narbonne."
The garments are fetched and given to William,
the count dons them, he looks for no excuse.
The robe is large, but it is not too long;   160
it is short by more than half a yard.

vii

The count is seated inside the cloister;
he has a large tonsure which the abbot cut,
and the fur he was given to wear
is too short for him, and the abbot laughs

and all the monks laugh at him as well.
As each one looks, he is delighted.
May the lord God protect him!

viii

Count William is shaved all around his head,
with that tonsure he looks like a prior;   170
not a monk or abbot or prior there
not shorter than he by half a foot and a hand.
The abbot regards him and says with love:
"You are a monk, in the name of our maker.
Now you must love us and show us respect,
and all the monks will treat you as a lord."
William answers: "You need not be afraid,
but you must tell the greatest and the least
not to be wicked or make me angry,
for I would frighten the most valiant so   180
that he might well say he had come on bad times."
William was in the order many days
and lived a holy life.

ix

The count is a monk, he has taken the robe;
most willingly he hears God's services,
he is not absent from mass or matins,
terce or nones or vespers or complines.
The other monks are quite jealous of him,
they tell each other: "This was real folly!
Our abbot committed a great outrage   190
when he received this man in our abbey.
An appetite like his I've never seen;
if we have a loaf and a half to eat,
he has three, he is never satisfied.
Curses on such a monk in an abbey!
Who brought him here, may God punish him,
he'll bring shame on us all!

x

If we have five yards of cloth in our robes,
he is so huge he has to have twelve,
with the hood and gown and the fur around.   200
He barely fasts from midday to nones;
in the morning he eats three good, huge loaves
so that not a crumb or a crust remains.
When we have beans, he asks for the beet-root
and demands fish and good wine besides;
of a huge barrel, not a drop remains.
When he is full, he chases us out,
he brings shame on us all."

xi

All the monks have entered the assembly
and begin to talk about Sir William.   210
One tells another: "Trouble is upon us;
if he lives long, we will all be starved."
But at these words the abbot appears:
"My lords," he says, "I see that you're worried.
Were you speaking now of William of the short nose,
who has given us such pain and trouble?"
"We cannot bear and endure him much longer,
when we converse, it does not please him,
he wants to strike or kick all of us.
His fists are huge, he might kill us with them;   220
the blows that he gives are to be feared.
When he's angry, he makes us all tremble—
there is no one who would dare say a word."
Just then the abbey's cellarer appears,
on crutches, so beaten he can scarcely stand.
He has been beaten by William of the short nose,
so that he cannot walk without aid.
"For God's sake, sir abbot, I come to complain
about your monk, may God punish him.

God confound whoever brought him in here!   230
I bring you the keys that protect your goods—
Let them be given to living devils!
Yesterday I was well, now I'm in pain,
because of that monk in here who is mad.
When he has fasted a little while,
he comes to the cellar and opens it quickly,
striking it with his foot to overturn it.
He comes for as much wine as he can find
and food, until he has had enough;
if you stop him, he strikes you straightway   240
or kicks you against the wall with his foot.
Yesterday Sir William of the short nose sat
and began to demand your wine from me;
I was a fool and refused to give it,
but he made me pay well for that folly.
Better for me if he were beyond the sea.
He leapt up and began to throw me
with such violence, that he hurled me
to my hurt, right against a pillar;
now I am forced to walk with crutches.   250
The other monks saw him throw me around
but harm would have come to whoever dared touch him.
Shame on a monk who is so to be feared!"
"My lords," says the abbot, "now hear my thought:
if all together you might agree,
we could certainly prevail on Sir William
so that he would be killed and quite destroyed.
Let us send him to fetch fish from the sea,
which he will carry on two pack-horses.
We shall give our money into his charge   260
and send a sergeant to accompany him
to conduct and lead the pack-animals.
Before they return they will be attacked,
murdered or captured, and we'll be set free.
There are robbers around who should be feared,
they live their lives by stealing and theft,

no man passes them without losing his robes.
We will have William ride his good charger
which they'll take away; he won't stand for it,
his heart is fierce, he will want to fight them, 270
and the robbers will swiftly destroy him.
Then we will be free of him forever.
If he returns, we'll discuss it again."
"It will be so, it will surely work out."
They send the prior to summon William
and he comes to them, he would not refuse.
William says: "Sir abbot, what do you wish?
I see that these monks are angry with me,
but by the apostle sought at Noiron,
if they make me the least bit angrier, 280
I will turn them upside down, inside out—
they won't have the heart to sing matins again,
or they'll do what I wish."
The monks hear him and begin to tremble.
One tells another: "We're in for trouble!
If he lives long, we will all be murdered."
The abbot says: "William, listen to me.
If you will do what is asked of you,
all the chapter will be grateful for it."
And William answers: "Yes, sire, in God's name." 290
"Sir William," says the abbot, "listen then.
You must go to the sea to get us fish
and take two pack-animals along;
you will also have our money in your charge,
so that you'll be able to buy the fish
and a sergeant will come to lead the horses.
But one thing I don't want you to forget:
one may not stray into another chapter.
You must go by the forest of Beaucler,
where there are robbers who must be feared, 300
who live entirely by stealing and theft.
No man passes them without losing his robes,
not even clerks or priests or tonsured monks.

If they should take your magnificent steed,
and all the garments that you are wearing,
Sir William, you must be very careful
not to allow yourself, sir, to fight back."
"God," says William, "I've never heard such words!
I have never been involved with trading,
selling or buying any kind of goods;	310
and if any thieves try to rob me,
I'll see that they die a miserable death."
"Silence," says the abbot, "don't think of that!
Since you're a monk blessed and consecrated,
you cannot wield a fatal weapon."
"God," says William, "then I will be murdered
and killed with great pain.

xii

By God, sir abbot, if they want my horse?
There's none better under heaven's mantle,
to carry arms in a full battle.	320
When you urge him on with the steel spurs,
he moves so quickly over land and rocks,
that no falcon or sparrow-hawk could catch him.
I won him from Aerofle, the fierce,
when, with my sword, I cut off his head.
If they take him from me, I will go mad."
And the abbot says: "Give him up willingly,
if they take him, you must not get angry.
You cannot fight."

xiii

And William asks: "If they take my gloves?"	330
The abbot answers: "Let them with good spirit,
give them up willingly and with a smile."
"Indeed," says William, "that would make me sad,
for by the apostle that pilgrims seek,
before I lost them, I'd make them suffer,
I think I'd kill them all."

xiv

And William asks: "If they take my boots?
And the wool tunic and the robe and cloak,
would I suffer them to beat me besides?
When it comes to beating, that's an ugly thing.   340
If I allow that, curses on my throat!
If I come upon thieves who take my clothes,
I tell you, by St. Peter, the apostle,
I'll hang them by the neck."

xv

And William asks: "If they take my pants,
the thing that we call the drawers?"
"Indeed," says the abbot, "that would be bad;
a thing like that ought to displease you.
Protect your drawers if you can work some harm,
with flesh and bone you may stand against them."   350
Then William says: "This pleases me well.
Since you give me permission to do that,
I swear to you by St. Hilaire's body,
if they do anything to annoy me,
they will find me fierce and cruel in my ways.
I'd be too ashamed to take off my pants.
Before they have them, I'll make several roar,
if God preserves my arms.

xvi

Count William, when he hears the decision
of his lord abbot, can only rejoice   360
that he is permitted to fight for his pants.
He goes to the city to have a belt made,
of the best silk cloth that can be bought;
he sends for a goldsmith to trim it well
with gold besants and buttons of pure gold.
And the wool weavers did praiseworthy work;
such needles were engaged in that labor,

that it cost him more than a hundred sous,
and when the count had gotten his belt,
he swiftly fastened it inside his pants.   370
"My belt," he says, "I will cherish you;
you cost me a lot of money to make.
If anyone, by St. Riquier's body,
who sees you should covet you,
so that he wants to get hold of my pants,
in my opinion, he'll pay well for it."
He goes to the abbot and addresses him:
"Sire," he says, "I shall go now on my way.
If they attack me, the miserable thieves,
and want to despoil me of my clothes,   380
I shall let them, to obey your command,
even the horse which I will be riding.
But the belt which I have had made,
if they try to take that, they will find me fierce.
Whoever attempts to get close to me,
know this for truth, he will pay well for it.
With my right fist on the top of his skull,
I will strike so his brains come pouring out
and all the others will be terrified."
The abbot hears and makes the sign of the cross   390
and the monks take counsel with one another:
"By St. Denis, he wants to run wild!
If the robbers cannot take care of him,
we'll be in trouble."

xvii

Count William has asked for leave to depart;
the abbot is willing and glad to grant it.
More than ten pounds the abbot has him take,
so that he'll be able to buy the fish,
and two pack-horses have been made ready,
and a sergeant who'll know how to lead them.   400
Count William has mounted on his charger,
he leaves the cloister, with no wish to stay.
The other monks, when they see he has left,

commend him straightway to the devils.
Had the worthy Sir William known of that,
he would have made them pay well for it.
The noble man has set out on the road,
the two pack-horses are led before him.
He begins to pray to Jesus in glory
to grant him a return healthy and safe. 410
He does not stop until he reaches Beaucler,
but not one of the thieves is to be found.
He passes beyond it and comes to the sea,
and there he begins to buy the fish:
pike and salmon, deserving of praise,
sturgeon and eels that will be salted.
He takes his chest and opens it quickly,
but it annoys him to count out the coins
so he throws them about by the handful.
One tells another: "Here's a good cleric. 420
Blessed be the soul who sent him to the sea.
If we had many men like this one,
we would be rich before a month passed;
he doesn't care how the grain is sold,
as long as his stomach is satisfied."
Count William will not argue with them,
he has no wish to dispute the peasants.
That night he finds himself very good lodging,
and eats several of the fish for his supper.
He doesn't forget to have good wine, either— 430
he does not intend to bring back any coins.
In great comfort, he rests that night
until the next day, when morning comes.
The count mounts, the horses are loaded;
he sets forth to return to the cloister
and does not stop until the woods of Beaucler.
Again he fails to encounter robbers.
As he is riding deep in the forest,
Count William is very noble and brave,
he looks at his sergeant and addresses him: 440
"Friend, sweet brother, can you sing anything?

You'd be foolish to be afraid of thieves.
Do you think that I will not protect you?"
In answer the sergeant begins to shout,
clear and loud he starts to sing:
"Would you hear about Sir Tiebaut the Slav,
and of William, marquis of the short nose,
how he captured the city of Orange,
and took Orable as his wife and peer,
and Gloriete the principal palace?   450
I cannot, sire, sing aloud any more—
this is where thieves usually gather,
who spend their days robbing and plundering.
If they see us, we will not escape.
No bishop or abbot could rescue us,
not a clerk or priest or a tonsured monk,
but we would quickly be hacked apart."
And William says: "You must not be afraid.
Do not stop singing because of the thieves,
for if they come, I know how to protect you.   460
The living devil must have carried them off,
for I cannot see or encounter one."
In answer, the sergeant begins to sing,
so loudly, does he make the woods resound,
that fifteen robbers have heard it clearly.
They are in the woods and about to eat;
they have their dinner laid out and prepared.
A hermitage they had recently robbed—
and strangled all the religious within—
then carried off their money and garments.   470
One tells another: "I hear a minstrel.
Listen to him sing of William Short-nose!"
And the leader says: "Make him come around here!
If he's carrying riches, he won't escape."
The others object: "Sire, let him be,
for no one should disturb a minstrel,
but all good men should love and honor them,
and give them money and clothes and food."
The leader says: "This is foolish talk;

if he comes through here, he must pay for it.   480
Before he has escaped from our hands,
he will be sorry he was ever born."
They all jump up and leap on their horses,
carrying weapons, they take to the road
and they don't stop until they reach William.
They shout at the count so violently
that they terrify the pack-animals,
and even Count William changes color.
From every side they shout at him:
"Stop, sir monk, you cannot get away!   490
If you go further you'll be cut to shreds."
Then William asks: "What do you want?
If you harm us, you won't gain anything,
instead you'll be excommunicated
by the abbot, the pope, and all the orders."
The leader says: "You're talking nonsense!
We wouldn't give a cent for any words
of a clerk or priest, bishop or abbot.
You are too rich and overburdened with goods;
you ought to give some to poorer people   500
and busy yourself amending your life.
You should keep your mind on singing matins
and let us think about robbing and theft.
You won't carry back as much as a cent,
of all the wealth you have brought this far."
They seize the sergeant and throw him down;
then they bind his feet and his hands tightly
and toss him upsidedown in a ditch.
And then they turn back to the count
and shout: "Sir monk, you won't get away."   510
May God protect him, in His great goodness,
he needs that help now.

xviii

The thieves are treacherous and hardened crooks,
they seize William from the front and the back,
holding his reins so that he cannot flee.

Some of them push him, the others pull.
One of them says: "This monk is a big one!"
"I'll say," says another, "his look is fierce.
Do you see how he rolls both his eyes!
If he gets angry, he'll do us some harm."   520
And a third says: "What rich gloves he has,
and trimmed with gold! You couldn't ask better."
He immediately demands William's gloves.
"Take them," he says, "I give them up sadly,
but I can see that I have no choice.
If you would now allow me to escape,
as God helps me, you will profit greatly."
But their chief says: "Your words are for nothing!
Of all the wealth you're carrying with you,
you won't take away as much as a glove."   530
"Indeed," says William, "this goes badly for me;
you're committing great sin."

xix

They demand from him the robe off his back,
and after that the wool tunic and gown,
and he gives them without asking mercy.
His body remains naked on the horse.
"God," says William, "what a fool I seem!
I have taken too much, by my faith to St. Paul,
I should have murdered four or five of them,
and killed them painfully."   540

xx

Astride the horse sits Sir William again,
naked and stripped, without a robe,
except for his pants, his stockings and boots.
The thieves are all around him in a ring,
they hold his reins so that he cannot turn.
"Robbers," he says, "what a foul lot you are!
You will yet be hung from a fearsome gallows,
it will happen if I can get away."

The leader swears by his chin and his throat
and St. Leonard, who is sought at Limoges: 550
"You will leave your horse and your boots to us
and those gauntlets you may give us as well."
The count gets down from his horse to the ground,
"Take him," he says, "for the apostle Peter!
It seems to me I have nothing left to pay,
except the pants that cover my thighs
and this belt that is poor and worthless."
But the leader says: "You'll give that up too."
William answers: "By the law of our order,
this is worth more than all the other clothes;   560
if you want it, you may get it too,
but I won't give it up."

xxi

"My lord robbers," says William of the fierce look,
"may God help me, you see a good belt here!
There's none better from here to Montpellier,
with gold bands and buttons of pure gold;
whoever has it ought to cherish it,
it cost more than seven pounds yesterday.
If you like it so much that you won't let it go,
you'll have to come a lot closer to me.   570
If I give it up, may God strike my head,
for I'll suffer the shame for it everywhere.
But let him come forward who would take it."
The leader of the thieves has seen the belt
and the precious stones and the gold gleaming;
by God he swears that he won't let it go.
He kneels down, for he wants to untie it,
so that he can pull it out of the pants.
The count watches him and can't help but rage:
"Ah God," he says, "now I must go mad,   580
these treacherous swine have captured me
and don't want to leave me even my pants!
I can see now that prayers would not help.

God confound me if I don't take revenge."
Could one but see him raising his head,
grinding his teeth and changing color,
he might well be afraid.

xxii

"God," says William, "now I see I'm in trouble.
I can't find any mercy or support.
My lord abbot, our master, commanded,   590
if I found a man who wanted my pants,
and tried to take off my belt by force,
then only could I get angry.
If I delay, I'd be better not born,
for these men are too evil and treacherous."
He raises his fist and strikes the leader;
he deals such a blow on the front of his face,
that he breaks the bone of his jaw in two
and throws him dead to the ground.

xxiii

Count William is furiously angry;   600
in his great rage he raises his right fist
and strikes another that stands before him,
completely shattering the bone of his throat.
He seizes two of them, one in each fist,
and hurls them together with such violence,
that they knock the brains from the other's head.
On the fifth man he lands such a blow
that he breaks his head into several pieces;
with his right fist he strikes another,
in the chest, so that he falls over,   610
and his heart cracks in his breast from the fall.
The seventh man he grabs by the hair,
swings him three times, at the fourth lets him go,
against an oak, that completely smashes him.
He says to himself: "When this one gets up,
he won't have any desire to sing.

He was a fool when he grabbed for my pants,
I haven't heard pants mentioned for a while—
if any one wants them, let him come here,
he will receive such good pay from my fists, 620
that he will not, I think, ever rob me
or any other man who takes this road."
When they hear him, they are all afraid;
one says to another: "What a devil!
If he keeps on, none of us will escape."
They rally together from all sides again
and throw what lances and darts they have.
God protects him, for he is not touched.
When the count sees this, he calls on God:
"As truly as You created the skies, 630
protect my body now, lord!"

XXIV

"God," says William, "as You are truly He,
protect my body from these stinking thieves.
Our blessed abbot committed a sin
when he sent me here so badly equipped
without my chain-mail or my Austrian blade,
my bright helmet or my Turkish spear.
Even if there were fifty-three of them,
they'd all be dead now, the cursed robbers.
I see so many good swords lying here, 640
I can't take them, because it's forbidden;
in the chapter the courteous abbot said
that I might use no arms but flesh and bone
to defend myself."

XXV

Count William begins to look around him;
nearby he sees his pack-horse standing,
one he had had loaded with fish.
The count tears off its legs to the haunch,
lifts it up and begins to advance.

He approaches the thieves and pays back the first 650
with such force that he knocks him over dead.
Then the worthy vassal strikes another
and then a third, he does not spare him.
He has killed three of the treacherous swine.
He strikes so hard, the noble, honored count,
that he kills them all, not one is left standing.
Now William has freed the road of those thieves;
no poor man will leave his goods there again.
Count William looks at the pack-animal,
from which he had taken the hoof and the leg, 660
"God," says the count, "by Your holy mercy,
restore, sire, this mutilated horse,
that I may see him healthy, whole and well."
Then he takes the haunch he had pulled off,
and the noble, worthy count puts it back
exactly where he had torn it loose.
In answer to the good, honored count's prayer,
God performed a miracle.

XXVI

When the good count has finished his prayer
he takes the leg of that good animal 670
and puts it back; immediately it heals.
With all his load, the horse turns around.
Count William now looks about him again,
sees his sergeant at the bottom of a ditch
where the robbers had hurled him earlier.
The noble count quickly sets him free
and then addresses these words to him:
"Friend, good brother, do you see all these horses,
sorrel or black and white, dark or dappled?
There are fifteen, I have counted them all. 680
Mount the best one and lead the others back."
The sergeant says: "Willingly, in God's name."
He seizes them, without wasting time.
The two of them start back on the road
straight to the abbey.

xxvii

Count William takes the fish that he bought
and he does not leave any horses behind.
The two leave the woods and ride to the abbey.
Three monks are at the gate as lookouts,
and beneath them they have bolted it well. 690
When they see William coming along the road,
they climb down quickly, and without delay,
go to the abbot and announce the news:
"William is coming with a great troop,
he's bringing Orcanie horses and steeds."
"God," says the abbot, "blessed lady Mary,
he could certainly not have earned all these goods;
he must have taken the lives of many,
and pillaged churches and monasteries.
Shut the gates, I want none of his folly, 700
this time we will not let him enter here."
"No, by God, sire," not one fails to say,
"he would beat us all and shame us badly."
William approaches and the sergeant, who shouts:
"Open the gates and take all this fish
and the horses; the abbey will be rich,
all through William, who had no help in it.
Now he has certainly deserved his keep,
it should not be denied him the rest of his life."
The monks hear him, they don't answer at all; 710
each one wishes he had never returned.
They cry out in high and clear voices:
"Stay out there, you will never enter here,
for you are a thief."

xxviii

The worthy William approaches the gate
which the gate-keeper has closed against him,
and bolted it shut and locked with great force.
Count William shouts at him and advises:
"Open the gate, God confound your throat!

Take the fish that these pack-horses carry;   720
there are good pike and a lot of fine shad
and excellent trout with enormous heads,
good sturgeon and fine salmon as well."
The gate-keeper says: "By Peter the apostle,
this time you will not enter this abbey.
The abbot himself had it closed to you."
"God," says William, "may your order be damned,
if you monks are going to bar my entrance.
But, by the faith that I bear St. Josse,
if I can get in by love or by force,   730
all the monks will pay for their actions.
I'll beat them all up."

XXIX

God," says William, "who governs all things,
in your goodness, give me counsel now.
I thought that I would remain with these monks—
damned be the abbot who won't let me in—
I can see now that they sent me on this trip
so that I would be destroyed by the thieves,
but the God of glory saved me from that.
Now I know that I won't find pity here   740
and my prayers won't gain me entry within."
The heart in his breast begins to heave
and his body to tremble with fury.
Standing beside him he sees a huge beam
which would have taken four peasants to lift.
In his anger, he grabs it with his fists
and begins to raise it high in the air;
with great vigor he stands before the gate
and begins to strike great blows upon it,
so that all the cloister resounds within.   750
Those blows could be heard from a league away.
The master gate is beaten to the ground
and the iron bars and the bolts are destroyed,
and a falling bar kills the gate-keeper.

All the monks have fled in terror,
scattering through the many chambers.
To the cloister comes Sir William the brave
and begins to shout at the monks inside,
telling them that they cannot escape.
If one could but see him crush to the ground   760
and strike so many rough blows with his fists!
He starts to grab each of them by the hood;
he gets hold of one who can't get away,
twirls him three times, at the fourth lets him go
so violently against a pillar
that both his eyes come flying from his head.
Then William shouts: "Come and talk to me now!"
He catches the abbot with a hard kick
that knocks him out, in the midst of the hall.
The other monks have all taken to flight.   770
If one could see Sir William the brave
running back and forth through the cloister,
into the kitchen and dormitory!
There is no room that he doesn't look into.
The monks that he finds he handles roughly,
by their hair, he throws one against another;
he beats them so hard they lose their senses
and flee for refuge to the great church.
One says to another: "We're in trouble.
We must give ourselves up to his mercy,   780
or we will be given up to torments."
They call William and throw themselves at his feet,
all together they beg him for mercy,
even the abbot who has just come to.
And William says: "You will all be spared,
but you must do what I have decided."
The monks answer: "Willingly and gladly."
And William says: "Then hear my demands:
fifteen horses I've presented to you,
and all the fish that I got at the sea;   790
but now I beg that I be forgiven

whatever offense or wrong I've done you.
For God's sake, sir abbot, I beg your mercy."
The abbot says: "It is all pardoned now,
Let the dead be buried immediately;
We will find other monks in good supply.
But now tell us, for Holy Charity,
about this wealth that you have acquired.
Did you go through the forest of Beaucler
and did you encounter the robbers there?"   800
William answers: "You will now hear the truth:
I did not meet any as I went through,
but when I came back they set upon me,
fifteen robbers I encountered there then;
they took my sergeant and tied his hands
and threw him upsidedown in a ditch.
I could not find any mercy in them,
but with flesh and bone I took care of them
so they will not trouble the road again,
and no poor man will lose his money there."   810
"O God," says the abbot, "be praised for this!
They never loved Jesus in his majesty.
Now may all your sins be forgiven you."
Then the abbot had the fish unloaded
and all the monks made their dinner of them.
Those who have died are quickly forgotten.
At the great table sits William the brave
and has as many good wines as he wishes,
all that he can drink.

XXX

That night as William the Fierce lies in bed,   820
an angel appears which God has sent.
He says to William: "Don't be amazed!
The glorious lord of heaven commands you
to take leave of the abbot in the morning,
carry your hauberk and your blade of steel,
all your armor—leave nothing behind—

mount and ride without delay
straight to the ruins near Montpellier.
In the wasteland near a sharp precipice,
there is a fountain beside a rock;   830
no Christian has ever lived a day there,
except a hermit who died yesterday,
cut to pieces by evil Saracens.
There you will find a dwelling and a church.
Be a hermit, for God has so decreed."
William answers, "I've no wish to delay."
The angel leaves and when it is day
Count William asks leave of the abbot,
who grants it; he is not angry,
and the other monks are extremely glad.   840
William goes to the stable and saddles his horse.
He never asks for a sergeant or squire.
When he has mounted he seizes his spear,
wearing his armor, leaving nothing behind.
The abbot gives him twenty pounds in coins
on the promise that he will not return.
Count William swears to that faithfully.
And now Sir William the fierce rides away,
straight to the ruins near Montpellier,
to the fountain that springs beside the cliff.   850
There he finds a dwelling place and a church,
which the Saracens had completely laid waste;
William enters there.

XXXI

Into the dwelling, William has entered;
inside he finds a chapel and altar.
A holy hermit had lived there long,
and then he died and went to his end.
There Sir William the worthy intends
to serve and honor almighty God
for the sins which encumber his soul.   860
He makes a collar from the hide of a deer,

and sets it on the neck of his fine horse.
Then he gathers a supply of stones
in order to rebuild the dwelling.
In a few months he has it well repaired
and enclosed and surrounded by a courtyard
where he plants many trees and herbs.
But still he fears Saracens and Slavs,
so he places a fort on top of a hill.
William of the short nose goes there to wait,   870
where they cannot harm him.

xxxii

William is deep in the desert,
by the dwelling where the fountain springs,
he plants herbs and trees in profusion,
and places a fortress high on the mountain.
There William waits for the foul Saracens.
It can still be seen by pilgrims who pass;
at St. William of the Desert they'll find
a small dwelling, where the other monks are.
Louis was in Paris with his household,   880
and he enjoyed himself like a scoundrel;
with him there was no count nor baron,
neither duke nor prince, not a knight or page,
who valued him as much as a button,
he was such a stingy fool.

xxxiii

Would it please you to hear how he was treated,
how he was loved and served by his men?
When he rides out from the city of Paris,
down to St. Lis where he normally lives,
or Orleans, or nearby to Chartres,   890
or to Laon or the city of Reims,
cursed be the count who'd accompany him.
No castellan, no prince, no life-vassal,
no chevalier who knew how to bear arms,

none of them thought the king worth a penny.
He had chased out all the men of good birth,
driven them out from his land and his court
and taken strangers for his councillors;
evil counsel they give him every day
and rob him and carry off all his wealth.   900
All his barons have now abandoned him;
none attends him for Easter or Nowell.
And beyond that, there is still more trouble—
he is beseiged by the pagan Ysoré.

[The text of the last thirty lines of the poem is damaged. Ysoré comes to Paris to avenge his father's death. The French are terrified, no one dares fight him. The Saracen army closes the city off completely. Louis has no one to turn to.]

Index